Yale Agrarian Studies

Peasant Power in China

The Era of Rural Reform,

1979–1989

Daniel Kelliher

Yale University Press

New Haven and London

This is a book in the Yale Agrarian
Studies series, James C. Scott, series
editor.

Designed by James J. Johnson.
Set in Stempel Garamond type by
Rainsford Type, Danbury, Connecticut.
Printed in the United States of America
by BookCrafters, Inc., Chelsea,
Michigan.

Library of Congress Cataloging-in-
Publication Data

Kelliher, Daniel Roy.
    Peasant power in China : the era of
rural reform, 1979–1989 /
Daniel Kelliher.
        p.   cm.
    Includes bibliographical references
and index.
    ISBN 0-300-05465-3 (alk. paper)
    1. Rural development—China—
History—20th century. 2. Rural
    development—Government policy—
China—History—20th century.
    3. Private plot agriculture—China—
History—20th century.
    4. China—Rural conditions. 5.
China—Politics and
    government—1976– I. Title.
    HN740.Z9C6388 1992
    307.1'412'0951—dc20   92-14883

10 9 8 7 6 5 4 3 2 1

For my mother and
my father

Contents

Preface

Between Deng Xiaoping's rise to power at the end of 1978 and the massacre in Beijing in 1989, a massive social change took place in rural China. During these years Deng Xiaoping mounted a hugely ambitious reform program. He aimed to modernize the entire nation and put its Maoist past to rest. In the countryside, however, Deng and his fellow reformers discovered that peasants had radical ideas of their own. Reform thus brought the state's plans up against a disorganized but effective expression of peasant power. My subject is this struggle between peasant and state for control over the transformation that swept rural China.

In seeking to understand the contest for power between state and peasant, I have used evidence from the entire era of reform. The last interviews in China that I did for this book took place in the summer of 1990. But the book concentrates particularly on the turbulent early period of reform, from 1979 to 1985. It was during these first years that the most startling changes occurred—the abandonment of the communes, the beginnings of family farming, and the wrenching movement toward privatization and free markets.

These changes eventually reached all of China, but they came earliest to southern China, in an atmosphere of heightened conflict and creativity. By focusing on the origins of reform, this book therefore reflects the experience of the south more than the north. This influence is all the stronger because the book itself began in Hubei, a south-central province at about the same latitude as Louisiana. I lived in Hubei at the height of its reform, in 1983 and 1984. The information I collected there came from holdings in the Wuhan University Library; formal interviews and visits at rural locales in central, southeastern, and western Hubei; discussions with university and government economists; and informal conversation with peasants, mainly in the area surrounding Wuhan.

Hubei neither ranked in the forefront of reform with Anhui and Sichuan provinces nor lagged behind with the recalcitrant provinces like Hebei. The relatively conservative leadership of Hubei tried to stay in the mainstream of reform throughout the 1980s, reading the confusing signals from Beijing and keeping as inconspicuous as possible. But peasants in Hubei—as in various villages across the entire south-central region of China—pushed for faster, more drastic change.

In this respect Hubei was part of a broader strain of peasant activism that influenced this book. Readers should note the regional character of this influence. Although most of the evidence I have gathered comes from beyond Hubei's borders, the preponderance is from Hubei's sister provinces, especially Anhui, Zhejiang, Jiangxi, Hunan, and Sichuan. This is significant, for all of these provinces lie in the broad south-central rice-growing region where the prospect of radical change away from the collective farm system was especially appealing to peasants. In the north, evidence of peasants agitating to break up the communes and push reform was slimmer. Farmers growing such crops as wheat on the North China Plain or in the vast flatlands of Manchuria were often more committed to collectivism, for they enjoyed greater advantages from consolidated fields and mechanization. Dividing the fields into small parcels for family farms struck many of them as irrational. In the south, however, where wet rice predominated, family farming was a passionate cause for many peasants. Wet rice was generally cultivated on small fields subdivided by dikes; it was not susceptible to easy mechanization; and its yields were extremely responsive to additions of human labor. For these reasons south-central rice farmers often jumped at the chance for family farming. This book reflects this regional setting. It does not capture the northerly instances of peasant indifference or resistance to reform as thoroughly, for the story it tells takes place in the ecological setting that encouraged the greatest peasant activism and inspired the most heated passions for change.

Because state-peasant conflict stands at the core of this book, I have purposely used a combination of sources that see rural politics along two different lines of vision—from the state center in Beijing and from the local standpoint. Aside from sources that see through the eyes of central state officials, I have relied on a number of publications that devote special attention to local politics. These include local and provincial Communist Party journals, national economic journals featuring detailed reports from rural localities, the provincial and municipal presses of Hubei and Wuhan, and publications of the Hubei Provincial Academy of Social Sciences. These sources were surprisingly candid about local problems. Local Party journals, for example, routinely reported troubles in carrying out policy, in order to alert cadres to difficulties that might arise in their own districts. News stories too small for the national press also found a place in local and provincial papers, making these papers an invaluable source on day-to-day confrontations between peasants and officials. Genuine disagreements over policy received freer expression in reporting with a local focus as well, especially in the national scholarly journals devoted to local investigations.

These sources on local politics have two large drawbacks. First, their information is spotty and unsystematic. Whereas China's national and provincial data on rural affairs are often so heavily aggregated as to be useless, local information suffers from the opposite defect: it is so disaggregated that drawing inferences from it can be hazardous. Most local studies from the 1980s covered a single village, township, commune, or county and offered precious little in the way of comparison with other units in the same jurisdiction. Assembling a coherent picture of rural politics with these isolated studies is akin to charting the night sky from random photographs of individual stars.

The second shortcoming is not limited just to these sources on local politics but extends to all normal research possibilities in China: the problem of finding a genuine voice for peasants. All my sanctioned interviews in China were restricted to rural officials; talks with ordinary peasants during official visits were usually chaperoned by cadres. Published sources are similarly weak in any direct form of peasant expression. When local studies quote peasants, it is sometimes difficult to distinguish what is genuine. The license that Chinese journalists and academics have to manufacture quotations from rural people is painfully obvious, particularly in the annoying habit of quoting peasants as if they spoke in jingles, sing-song rhymes, and couplets. Sifting through quotations from peasants for those that ring true obviously involves critical judgments and subjective choices. In this work I was aided by many expeditions in what the sociologist Thomas B. Gold has called "guerrilla interviewing"—that is, I went off alone by bicycle and engaged farmers in conversation. Nowhere in this book do I cite these conversations as sources (indeed, nearly every citation is to a published source), but I believe this guerrilla interviewing nonetheless engendered a better instinct for distinguishing what is authentic in quoted speech attributed to peasants.

In spite of their shortcomings, local sources provide an indispensable balance against national newspaper editorials, central documents issued by the state in Beijing, and the speeches of the mighty. This contrast is especially useful in grasping state-peasant relations, for it shows that politics is not solely what the state center proclaims, and rural reality is not always what state leaders believe. The interplay between central and local sources helps create the tension at the heart of this book, between the desires of peasants and the power of the state.

Acknowledgments

My greatest intellectual debt is to Vivienne Shue and James C. Scott. As teachers, they guided me through the earliest stages of this project. Although perhaps only a third of this book comes from the dissertation that they oversaw, the spirit of their thinking stayed with me through later years of research and writing, to this day.

Many of the ideas that I worked out in this book originated in conversations with Kevin O'Brien, Barry Naughton, Arlene Elowe MacLeod, and Margaret Pearson. On an early draft I received very helpful suggestions on dealing with the Chinese state from Hong Yung Lee. Nicholas Lardy also helped me to comprehend China's procurement system. In later stages of manuscript preparation I received careful readings from Marc Blecher, Valerie Bunce, James Farr, W. Phillips Shively, and David Sylvan.

Funding for research in China and Hong Kong came jointly from the Social Science Research Council and the American Council of Learned Societies, under a grant from the Ford Foundation. At the Social Science Research Council I was very fortunate to deal with Sophie Sa, who came up with resourceful solutions to problems I ran into in the field in China. For enabling me to do research in Hong Kong I thank the Universities Service Centre and, especially, Eric Goldman. Wuhan University hosted me for my research in Hubei Province. At Wuhan I received the warmest support from Gao Shang-yin, who was a genuine friend to scholarly exchange. For financing my research in Hebei Province, I am grateful to the political science department at the University of Minnesota and to Patricia Needle and the China Center, also at Minnesota.

The Center for Chinese Studies at the University of California at Berkeley financed research for this book in the United States. The Center was unfailingly welcoming during my repeated visits in the late 1980s. For this hospitality I thank Joyce Kallgren and David Keightley. I am also grateful to C. P. Chen and Annie Chang of the Center for Chinese Studies Library, the two most off-beat, open-minded, and resourceful librarians I have ever met.

John Covell and Leslie A. Nelson at Yale University Press steered the work through its last steps toward publication. I thank them especially for the enthusiasm that they shared with me for the book. At the very end of this project I also received particularly close readings from two other people. Mark Selden was one, and I am grateful to him for detailed, tough criticism and for a barrage of ideas. The other was Randall E. Stross. Here I want to register my admiration for Randy's ruthless, hilarious style of editing.

And to Pamela Hoopes—well, on with the merry chase.

Chronology

1949	Liberation; People's Republic of China established
1946–52	Land Reform
1955–56	Collectivization of farming
1958–60	Great Leap Forward; rural people's communes set up
1959–61	The "three hard years"; severe famine
1966–76	Cultural Revolution
1976	Mao Zedong dies; fall of leftist Gang of Four
1978	Deng Xiaoping's reform coalition consolidates power
1979	Rural reform begins; major rise in farm-gate prices
1982	Family farming on a wide scale officially approved
1983	Private entrepreneurship wins official backing
1983–84	Communes disbanded
1985	Procurement reform; open conflict within reform coalition
1987	Hu Yaobang deposed as head of Communist Party; conservative reformers gain strength
1989	Democracy movement suppressed; Zhao Ziyang deposed; conservatives dominate Communist Party

Administrative Levels

The state (government and Communist Party)
- Center
- Province
- Prefecture
- County

Communes (1958–84)
- Commune
- Brigade
- Team

Rural administration after reform
- *Xiang* (township)
- Village people's committee
- Village small group (often not organized)

During the reform period, a successful county could be designated a "municipality" (*shi*), and a successful *xiang* could be designated a "town" (*zhen*). Such name changes were mainly honorific, however, indicating little change in practical administration.

Editorial Notes

Citations

Because Chinese journals do not conform to a system of volume and issue numbers, most journal citations here will give the year plus the issue number for that year, as in "1992: 10." Unless otherwise noted, the issue number also corresponds to the month of publication—hence "1992: 10" also indicates October of 1992.

Citations to JPRS refer to the Joint Publications Research Service in Washington, D.C. These citations follow the JPRS notation system, in which "JPRS-CAG" indicates the series entitled *China Report: Agriculture,* and "JPRS-CAR" indicates the *China* area-report series.

Transliteration

Pinyin is used for all transliteration of Chinese, except for a few place names familiar in the West in other transliterations, such as Yangtze River. In citations to English-language publications, Wade-Giles transliterations in titles and authors' names have been left unaltered.

Measures

Most of the measures used in this book are metric. *Tons,* for example, refers to metric tons (1,000 kilograms). Sometimes in quoted material other measures appear, for which the following guide may be helpful:

1 *mu* = one-fifteenth (0.067) hectare = 0.165 acres
1 acre = 0.405 hectare
1 *jin* = 0.5 kilogram = 1.1 pound
1 *yuan* = the monetary unit of China. The yuan declined against the American dollar in the years 1979–89, from a high of roughly U.S. $0.65 to a low of roughly U.S. $0.27. It was generally agreed that the official rate exaggerated the value of the yuan through most of this period.

Chinese
Newspapers and
Journals Cited

Newspapers

Anhui ribao (Anhui Daily), Hefei
Changjiang ribao (Yangtze River Daily), Hankou
Guangming ribao (Bright Daily), Beijing
Hubei ribao (Hubei Daily), Wuchang
Jingji ribao (Economic Daily), Beijing
Jingjixue zhoubao (Economics Weekly), Beijing
Nanfang ribao (Southern Daily), Guangzhou
Nongmin ribao (Peasant Daily), Beijing
Renmin ribao (People's Daily), Beijing
Zhejiang ribao (Zhejiang Daily), Hangzhou

Journals

Dangyuan shenghuo (Party Member's Life), Wuchang
Hongqi (Red Flag), Beijing
Hubei caijing xueyuan xuebao (Journal of the Hubei Institute of Finance and Economics), Wuchang
Hubei nongye kexue (Hubei Agricultural Science), Wuchang
Jiage lilun yu shijian (Price Theory and Practice), Beijing
Jihua jingji yanjiu (Planned Economy Research), Beijing
Jingji cankao (Economic Reference), Beijing
Jingji guanli (Economic Management), Beijing
Jingji kexue (Economic Science), Beijing
Jingji wenti (Problems of Economics), Taiyuan

Jingji xueshu ziliao (Economic Science Materials), Shanghai
Jingji yanjiu (Economic Research), Beijing
Jingji yanjiu cankao ziliao (Economic Research Reference Materials),
  Beijing
Jingji yanjiu ziliao (Economic Research Materials), Beijing
Jingjixue dongtai (Developments in Economics), Beijing
Liaowang (Outlook), Beijing
Lilun yu shijian (Theory and Practice), Shenyang
Lilun zhanxian (Battlefront of Theory), Hefei
Lishi yanjiu (Historical Research), Beijing
Nongcun gongzuo tongxun (Rural Work Newsletter), Beijing
Nongcun jinrong (Rural Finance), Beijing
Nongye jingji congkan (Collected Works on Agricultural Economics),
  Beijing
Nongye jingji wenti (Problems of Agricultural Economics), Beijing
Nongye jishu jingji (Economics of Agricultural Technology), Beijing
Shangye gongzuo (Commercial Work), Beijing
Shehui kexue dongtai (Developments in Social Science), Wuhan
Wuhan daxue xuebao (Journal of Wuhan University), Wuchang
Xinhua wenzhai (Xinhua Digest), Beijing
Zhonggong yanjiu (Research on Chinese Communism), Taibei
  [Taipei]

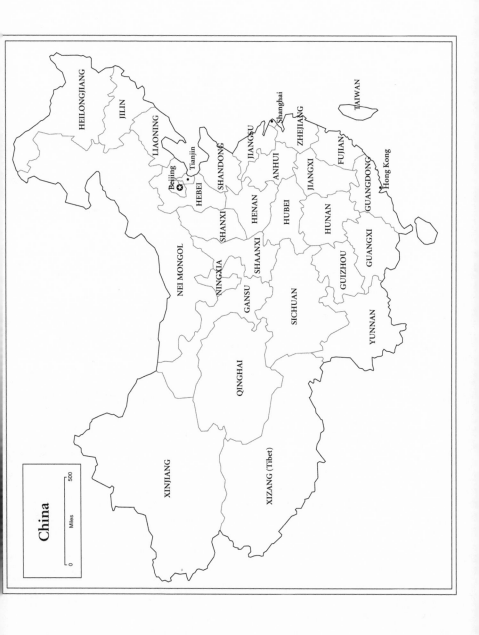

China

Miles

0   500

HEILONGJIANG

JILIN

LIAONING

NEI MONGOL

Beijing
Tianjin

HEBEI

SHANDONG

SHANXI

NINGXIA

GANSU

SHAANXI

HENAN

JIANGSU

Shanghai

ANHUI

ZHEJIANG

HUBEI

JIANGXI

FUJIAN

TAIWAN

GUANGDONG

Hong Kong

HUNAN

GUIZHOU

GUANGXI

SICHUAN

YUNNAN

QINGHAI

XINJIANG

XIZANG (Tibet)

Chapter One

On the Eve
of Reform

By mid-December 1978, Beijing residents could sense a big change coming. For weeks the press had been alive with stunning condemnations of the Cultural Revolution and hints of a raging leadership struggle. Swarms of elite Red Flag limousines with their black-tinted windows and anonymous passengers had assembled daily in the heart of the capital for the past month—the usual sign of a work conference of the Chinese Communist Party's highest leaders. In mid-December these weeks of rumors and secret meetings culminated in a five-day gathering of the Party's governing body, the Central Committee. Like all plenary sessions of the Central Committee, this one—known as the Third Plenum[1]—would not be announced to the populace until it was over. Behind the closed doors of the Third Plenum, a victorious coalition of Mao Zedong's opponents was ratifying a sweeping set of policy changes. Mao, the supreme Chinese leader since 1949, had been dead for two years, but his policies had lived on until this December meeting. Now two people who had opposed Mao for over a decade were about to triumph. Deng Xiaoping had seized political control over the Party, and Chen Yun, the man behind the most sustained critique of Maoist development strategy, would finally have the chance to see his radical economic reforms put into action. For these two architects of China's reform coalition, the Third Plenum marked the beginning of their attempt to modernize China.[2]

1. Short for the Third Plenum of the Eleventh Central Committee of the Chinese Communist Party.
2. For a firsthand account of the atmosphere in Beijing at the time, see

As the Party leaders met in Beijing, a very different kind of gathering was taking place in villages all over China. These modest village meetings possessed none of the historic quality now associated with the Third Plenum, but for the peasants in attendance they had far more immediacy and significance than the big meeting in the capital. The harvest was over; the business at hand was for each peasant collective to divide the year's cash income among its members.

One of the thousands of places where such a meeting took place that December was Tongjianyi, a village in the Han River Valley of Hubei Province. On the appointed day, the Tongjianyi peasants assembled in their brigade conference hall for the ritualized payday that came only once a year. Four long wooden tables stood in the center of the unheated hall with bundles of cash arranged on them. Each bundle was wrapped in red paper. Red, the traditional color of success, suited the occasion. The year 1978 was a good one in Tongjianyi—or at least it was better than 1977, which had passed without any year-end meeting like this one because the collective had had no cash to distribute. This year, however, the second rice crop was outstanding, and net per capita income would reach 110 *yuan*—equivalent to about seventy American dollars.

Such miserably small income was barely below average for rural China in 1978. Chinese peasants lived in dark dwellings constructed mostly of mud bricks and thatch. Their ordinary diet consisted almost entirely of grain, and for many millions of peasants hunger was routine. The infant mortality rate among peasants was twice that of China's city-dwellers.[3] For children and adults alike, farm work was grueling. The two main sources of energy were animal power and human muscle. Barely half of all peasants finished elementary school, and the schools were so bad that, as one Chinese lamented, "each year a new batch of illiterate or semi-literate children is produced."[4] With

---

Roger Garside, *Coming Alive: China After Mao* (New York: McGraw-Hill, 1981), chap. 9.

3. Guo Zonghe, "Cheng xiang jumin wuzhi wenhua shenghuo shuiping de bijiao" (A comparison of urban and rural residents' material and cultural standards of living), *Nongye jingji congkan* 1982: 1, p. 55.

4. Ren Qiang, "Puji xiaoxue jiaoyu de jige wenti" (Some problems with universal elementary education), *Jihua jingji yanjiu* 1983: 27 (Sept. 25), p. 35.

migration to the cities prohibited, most peasants could hope for better lives only through a reinvigoration of the rural economy.

For the villagers gathered in Tongjianyi to collect their meager cash, the need to enliven the stagnant farm economy was as imperative as anywhere in China. With winter descending on their valley east of the dark Wudangshan Mountains, many families in Tongjianyi had neither winter clothing nor cotton quilts. So as the accountants handed out the red packets of cash from the tables one by one, the inhabitants of Tongjianyi faced two difficulties: how to endure another winter, and how to make the red bundles fatter.[5]

Four months later, as Tongjianyi's farmers were transplanting the first rice crop of 1979, Chen Yun was at the next Party work conference in Beijing. After more than a decade without real power, Chen was suddenly thrust back into the center of economic policy–making, at the right hand of Deng Xiaoping. A self-taught economist, he had directed China's enormous economic expansion in the first decade after Liberation, 1949–59, a period the Chinese proudly labeled the "ten great years" (*weida de shi nian*). But after Chen's tacit opposition to the catastrophic Great Leap Forward at the end of that decade, he had faded from power.[6] Now, in 1979, Chen was seventy-four years old. Hoping at last for the chance to see his ideas for modernizing China put into practice, he used his speech at the conference to muse about the Four Modernizations—China's ambitious new economic program for modernizing agriculture, industry, science, and defense: "It would make a most beautiful picture if the targets of the Four Modernizations can be fulfilled [by the year 2000]. I also hope to be able to live another twenty years. I shall die contented if I can hear about it—I don't have to see it—one moment before my eyes are closed."[7]

5. This was in Gucheng County. On Tongjianyi see *Hubei ribao*, Jan. 2, 1979, p. 2; on Gucheng's cash-distribution meetings, see *Hubei ribao*, Jan. 2, 1981, p. 2.

6. Chen was the preeminent economic policy maker in the first four years of the People's Republic, 1949–52. After losing ground to Gao Gang in 1953, Chen regained his influence until the late 1950s. Chen was again at the center of economic policy in the aftermath of the Great Leap, but clashes with Mao over agricultural policy drove him into effective retirement from 1962 to 1978. See David M. Bachman, *Chen Yun and the Chinese Political System*, China Research Monographs no. 29 (Berkeley: Institute of East Asian Studies, 1985), chap. 2.

7. Chen's comments came in a rambling speech at the Central Committee

Wistful as Chen's vision of China at the millennium may have sounded, he was still hard-nosed about how to make it come true. He went on to taunt his colleagues about the resources that China still lacked to accomplish the vision: "I want to ask whether we have accumulated the labor force, the materials, the capital, the experience and the technology needed for the realization of the Four Modernizations? Have we or not? Speak up! No, I don't mean some time in the future, I mean now, today! Have we? Why not? You dare not say?"[8] Chen's exasperation came from years of watching as grandiose plans for China's future were drawn up and then abandoned. If the new Four Modernizations program was to be different, it would have to be nourished with great quantities of capital. In the rest of his speech, Chen made it clear where that capital must come from: the state would extract it from the countryside. The other leaders trying to make out Chen's "most beautiful picture" of a modernized China twenty years in the future may have envisioned complex technology and roaring industry. But Chen forced them to see that bringing the vision to pass meant facing the mundane and mammoth task of reviving Chinese agriculture. China's relatively backward economy still had to rely on agriculture to provide foreign exchange earnings, raw materials for light industry, and capital accumulation. For the officials at the state center,[9] no less than for China's ordinary villagers, dreams for the future—large and small—had to start down on the farm.

Thus central leaders like Chen Yun and millions of peasants like those in Tongjianyi arrived at the eve of China's rural reform with hopes to make farm output abundant. These parallel aspirations— rather grand among state officials, more modest and urgent among the peasants—created a decade of drastic change after 1978. Separate moti-

---

Work Conference in April 1979. At that time he was a vice-chairman of the Party and a member of the Standing Committee of the Politburo. Three months later he became a vice-premier of the State Council and chairman of the Financial and Economic Commission. The quotation is from Chen Yun, "Chen Yun's Speech at the CCP Central Committee Work Conference," translated in *Issues and Studies* 16 (April 1980), p. 90.

8. Ibid. I have made slight corrections in a garbled translation here.

9. The terms *center* and *central* refer to the highest level of the political hierarchy in China, including both government and Party organs, with headquarters in Beijing.

vations drove the two groups toward reform. Central leaders wanted to increase the state's claim on farm output to pay for an expensive modernization scheme. Peasants wanted richer harvests for themselves, to ease their unrelenting poverty. Searching desperately for new solutions, they pushed unsanctioned changes that radicalized the leaders' reform plans beyond recognition. Locked in a struggle against each other, state and peasant together changed the face of rural China.

This book is about that struggle between state and peasant, and the enormous social change it produced. In the years 1979–89, state and peasant fought, cooperated, cheated, stumbled, lied, and compromised their way toward reform of everything fundamental in rural life. They dismantled the commune, China's core structure of rural governance and management, and sliced the landscape into an uncountable profusion of tiny family farms. They loosened government domination of commerce and enterprise, reducing central planning and bringing to life a vast array of entrepreneurial ventures. With this creation of individual farms and businesses along with free markets in goods, credit, and labor, China's rural reform was the most massive single act of privatization in history. Wrapped within these changes were the seeds of a new life for hundreds of millions of people. The restoration of markets and family farms was at once enlivening and frightening to rural people. While the general standard of living for peasants made an astounding upward jump, people feared that a revived private economy might be inhumane to the poorer villagers. The changed development strategy also portended new tensions in the equation of rural power. The ground under the feet of state and peasantry changed as a result, altering the terrain of their perpetual contest to control rural life.

The importance of what happened in the countryside for the larger study of Chinese politics is self-evident. The rural reforms were so radical—and transformed so vast a sphere of Chinese life—that to investigate how they came about is practically to ask what drives political change in China. To answer this first large question I have used interpretive histories of the three major areas of rural reform: family farming (chapters 3 and 4); marketing (chapters 5 and 6); and privatization in land tenure, credit, labor, and entrepreneurship (chapters

7 and 8). These histories trace the tumultuous interaction between the peasantry and the state. The goal of this book is to understand how the intertwined acts of the complex state apparatus and millions of peasants transformed rural China, and how this great transformation in turn changed the political relationship between state and peasant.

The second aim, equal in weight, is to map out how China's reform experience alters our wider theoretical understanding of peasant politics and state socialism. Rather than treating China as an exotic case, I attempt to connect it to broader theories of politics. Although social scientists are in the habit of seeing China as a case by itself (and thus interesting but convenient to set aside), it would be a mistake to dismiss the rural reforms as another Chinese anomaly. The same elements that dominated China's transformation were the driving forces behind political change in other parts of the world in the late twentieth century. What were these elements? First, a struggle for power between peasant and state. Second, the reform of a state-socialist system. Third, the movement toward privatization. The second purpose of this book, therefore, is to use the Chinese case to elucidate three worldwide political phenomena: state-peasant relations, reform within state socialism, and privatization.

In China's struggle over reform, peasants demonstrated a greater capability for influencing state policy than the literature on peasant politics generally grants them. This power to influence the state is surprising since rural Chinese were living under a state-socialist system. (By state socialism, I mean nondemocratic socialism with central planning and unitary state-Party power.) State socialism places rural citizens in a position that is particularly weak, even for peasants. In capitalist societies, whether oppressive or democratic, rural people nearly always have alternative organizations and norms that compete with the state, often thwarting or skewing the state's desires. State socialism, in contrast, deprives peasants of these alternative sources of power, leaving them no open channel through which to influence politics. Yet in spite of these unfavorable conditions, Chinese peasants altered major political outcomes during Deng's rule, and on no modest scale. The most dramatic example of peasant power during the reforms was the rise of family farms. In re-creating the family farm, peasants succeeded in seizing the initiative and turning the main thrust of reform to their own ends. This is not to say that the peasantry suddenly faced down the might of the state. On the contrary, as the record of the struggle over marketing reform will show, peasant power thrived only within narrow limits. But the main point here is not peasants' customary weakness; rather, it is their surprising, significant strength. The first theoretical problem, therefore, will be how peasant power can arise under the strong state that dominates state socialism.

State socialism has generally been interpreted as an inflexible, tightly controlled system of rule. Yet, once begun, reform in state-socialist systems tends to career beyond state leaders' intentions. In China, Deng's rural reform lunged out of his government's control right from the beginning. Measures instituted as supposedly discrete adjustments had an overwhelming tendency to leap ahead to other, unplanned changes. To explain this phenomenon I will introduce the idea of reform as normal trauma in state socialism. Because of the rigid, compartmentalized structure of power in state-socialist systems, necessary changes and adjustments get bottled up and postponed, until a small, innocuous reform sets off a chain reaction of other reforms. Every change that was waiting to happen occurs in an explosive rush. Reform thus takes on a cataclysmic appearance and seems to destabilize features of the state-socialist system once believed to be unshakable. The evidence from China suggests that such traumatic outbursts are not anomalous but a recurring feature of state socialism—normal traumas. The second theoretical aim, then, is to use China's rural transformation to understand why reform takes on a life of its own in state-socialist systems.

The tendency of reform to snowball is most pronounced in the case of privatization, which poses the third theoretical problem of China's reform. The question here is why state socialism—a system ostensibly committed to collectivism—gives rise to privatization. Privatization blazed across rural China in the reform years. Once it was set loose in the realm of land tenure, it stormed through China's policies on credit, labor, and rural enterprise as well. The result was more radical change than anyone in the leadership or in the villages could have foreseen. Behind this rampaging action is a process in which each step of privatization proves economically salutary only if the next successive step is taken. Privatization thus begets more privatization, which rolls over one part of the collective economy after another. In China a conservative coalition did try to arrest this dynamic, and it succeeded in part. But the question remains: Why was privatization allowed to go as far as it did in an avowedly socialist system? China's reform suggests that privatization can be very attractive to ruling communist parties, for it helps to create powerful constituencies in society. Historically state-socialist systems have suffered from weak bases of popular support, a shortcoming that proved lethal to the Soviet-style governments of Eastern Europe. By privatizing agriculture, reform-minded governments can make allies of richer farmers, merchants, and rural entrepreneurs. Privatization can thus carve out the constituencies of social support that state-socialist systems so sorely lack.

These three theoretical problems—state-peasant relations, reform within state socialism, and privatization—all need to be carefully elaborated. That will be the task of the next chapter, where I will try to bridge the gap between two different readerships—those whose main interest is China, and those who care about China only insofar as it illuminates the rest of the world. Developing the three theoretical problems further will show why China's reform period is so rich a source for the broader analysis of social change. Assuming that not all readers have an intimate knowledge of Chinese politics, I will devote the rest of this chapter to drawing the background of the reform era.

Rural Policy under Mao Zedong

The radical changes of the reform era swept aside the world created by Mao Zedong, who dominated rural affairs from Liberation in 1949 to his death in 1976. Mao was committed to rapid industrialization and progressive rural politics, and he believed China could achieve both of these without sacrificing agricultural growth. In actual practice, however, Mao and his followers often treated farm growth as a distant third goal behind the priorities of industrialization and social change. Especially after 1966, the Maoist leadership displayed little concern with farm output, trying instead to make peasants' day-to-day life ideologically correct. This fixation on politics (as opposed to output) and industry (as opposed to agriculture) made it difficult for dissatisfied peasants or poor farm performance to influence the state. Despite Mao's lifelong dedication to peasant interests, his government eventually became all but deaf to peasant complaints of deprivation.

The first decade of Maoist rule had been more promising. Mao destroyed the pre-Liberation private farm economy, notorious for its mediocre productivity and stomach-wrenching cruelty toward Chinese peasants. After completing the enormously popular Land Reform in 1952, Mao followed up with the collectivization of farm land and, in 1958, the commune system—the basic collective farm structure that Deng Xiaoping's reforms would attack some twenty years later. At the bottom of the commune system was the production team. A team contained one or two hundred people from the same village (or sometimes several small hamlets) who owned the land collectively and shared both the work and the output. Anywhere from two to two dozen teams comprised the next-higher unit, the brigade, which ran most rural industry. At the top of the structure, overseeing roughly ten to twenty brigades and answering to outside officials, was the commune itself. The commune performed administrative duties and saw that the brigades and teams delivered their production quotas to the state.

This uniform collective structure provided a framework through which Mao's leftist leadership could pursue its consuming passion for political change. The collective organization campaigned against all the countryside's infamous social problems, including illiteracy, male supremacy, and wretched health care. The collective structure also insured a rough equality within administrative units. All the families in a production team, for example, shared in their village's wealth or poverty. Across units, however, and even more across regions, the commune system consolidated inequalities by demanding that every team, brigade, and commune be economically self-sufficient. Self-sufficiency was supposed to aid national defense and encourage local resourcefulness, but it also stifled market development. Markets for labor, credit, or goods were scarce, so people in a poor unit had little chance to find work elsewhere, to start a business, or to sell extra output outside the state plan.

These inflexible features of the commune system grew worse

during the Cultural Revolution (1966–76). Although the Cultural Revolution was mainly an urban event, its ideological rigidity seized the countryside as well. The practice of "putting politics in command" placed social and ideological priorities ahead of farm production. The leaders of the Cultural Revolution, who helped Mao to overthrow the Party's old guard, launched rural China on an exhausting effort at social transformation, with some success. Before Mao's death China established one of the best rural health-care systems in the third world. In other policy areas, though, such as rural education and women's rights, the progress was disappointing. Meanwhile, with politics in command, the Left dismissed concerns about farm output as parochial and secondary. The leadership was especially hostile to small-scale peasant production—endeavors like private vegetable plots and family enterprises. In its insistence on anticapitalist purity, the Left cut off these meager opportunities for peasants to raise their noncollective income.

Late Maoism's ambivalence about farm production had a decisive political effect as well. Devaluing farm production as secondary to other goals inoculated the state against any economic threat posed by peasants. By affecting farm output, peasant dissatisfaction can endanger state goals—provided state leaders care about rural economic performance. Peasants then possess some potential for economic blackmail. But in late Maoism the leaders were peculiarly uninterested in farm production, no matter how many declarations they churned out in support of agriculture. Deng Xiaoping, on the other hand, placed the economy as a whole first. He needed a dramatic revival in agriculture for his economic ambitions to triumph, and that need made his government vulnerable to peasant pressure. Peasants thus had the chance to influence state policy that late Maoism had denied them.

The Reform Coalition

Two years after Mao's death his opponents squeezed out his designated successor, Hua Guofeng, and took over China. At the Third Plenum in 1978 and at later high-level meetings, the main state apparatus (including the Communist Party, the State Council, and the Military Affairs Commission) fell under control of leaders aching to change the course of Chinese development. This reform-minded leadership was neither a single faction nor a loyal following obedient to a supreme leader. It was a coalition of groups bound by a common dismay with what had become of China since the economic disaster of the Great Leap Forward (1958–60). The new leaders were nearly unanimous in blaming their Maoist predecessors for the two subsequent decades of lost chances. Later, in the 1980s, divisions over politics and economics would embitter the coalition. Some leaders would feel betrayed by what became of the reforms; others would be thrown into disgrace from positions at the very top. But at least in the beginning the coalition enjoyed enough cohesion to launch the initial rural changes at the Third Plenum.

This reform coalition, which ruled China from the end of 1978 to 1989, brought together two main groups. The first was dominated by the Party old guard, conservative reformers whom Deng courted heavily throughout the 1970s to back his own political resurrection. Most of the people in this group (which included Chen Yun, Li Xiannian, Peng Zhen, Hu Qiaomu, and Yao Yilin) had achieved prominence in the 1950s but were later attacked or discarded in the Cultural Revolution. These conservatives looked back to the 1950s as China's golden age of deliberate, steady growth. They wanted to restore the prestige the Party had once enjoyed among the people. Within the Party they aimed to reinstate the old norms of discussion and consensus that were first eroded in the Great Leap, then obliterated by the Cultural Revolution. And in economics the old guard sought a return to the 1950s model of a planned economy, but this time with more flexibility, enabling farmers and enterprises to respond to price signals. The conservatives took their intellectual lead from Chen Yun and his critique of Maoist economic strategy.

The second group in the coalition agreed with the old guard's economic critique as far as it went, but was prepared for more radical experiments with markets, private enterprise, and income differentials. This group of economic liberals (which included Wan Li, Hu Yaobang, and Zhao Ziyang) was less wedded than the old guard to orthodoxies of either planning or ideology. They placed practical economic results before nearly all ideological questions, adhering to Deng's famous observation, "White cat, black cat—as long as it catches mice it's a good cat."[10] Zhao Ziyang—who rose to premier (1980) and Party general secretary (1987) before falling in the political crisis of 1989—exemplified this pragmatic approach early in the reform years as first Party secretary of Sichuan Province (1975–80). During the later part of Zhao's tenure in Sichuan, if a rural innovation was robust enough to survive and deliver economic results, then it won his support. Other leaders shared Zhao's view that economic performance should be the main criterion for reform policy. Together they composed the group that backed the more extreme economic reforms, including freer markets, drastic reductions in the scope of central planning, and autonomy for all manner of enterprises, both public and private.

The key figure joining the two parts of the coalition was Deng Xiaoping. Deng shared the old Party values of the conservatives, but he had an openness to experimentation that tied him to the market-oriented liberals as well. In the heyday of the reform coalition in the late 1970s and first half of the 1980s, Deng's personal backing was instrumental in bringing more liberal leaders into top positions, including Hu Yaobang as Party general secretary, Zhao Ziyang as premier, and Wan Li as head of the National People's Congress. When the coalition disintegrated in the late 1980s over questions of political reform, Deng's decision not to support some of these leaders sealed their downfall as well. For at least seven years, however, from 1978 until the beginnings of trouble in 1985, Deng held the coalition together with his vision of new possibilities for the Chinese countryside.

Deng Xiaoping versus the Left

Ambitious thinking drove both Deng and his reform program. Deng's personal style belied his ambition, and this at first made his leadership difficult to interpret. He made a fetish of appearing modest in his leadership role as well as in his goals for China. He did not seek to elevate himself above his col-

10. Quoted in Chi Hsin, *Teng Hsiao-ping: A Political Biography* (Hong Kong: Cosmos Books, 1978), pp. 38–39.

leagues with preeminent rank in Party or government. He was never premier or head of state, and did not covet the title of Party chairman or general secretary.[11] He eschewed grandiose plans. Not even his all-embracing reform program received a properly imposing name; it went by an old name used for earlier policy packages—the Four Modernizations.[12]

This apparent modesty built Deng's image as a practical leader, and for years his name appeared in the American press tied to the inevitable adjective "pragmatic." Deng's famed pragmatism meant a tough-minded economic approach to China's problems, in contrast to the millennial visions of perfection and equality pursued by China's Left. But the impression that he had more modest aims than his Maoist predecessors was misleading. In fact Deng's ambition was immense. As the reform coalition's paramount enforcer, power broker, and final arbiter, Deng mounted a program for change that matched the scope of such massive movements as the Great Leap Forward. In a single decade after 1978 he attempted to transform China's relation to the world economy, to achieve both industrial and macroeconomic reform, to modernize the army, to rescue the Party from ruinous internal struggles, and to revivify Chinese agriculture. Of all these problems the most overwhelming was agriculture.

And it was there that Deng's supposed modesty was most misleading. In a characteristically practical shift, he jettisoned the socialist ideals of the Left and concentrated on two concrete goals for agriculture: increasing production and procuring more of the farm product for the state. The blunt resolve with which Deng pursued these goals enhanced his reputation as a pragmatist but gave the false impression that his rural reform program would be modest and straightforward. In fact, making production and procurement paramount—superseding all other rural policy goals—opened the door to rural change of

11. Deng headed the Party Secretariat before his fall in the Cultural Revolution, but never took the position back when he was rehabilitated.

12. Zhou Enlai had originally coined the slogan "Four Modernizations" in 1975. Hua Guofeng, who succeeded Mao and was overthrown by Deng, inherited the term, promoting his quasi-Maoist policies as the Four Modernizations. As much as Deng scorned Hua Guofeng, after deposing him he nevertheless kept the same title for his own anti-Maoist program rather than christening it with something appropriately bombastic.

an all-encompassing nature. As long as production and procurement stood to gain, no change was out of bounds and no traditional socialist goal was sacred. Thus the apparently narrow, economic focus of reform was a license for unprecedented change: it meant relinquishing the fundamental aims that ostensibly had guided rural policy for decades. Social welfare, income equality among villagers, medical extension programs, women's rights, and rural education all became secondary to economic ends.

The enormity of this change was sometimes lost on Westerners, to whom pragmatism, nonideological incentives, and a market-oriented farm economy seemed only natural. But to Chinese the trend toward privatization and ruthless competition was almost unthinkable in light of what rural policy had been before the reforms. The emphasis of late Maoism on rural social change was so extreme that some leaders came to regard economic questions as epiphenomenal. It was thought that as long as the political situation was in order, production would take care of itself. A theoretical article written in the early 1970s in the murky prose typical of that period explained the relation between politics and economics: "Where the revolution is grasped well and the Party line and policies are thoroughly implemented, with the contradictions between the enemy and ourselves and contradictions among the people correctly handled, the socialist consciousness of the masses raised and all positive factors brought into full play, it follows that production will develop at full speed."[13] With this cavalier attitude toward the economy, the Left was free to look upon rural China as the grand stage of social experimentation.

The contrast with Deng Xiaoping could not have been more stark. Deng's view of rural China had nothing to do with social progress, equality, or other traditional goals of socialism. He saw the countryside as a desperately poor place that needed to be enriched. He also regarded agriculture as China's only source for the raw materials, capital, food, and markets required to achieve the Four Modernizations. Although the social program of his leftist rivals may have been tinged with grandiosity, Deng appeared to have no social goals

13. Li Chien, "Attach Importance to the Revolution in the Superstructure," *Peking Review* 16 (Aug. 24, 1973), p. 6.

for rural China at all. And while the Left had adopted super-heroic production targets to encourage people to overreach themselves, Deng set about the business of figuring out exactly what the state could get out of the countryside. Consequently, if one set the Left's stated objectives against Deng's targets for the Four Modernizations, Deng looked restrained and pragmatic indeed. But in reality his rural economic program was the more ambitious of the two, for he took its targets seriously. Nowhere did Deng's ambition to modernize China demand more than from agriculture.

Chen Yun and the Opening Strategy for Reform

For the economic strategy to revive agriculture and bring his wider ambitions to life, Deng Xiaoping turned in 1978 to Chen Yun. Chen's critique of Maoist development strategy provided the initial intellectual foundation for reform.[14] Like virtually all the reform leaders, Chen believed that unless the farm economy was wrenched from its depression, there would be no Four Modernizations. Chen's first goal was to free agriculture from its peculiar status in the legacy of Mao Zedong.

Mao had seen himself as the originator of a non-Soviet development strategy that raised agriculture from the degradation to which Stalin had consigned it. Stalin bled Soviet agriculture mercilessly in the service of industry. Mao claimed (though his practice deviated sharply from his theory) that he was attempting to create a more balanced economy with stout backing for rural development. By the time of Mao's death, however, the Chinese economy had become a crossbreed of Soviet and anti-Soviet features that gave little support to ag-

14. Chen Yun was the most influential of the thinkers whose critique of Maoist economic strategy shaped the reforms. Others in this tradition included Sun Yefang, Xue Muqiao, Hu Qiaomu, and the already deceased Deng Zihui. For a sense of this critique, the most easily accessible works are the collection of Chen Yun's writings in Nicholas R. Lardy and Kenneth Lieberthal, eds., *Chen Yun's Strategy for China's Development: A Non-Maoist Alternative* (Armonk, N.Y.: M. E. Sharpe, 1983), and Xue Muqiao's book, *China's Socialist Economy* (Beijing: Foreign Languages Press, 1981). Also see Bachman, *Chen Yun,* which includes an extensive bibliography of Chen's works.

riculture. From the Soviet side China inherited central planning, high rates of nonfarm investment, collectivized agriculture, and a diversion of resources to heavy industry. From Maoist thinking China acquired a distrust of markets, private property, and material incentives, plus a tendency to use economic organization to promote socialist consciousness. Combining these Soviet and Maoist traits had produced an offspring with unnatural proportions. The agricultural limb of this hybrid was stunted. The industrial limb was heavy with unchecked growth.

Chen believed this blend of features retarded China's overall growth by crippling agriculture.[15] The fundamental problem, as he saw it, was low agricultural incentives and high state investment. The investment rate was excessive, with funding skewed to heavy industry. This encouraged rapid expansion of the urban work force and pressed agriculture to supply and feed the workers cheaply. Agriculture could not carry these burdens, not only because it had been denied investment funds, but because incentives for farmers to produce the surplus demanded by the state were too small. Farm-good procurement prices were set too low. Furthermore, central planning was so heavy-handed and inflexible that it prevented farmers from pursuing the subsidiary production that might have elicited their enthusiasm. And finally, since light industry had also been slighted, farmers had little reason to want to make more money even if they could: there were hardly any consumer goods to spend it on.

Returned to power with the reform coalition in 1978, Chen Yun opened his long-deferred attack on this malaise. His strategy for restoring agriculture's role in a balanced economy embraced three sets of tactics: one in the economy as a whole, a second in agriculture, and a third in central planning. The macroeconomic tactic was to reduce the rate of investment while shifting funds from heavy industry into light industry and, to a smaller extent, into agriculture—a shift known in Chinese parlance as "readjustment." At the same time, he

15. I have concentrated on Chen Yun here because of the remarkable degree to which the Third Plenum reforms reflected his economic thought. For an analysis of the consistency in Chen's thought over the decades, as well as the influence of his ideas in the early reforms, see Nicholas R. Lardy and Kenneth Lieberthal's introduction to *Chen Yun's Strategy.*

sought to limit the influence of the heavy-industry ministries in the State Planning Commission. This first set of changes was meant to bolster agriculture's position in the economy. Chen complemented this "readjustment" with a second set of policies to boost material incentives to farmers. He dispensed with appeals to farmers' socialist consciousness, offering instead higher procurement prices on farm goods. To connect farmers' income more directly with their individual work effort, the level of accounting in the communes was lowered from production teams to small work groups of a few families. In work groups, farmers drew their pay from the collective output of a much smaller number of people. They could more easily see a personal reward for working harder. Farmers also got the chance to supplement income with produce from enlarged private plots. As his third tactic, Chen engineered a switch from production planning to price planning—that is, using relative price differentials to obtain a given crop mix instead of commanding cropping areas by fiat. This more flexible planning system allowed each farming area to plant more lucrative crops suited to its own ecological conditions. Chen hoped that these three sets of reforms would encourage peasants to see their personal interests as intimately bound up with a rebirth in the rural sector. And with a healthy farm sector, Chen believed, China could achieve the balanced growth it needed to modernize. In a sweeping political victory, Deng Xiaoping succeeded in winning the support of the Third Plenum for all of Chen Yun's reforms.

Had the changes in China's countryside gone no further than this initial program, the adoption of Chen's policy package would have been a textbook case in meticulous, successful reform. But this original plan—the crowning achievement of the Third Plenum—was only a shadow of the radical reforms to come. To Chen's dismay, rural change immediately lurched ahead of what the Third Plenum had mandated. Even before the documents announcing the reforms arrived at the local level in 1979, many villages had undertaken changes that made the new policies redundant or obsolete. The initiative had already passed from the state center to peasants, local cadres, and a few maverick provincial leaders. The storm of change that followed swept everything with it, as if it were an uncontrollable natural force.

The main blast passed by the end of 1985. Although smaller squalls were still swirling in certain areas of rural life at the end of the 1980s, by then it was possible to see how much the reforms had altered the countryside.

The change was astounding. Land tenure, rent, taxation, the sexual division of labor, inheritance, credit, religious practices, income, private enterprise, collectivism, migration—hardly anything that mattered in rural life emerged untouched. The reformers could be justly proud of what came to pass by 1985: record leaps in farm output, with a richer share of procurements for the state; dazzling diversification of the rural economy; and huge increases in peasant income, matched with new supplies of consumer goods reaching the villages. Yet Chen and his old-guard allies were not pleased. On the contrary, they were shaken, hardly able to believe all that the storm had simultaneously taken with it. Before the 1980s ended, the communes were gone, peasants had fought the state plan to a standoff, and the internal logic of privatization was driving state policy in directions no one could have imagined at the time of Chen's policy triumph in 1978.

China's rural reform brought a time of uncertainty, an era open to new possibilities beyond the expectations of even the most powerful people. Farmers, local officials, bureaucrats, and state leaders tried to control the day-to-day changes that were altering a way of life. They all took part in the contest between ordinary people and a strong centralized government, with both sides trying to remake the Chinese countryside.

Chapter Two

Bases of Interpretation

China's era of rural reform raises many theoretical problems, but three stand out: state-peasant relations, reform under state socialism, and privatization. Each of these problems cuts close to the heart of what drove reform in China, yet each is anchored in a crucial issue of world politics.

Peasant and State

A basic question raised by China's reform is whether peasants have a significant influence on political and social change under a strong state.[1] My research indicates that peas-

---

1. A note on what I mean by *state* and *peasant* might prevent later confusion. This book uses the Weberian concept of the state: the totality of administrative, bureaucratic, and coercive apparatuses. In ordinary speech, Chinese customarily refer to "the party" (*dang*) or "the government" (*zhengfu*). These two structures, along with the military, are the main components of the Chinese state. To capture this totality, from the highest reaches of power down to the local official presence, Chinese speak of "the state" quite commonly and naturally in a way that Americans (except for academics) do not. For this purpose they use the word *guojia*, which in certain contexts may also mean "country" or "nation."

Peasant in this book follows the meaning of the Chinese word for peasant, *nongmin*. Taken narrowly, *nongmin* can be a synonym for *farmer*. But its general meaning is much broader, encompassing nearly all ordinary rural people, whether they are farmers, laborers, fishermen, truck-drivers, or even village factory workers. Here I intend this broader meaning for the word *peasant*. The term in Chinese also implies a separateness from urban society and can carry a derogatory flavor (like its English counterpart) on the lips of city people. That sense of separateness

ants living in ordinary, nonrevolutionary circumstances have a greater capacity to change political outcomes than they are generally given credit for. Under certain conditions of state-peasant interaction— conditions the Chinese case helps to specify—this capacity is not limited to resistance against state policy but can attain a significant level of creativity, in effect contributing to the making of policy. Given the Chinese state's putative strength and the obvious political weakness of the peasantry, this finding is counterintuitive.

The idea that peasants could play any decisive role in creating rural reform challenges the long-standing pattern of state-peasant relations in the People's Republic of China. Peasants may have made the Chinese Revolution that finally triumphed in 1949, but the Revolution did not empower them. Like the rest of society in the decades after 1949, the peasantry had little strength against the power of the postrevolutionary state. By the late 1970s this pattern of state domination of peasants was firmly established. Therefore analysts have generally assumed that a change of the magnitude of Deng Xiaoping's reforms could occur only under state control. Two compelling types of reasoning underlie this expectation of a domineering state: theoretical reasoning and reasoning from the historical record.

Theoretical Reasons for Assuming Peasant Weakness

Theoretically, one way of assessing the expected distribution of power between Chinese peasants and the Party-state apparatus is by analyzing the relative strength of state and society.[2] The relevant variant of this body of theory sees a mutual, reciprocal relation between state and society. The domestic political powers of state and society are interactive and define each other.[3] Under criteria devised by theorists

---

is also intended here. Culturally, hierarchically, and in the realm of life chances, peasants live a different life from other people in China.

   2. The broader tradition from which this line of thinking comes is the analysis of civil society and the state, with roots stretching from Weber and Marx back to Hobbes and Locke.

   3. Of the various analysts of state power, Alfred Stepan is clearest on this point. See his "State Power and the Strength of Civil Society in the Southern Cone of Latin America," in Peter B. Evans, Dietrich Rueschemeyer, and Theda Skocpol, eds., *Bringing the State Back In* (Cambridge: Cambridge University Press, 1985), pp. 317–43.

in this tradition, China would be classified as having a strong state and a weak society—the worst possible combination for the growth of peasant power. The Chinese state fits Stephen Krasner's definition of a strong state as "one that is able to remake the society and culture in which it exists."[4] The People's Republic demonstrated this ability in a sustained series of massive intrusions into society, at once creative and devastating. These included Land Reform, collectivization, the Great Leap Forward, and the Cultural Revolution. Having executed these wrenching transformations, the Chinese state clearly merits inclusion among the strongest states—those that can "change economic institutions, values, and patterns of interaction among private groups."[5] The state's interventions after the Revolution increased its relative power both by eliminating rival claims from "enemy" classes in society and by winning the respect and support of the surviving classes. Land Reform, for example, destroyed the landlord class. At the same time it won from the peasantry such immense good will that only two decades of catastrophic blunders, beginning with the Great Leap, could dissipate it. (Enthusiasm for Land Reform was especially strong in southern China, where peasants lived with extremely high tenancy rates.)

This achievement of legitimacy gave the Party elite enormous power over Chinese society. In assessing strategic elites who attempt "a new pattern of relationships between the state and civil society,"[6] Alfred Stepan identifies as strongest those that go beyond coercion as a means of habituating society to obedience. They succeed in the "installation of new state structures that achieve what Antonio Gramsci would term 'hegemonic' acceptance in civil society."[7] The new Chinese state not only possessed the power to restructure society, but also secured the people's belief that its actions were correct and legitimate.

On the opposite side of this relationship, Chinese society has been extremely weak. One useful measure of a society's strength is its

---

4. Stephen D. Krasner, *Defending the National Interest* (Princeton: Princeton University Press, 1978), p. 56.

5. Ibid.

6. Alfred Stepan, *The State and Society: Peru in Comparative Perspective* (Princeton: Princeton University Press, 1978), p. xiii.

7. Ibid.

richness in organizations competing with the state for people's allegiance. Joel Migdal has shown that strong third-world societies, for example, are suffused with "tenacious elements blocking state aspirations,"[8] usually organizations with alternative sets of rules regulating behavior. Such organizations not only enforce separate, nonstate norms with rewards and sanctions, but also give meaning to people's lives through alternative symbols, myths, or ideologies.

Alternative organizations of this sort were once numerous and formidable in China. Clans, secret societies, private companies, foreign enterprises, patron-client relationships, religious organizations, and solidary villages all commanded people's loyalty to varying degrees. But as these organizations repeatedly failed to protect people during more than a century of rural crisis, peasants switched loyalty to one organization that did offer protection: the Communist Party. (In this case, the Party earned the strongest loyalties in northern China, where its long presence during revolution and Japanese invasion won peasant gratitude.) The alternative repositories of peasant loyalty fared badly after the Revolution. The great exception was patron-client relationships, which thrived in the bureaucratized life of the People's Republic. But the Communist Party was exceedingly jealous of loyalties to large alternative organizations and completely destroyed some of them. Only a few larger associations remained strong, as family organizations did, though they lived a shadowy existence on the edge of legitimacy. Most alternative organizations were suppressed, surviving only underground or behind the closed doors of private homes. Peasants were left standing alone to face the new state they had brought to power. While saving itself from destruction, rural society created a state against which it was almost powerless.

China would therefore be classified as a rare third-world case of a weak society and a strong state. Many analysts have argued that such maximal state power occurs only in the period immediately after a revolution. As Krasner observed, "It is not that the state is so strong during such periods, but that the society is weak because existing patterns

---

8. Joel S. Migdal, *Strong Societies and Weak States: State-Society Relations and State Capabilities in the Third World* (Princeton: Princeton University Press, 1988), p. 25.

of behavior have been shattered."[9] In China, this period of shattered norms has lasted since the Revolution. Living in a society bereft of non-state organizations to uphold alternative norms, Chinese peasants should, according to theory, also suffer a crippling poverty of power.

Historical Reasons for Assuming Peasant Weakness

In this theoretical setting of a strong state and a weak society, rural change would be expected to occur only under state initiative and control. Indeed, the historical record fits this prediction—at least until the time of Deng Xiaoping's reforms. Most China experts have adhered (quite correctly) to a general image of the state as instigator of change. The totalitarian school promotes this image in its crudest form, with a rural populace "mobilized" to perform the will of the state center and its dictator. But even the most subtle analysts with an intimate, sympathetic knowledge of the peasantry present a composite picture of unrestrained state power becoming ever more insensitive to peasants. At first, with the Revolution finally won, the Communist Party seemed to pursue the will of the majority of peasants. For example, William Hinton describes in *Fanshen* a partnership between the peasantry and the Communist Party that is genuinely in the peasants' interests, at the time of Land Reform in the late 1940s.[10] Among the throngs of rural poor, Land Reform was hugely popular. Hinton's book conveys the exhilaration of this first step toward empowerment of peasants and suggests the potential for this process to continue after Land Reform. But even in the historical moment captured in *Fanshen*, the roles in the partnership are clearly defined: though the peasants' power is at long last realized, leadership belongs to the Party. In fact, without conscious control and direction of peasant energies by the Party, Hinton says, Land Reform could not have succeeded: "The military potential, the productive capacity, and the political genius of the peasants had to be cultivated, mobilized, and organized, not simply 'liberated.' "[11]

9. Krasner, *Defending the National Interest*, p. 56.

10. William Hinton, *Fanshen: A Documentary of Revolution in a Chinese Village* (New York: Vintage Books, 1966). I refer to "Party" rather than "state" in discussing Hinton's work because he was investigating Land Reform at an early stage in a liberated area just before the establishment of the People's Republic.

11. Ibid., p. 605.

Such "liberation"—with peasants autonomously in control—never occurred.[12] Instead, as the state became more adept at harnessing and steering peasant proclivities, peasants became the objects rather than the subjects of rural transformation. In Vivienne Shue's definitive study of farm collectivization in the 1950s, the image is still of a relatively benign state working in the peasants' interests, but with far more sophisticated methods than in Land Reform.[13] Here, midway through the first decade of the People's Republic, we see the state using tax policy, carefully crafted material rewards, preferential contracts, and credit management to shape the economic landscape. With these refined incentives, the state induces peasants to choose collectivization as the fulfillment of their self-interest. Shue explicitly rejects the idea of a strong state coercing a weak society. The socialist transformation of agriculture, she says, cannot be explained "as the sheer imposition by organized force of new values and systems on a feeble (or defiant) old natural society."[14] Yet the image of peasant and state she presents has already changed from the unequal partnership seen in *Fanshen*. Empowerment is no longer on the agenda. In the immense movement to collectivize agriculture that Shue describes, the subject is clearly the Party-state. Her analysis focuses on the Party's masterful policy implementation and shaping of peasant choices. Shue emphasizes the ability of peasant cadres to obstruct or accelerate the progress of collectivization, to be sure, as well as the Party's vigilant monitoring of local desires. But the instigator of change is the Party. Peasants, although canny and alert to their own interests, are mostly the object of the Party's growing political skill.

After the Great Leap Forward, which left 20 million dead from famine,[15] the partnership between peasant and state dissolved com-

12. For an explanation of declining Party responsiveness to peasants after the Revolution, see Brantly Womack, "The Party and the People: Revolutionary and Postrevolutionary Politics in China and Vietnam," *World Politics* 39 (July 1987), pp. 479–507.

13. Vivienne Shue, *Peasant China in Transition: The Dynamics of Development toward Socialism, 1949–1956* (Berkeley: University of California Press, 1980).

14. Ibid., pp. 333–34.

15. This estimate of mortality is in the low to middle range. See Penny Kane, *Famine in China, 1959–61: Demographic and Social Implications* (New York: St. Martin's Press, 1988).

pletely. Accordingly, in intimate portraits of post-Leap rural politics, the image of peasant powerlessness against the state's will is firmly in place. In *Chen Village*, the highly praised chronicle of one peasant community through the 1960s and 1970s, for example, an erratic state makes peasants the target of its mania for ideological correctness.[16] The state's relentless ideological assault, as portrayed in this book, corrupts peasants by teaching them to conspire in the manipulation of the official political vocabulary to win personal advantage. By the late 1970s, according to the authors, "the peasantry had become exhausted with a political rhetoric that all too often had been employed to bludgeon a minority of villagers and to enforce reticence and conformity among the majority."[17]

Thus there are two sets of reasons driving an expectation that Deng Xiaoping's reforms would be state-led, with peasants following, obeying, and responding to the state's will. From a theoretical point of view, the peasantry was embedded in a weak society facing an exceptionally strong state. And in the historical record of the People's Republic, peasants had been steadily diminished into the object—not the subject—of rural change. In this theoretical and historical setting, the capacity of peasants to control their own lives, much less to alter the direction of the state's rural policy, appeared minuscule.

The Source of Peasant Power

Contrary to these expectations, peasants played an active, creative role in the reform era. Although they never possessed a coercive capacity to make the state act against its will, they nevertheless asserted their power to influence, alter, and even create the substance of fundamental rural policies. Under Deng, peasants exercised this narrow species of power, creating possibilities that state leaders had not conceived of and leading the state to choose these peasant creations as policy. At the lowest magnitude of influence, Chinese peasants manipulated the state's reform package, shifting the effect of new policies to benefit farmers more than the state. Reform of the procurement

16. Anita Chan, Richard Madsen, and Jonathan Unger, *Chen Village: The Recent History of a Peasant Community in Mao's China* (Berkeley: University of California Press, 1984).
17. Ibid., p. 281.

and marketing system is the outstanding example of such manipulation.

At the next level of influence, peasants pushed certain reforms much farther than they were meant to go, forcing state leaders to stretch policy far beyond their original intentions. This took place in the first reorganization of collective work and in the later reform of credit, labor, and land alienation. And at their peak influence, peasants wrested the initiative from the state: they created social and economic changes on their own, which the state adopted as official policy after the fact. This assertion of peasant will occurred in the early movement that radicalized the entire reform era—the reinvention of family farms.

How could any of this happen? How could a quiescent peasant society assert itself against the same state that had overpowered it for decades? And what are the limits to such peasant power? The evidence from the reform period shows that Chinese peasants gained the chance to assert some control over their lives because they were able to make a hostage of the state's primary domestic policy goal, the economic program known as the Four Modernizations.

To understand how Chinese peasants could attain this position of limited strength, we can examine the potential sources of peasant power in a state-peasant relationship. Consider the opening position between peasant and state. Under conditions of a strong state and a weak society, the peasantry has only one essential asset: initial control over the harvest. If society is truly weak, then peasants lack the political assets that have given them their famous place in the history of resistance—intransigent clan organizations, millenarian fervor, secret societies, social banditry, and revolutionary base areas. The one source of power remaining to them is their primary position in agriculture. Peasants plant the crops, and their hands are the first to touch the harvest. State socialism does nothing to alter this fundamental premise of peasant political life. In China no system of collectivization has ever changed the fact that peasants reap the grain and pile it on the village threshing floor. It is up to the state to wrest the harvest from the peasants. The state needs the farm product to feed the cities, to earn foreign exchange, to accumulate capital, and to supply industry with raw materials. In the game of state-peasant relations, therefore, the state must make the first move to challenge the position of the peasants.

The state has several means available to seize the farm product. In addition to taxation and price manipulation, many strong states have recourse to compulsory procurements of farm goods under central planning.[18] But more important than the method is the question of how aggressively the state squeezes farmers. The assault on the harvest may be mild or vicious, depending upon the state's ultimate goals. Even among socialist countries, state goals—that is, the state's basic domestic project—can vary enormously. Certain types of basic project are relatively impervious to the threat implied by peasants' initial control over the harvest; the state can grab farm output as aggressively as it likes. But, as I will explain below, there are also basic projects that are acutely vulnerable to sabotage if peasants exploit their position in agriculture as a weapon against the state. And this is why peasant power flourished in China's reform era. When balanced growth is the state's ultimate domestic goal, as it was under Deng, it maximizes the potency of the peasants' one political asset—their primary place in agriculture.

To clarify this explanation of peasant power under a strong state, let me suggest three ideal types of state project, each with its own goals in the countryside: (1) social transformation, (2) rapid industrialization, and (3) balanced economic growth. Naturally, these projects may overlap in practice, but here I want to consider them separately. Each project contains an inherent stance toward peasant control of the harvest and therefore implies a different limit on the state's aggressiveness in responding to peasant power.

If the state's basic project is social transformation of the countryside—promoting equality, changing gender roles, altering attitudes, or creating a fundamental change in social organization—then peasant power is likely to be small. This follows logically from the assumption that peasants' main asset is their primacy in agriculture: a state that prizes social goals above economic growth will not be threatened by

18. This is because nearly all contemporary strong states with large peasantries sprang from revolutions, and many such states, like the Soviet Union and China, attempted some form of socialist development with central procurement systems.

peasant influence over agricultural output. Peasants will retain some measure of power only if their voluntary cooperation is required to implement the state's social program, as was the case during Land Reform in China. But for less popular social changes, or for transformations forced upon an unwilling countryside, the state can proceed without peasant cooperation. Alienating the peasantry with an unpopular social program may have high economic costs, including farm stagnation or reduced extraction of rural surpluses, but if the state counts up its successes by noneconomic criteria these costs can be absorbed. Such a state may antagonize peasants in pursuit of its social or ideological agenda without endangering its main project. Thus in China it has been during periods of leftist concern with progressive forms of social organization that peasants have had the least power over their lives. For instance, the leaders who held sway through most of the Cultural Revolution decade cared fervently about creating an ideologically correct rural society but disdained wearisome farm production figures. To them politics superseded everything, including pedestrian economic questions. They therefore scorned any economic threat posed by discontented peasants, and peasant dissatisfaction swelled dismally under their rule.

Peasant power is also very low when the state's basic project is rapid industrialization. Here peasants' control over the primary source of capital accumulation represents a menace to the state's project. Outright hostility toward the peasantry is therefore the hallmark of the pure form of rapid industrialization, Stalinism. Stalinism reduces the countryside to a target of accumulation, pressed mercilessly in the service of industry. Thus farm collectivization becomes a matter not of social transformation but of political conquest. Procurements of agricultural goods become predatory, brutally expanded both to obtain more of the farm product and to subdue the producers. Peasant power withers under this condition because the state mounts a relentless attack upon the peasants' main political asset: control over the harvest. Under the state bent on social transformation, this asset is merely irrelevant to state goals. But under the Stalinist state, this control so threatens the state's basic project that it becomes a provocation, grounds for war against the peasants. The Stalinist state seeks to eradicate it. Although China has never experienced pure Stalinism, it approached this condition in the bleeding of the countryside in the Great Leap Forward. Peasant helplessness against the state was reflected in the horrible famine that followed.[19]

In contrast, when the state chooses balanced economic growth as its basic project, it maximizes the power peasants derive from their primacy in agriculture. Balanced economic growth means two things. First, that the state genuinely cares about economic growth—not just empty slogans or fanfare celebrating economic plans that never come to pass. This focus on real growth also implies that the state prizes economic expansion above other concerns, such as ideological correctness or social progress. Here balanced growth might be distinguished from the intermittent leftist swings of the Maoist era, when leaders paid less attention to the economy as a whole than to political issues. Second, a basic project of balanced economic growth means that no major sector of the economy will be slighted to promote exclusive development of another sector. Here again, balanced growth contrasts with the programs of the Maoist era, which (despite the rhetoric) skewed investment to heavy industry while slighting light industry, consumer goods, and especially agriculture. A project of balanced growth necessarily treats agriculture more kindly, not only for the health of the farm sector itself but because agriculture must flourish to provide new stores of raw materials needed for light industry and for consumer goods (such as clothing and foodstuffs).

A state that makes balanced growth its basic project is therefore forced to treat the peasants' position in agriculture with respect. Obtaining a larger farm product without harming the (often fragile) health of a farm economy is crucial to the state's enterprise. That means loosening peasants' initial control over the harvest without alienating them. Instead of wrenching crops away by force, the state will choose milder means like raising farm-gate prices. The state must take pains to win peasants' enthusiasm, encouraging creativity to diversify the rural economy. Under these conditions, the peasantry's power against the state reaches its zenith. The state will handle this

19. See Thomas P. Bernstein, "Stalinism, Famine, and Chinese Peasants: Grain Procurements during the Great Leap Forward," *Theory and Society* 13 (May 1984), pp. 339–77.

power gingerly, displaying unwonted sensitivity to peasant dissatisfaction and openness to peasant initiatives.

This is precisely the condition that prevailed in China under
Deng Xiaoping. Having made the economic goals of the Four Modernizations their exclusive priority, the leaders feared the reaction of
the peasantry if they continued the draconian, extortionate rural policies of the past. Deng's new program required not only the peasants'
goods but their cooperation. Force would have been counterproductive, crushing the very peasant energies the state needed to elicit. They
therefore gave peasants unprecedented leeway to experiment, then
followed the peasants' lead in one policy area after another. The state
did not always willingly grant this license to innovate; peasants often
had to seize the initiative, pressing policy beyond the timid intentions
of the leaders. The acquiescence of the state derived from its need for
balanced economic growth, not from a lack of stomach. As the 1989
slaughter in Beijing testifies, the state was still capable of ruthlessness;
a ruthless assault on the peasants' position in the heart of the agricultural economy, however, would have been self-defeating. With the
state bent on growth, peasant power was at its peak.

The Irony of State Socialism

Specifying the conditions that maximize the *potential* of peasant
power still leaves a question—how could peasants *actually* exercise
power? In a weak society, how could they assert themselves in any
coherent way? The logical assumption is that without organization,
peasants would squander their potential influence in a random expenditure of individual energies. Without farmers' unions, political
organizations, strong clans, religious identities, and the like, there is
nothing to bind peasant desires into a cohesive drive. In China especially, where state socialism systematically suppressed alternative organizations and identities, the notion of peasants influencing politics
would appear to be hopeless—regardless of their strategic position in
agriculture. The question, therefore, is what enabled peasants to realize their potential influence in the reform years? The answer, oddly
enough, is the structure of state socialism itself.

Analysts of the totalitarian school have long argued that state
socialism atomizes people, isolating them as individuals helpless
against an all-powerful state. But the essential point that eludes the

totalitarian school is that people are atomized as members of a class. Workers under state socialism live lives defined by the state as appropriate for workers. Peasants live within the social forms approved for peasants. Intellectuals likewise have their prescribed role and way of life. The consequence is that class assumes extraordinary importance in social existence. With great numbers of people thrown into the same social circumstances—that is, the way of life prescribed for their class—class becomes the very definition of the individual's relation to society and the state. The irony, of course, is that state socialism, far from liberating people from class, makes class a more salient feature of social existence than under many forms of capitalism. And there is a further twist in this irony. By placing great numbers of people in very similar, prescribed circumstances, state socialism unwittingly creates the possibility of mass action by disorganized, atomized individuals. The individuals may indeed be isolated and feel helpless, but because so many have been reduced to the same status and face the same conditions, they may unintentionally react to openings for change with overwhelming unity and in overwhelming numbers.

This atomized mass action occurred in China during the reform years. Peasants with no plan, no communication, and often no knowledge of each other's actions behaved as if acting in concert. Unanimity of action came from sameness of circumstance. For years China had imposed uniform policies on an exquisitely varied farm ecology. People tilling wet rice in the hilly south were locked into the same commune structure as farmers growing wheat on the North China Plain. The miserably poor communes of Gansu had to follow the same models as the rich suburban communes of Shanghai. Toward the end of Mao's life, during the heyday of the Left, this enforced uniformity grew still more rigid. When the state's grip loosened slightly after Mao died in 1976, the peasant backlash in certain regions was strangely united. In the villages that had hurt most under the Left—in poor districts, in mountainous areas, and all across the rice lands from Sichuan to Anhui—peasants pushed state policy in certain common directions. These peasants were in no way organized. What they lacked in organization they made up in sheer numbers. Though peasants were atomized, the body of rural China moved because so many of its atoms lunged in the same direction at the same time.

In this way the potential for peasant power was realized where no one would have thought it possible. Given their key position at the harvest, their strength as a class under state socialism, and the state's desire for balanced growth, Chinese peasants were able to change rural life as actively and effectively as the state did, so that neither side was fully in control of the outcome.

Reform under State Socialism

The second theoretical problem raised by China's rural transformation is why reform is so volatile in state socialist systems. The Chinese case shows that reform in state socialism tends to multiply in a compulsion for further reform, outrunning the intentions of the nominal policy-makers. Deng's government had to contend not only with peasant power but with this self-propelling tendency of reform. This idea that broad, state-initiated change can escape the state's control goes against common assumptions about the exercise of power in state socialism.

No school of thought has influenced Western perceptions of state socialism so deeply as the totalitarian school, in spite of all the evidence contradicting its premises.[20] This influence has resulted in a predilection to see power—including the power to steer reform—as lodged almost exclusively at the top of the state-socialist hierarchy. The main challenge to such a totalitarian interpretation of China came with the Cultural Revolution, when chaos and mass attacks on the Communist Party undermined the totalitarian-school premise of complete state control over society. Yet the image of Mao Zedong as supreme leader—both above the fray of the Cultural Revolution and somehow behind it all—gave continuing credence to the totalitarian notion that all real power was concentrated at the highest reaches of the system. When Deng Xiaoping finally succeeded Mao, he inherited the aura of all-powerful leader, an image the Western press promoted as actively as the Chinese press did. Although some Western scholars pointed out that Deng was likely to practice a more collegial leader-

---

20. The events of 1989–91 in Eastern Europe and the Soviet Union are only the most recent and dramatic instances of actual practice defying the totalitarian model.

ship style than Mao, our popular press portrayed him as China's next dictator—although a strangely benign one, committed to massive reform. Upon reaching the pinnacle of leadership, Deng became the West's preferred version of Mao, an enlightened despot atop a command structure that would remake Chinese society in a quasi-Western guise: pragmatic, capitalist, open to world trade, nonideological. Yet even as the Western press cheered the change, its interpretation of Deng's power to inculcate these new "Western" values throughout the Chinese populace remained peculiarly the same. The totalitarian image survived: the supreme leader of the all-powerful state center could command a uniform response by society. Only this time, the command was to reform.

This image of reform blossomed in such Western publications as *Time* magazine. Deng Xiaoping was *Time*'s Man of the Year in 1979 and again in 1986. But when the desire for change in China outstripped Deng's limited vision in 1989, he slaughtered democracy activists—to the disappointment of *Time*'s publishers, who quickly anointed Mikhail Gorbachev Man of the Decade. The error here is not in commending reformers; rather, the problem lies in reinforcing the totalitarian image of reform as a controlled process proceeding under the deft hand of a dictator. No "great leader," not even Gorbachev or the once-applauded Deng, could simply command reform of a state-socialist system. Instead, the imperative for reform builds up within the system and, once released, becomes a force that the national leaders can barely cope with.

Why does reform have this tendency to take on a life of its own? The unpredictable, volatile behavior of reform derives from the rigidity of state socialism. This rigidity has a paradoxical result: it causes reform to be a normal part of the system, yet guarantees that when it does occur it will be traumatic.

The rigidities of state socialism that make reform hard to control are built into the system, beginning with central planning. Because of the critical position of agriculture, the basic time unit of central planning tends to be one year (as in farming) rather than a shorter cycle. This annual cycle makes short-term adjustments difficult. The consequent periodic shortages of resources lead to hoarding, which is carried out on a grand scale by such geographic or economic units as provinces, counties, factories, and communes. An inflexible planning system thus fortifies a set of rigid administrative boundaries, as each unit tries to retain scarce resources. The central leadership has two choices for coping with this intransigent system. One is to decentralize, a move that usually ends in a local accumulation of power that the center cannot abide. More common is to try to wrestle the whole system into submission with commands from the state center to be obeyed uniformly nationwide, which only reinforces the system's rigidity. To make things worse, the chain of command below the state center is studded top to bottom with power-holders who resist any change, especially reform. Officials at lower levels have a conscious or intuitive sense of danger about seemingly innocuous, modest, one-time-only reform. They recognize a small change as one that can bring down the world they have carefully constructed to protect themselves amid material shortage and political danger. Supple socioeconomic systems can make piecemeal changes and constant adjustments more easily. In contrast, the rigidity of state socialism makes any change difficult, dangerous, and vulnerable to bureaucratic sabotage.

This rigidity provided the evidence that analysts in the totalitarian and functionalist[21] schools needed to portray state-socialist systems as monolithic, unchangeable, and complete in themselves. However, the evidence from China's period of jarring, precipitous rural reform suggests a different view of state-socialist systems, based on a different assumption—namely, that the impetus for socioeconomic change is ever-present. State socialism only arrests this impetus until something must give. Where there is no tolerance for change built into the structure, one real change will have overpowering amplifier effects, as all the related changes waiting to happen tumble forth. Thus if one reform shatters the status quo, as family farming did in rural China, it draws many others behind it. Once this snowballing begins, the reform-minded state may intend each subsequent change to be discrete, perhaps the final bit of tinkering—only to see it beget not only another reform, but cascades of reforms. Reform in

---

21. Probably the finest book on any subject in the functionalist tradition was on China: Franz Schurmann, *Ideology and Organization in Communist China* (Berkeley: University of California Press, 1966).

state socialism therefore appears to be cataclysmic and abnormal, as it did under Gomulka, Khrushchev, Kadar, Dubcek, Gierek, and Deng. But in fact, while reform may be irregular and spasmodic, it is also a normal part of state-socialist development: a normal trauma.

China under Deng offers a spectacular example of state-socialist reform running out of control. What seemed in 1978 to be innocuous reforms in commune organization and price policy gave way to then-unimaginable changes. Whole series of pent-up changes burst forth, dragging in their wake further lines of reform. The people who composed state and society were not the only actors in the Chinese reform. Reform took on a life of its own once it was loosed in rural China, driving the actions of state and peasant alike before its own internal logic.

Privatization

The internal logic of reform is particularly strong in the case of privatization—the third theoretical problem raised by Deng's reforms.[22] In the 1980s privatization whipped through China's farm sector, converting huge portions of land, capital goods, labor, marketing, and credit to private control. The issue here—why a socialist system would be susceptible to this sudden, wrenching change of direction, allowing privatization to seize upon every fundamental part of the farm economy—has two components. The economic question is how privatization could attain this compelling force in a collective economy. And the political question is why a leadership publicly committed to collectivism would endorse such a surge of privatization at all.

From an economic point of view, the Chinese case suggests that privatization is compelling because of its step-by-step logic: each act of privatization seems to require another in order to protect economic gains. With this tendency to reproduce itself, privatization becomes overwhelming once the first essential aspect of a collective economy is converted to private control. For example, when usufruct rights on

22. Privatization here refers to the shift of control over any economic practice or resource from the public to the private domain.

land become private and individual, as they did early in China's reforms, great pressure builds for further privatization in related aspects of land tenure. Almost immediately, private usufruct rights become cumbersome without private transfer mechanisms like land rent and land sale. Mortgages are a logical extension of privatization in land tenure, because private tilling is impractical without credit. Soon the newly independent farmers realize that private transactions going beyond land tenure have become practical necessities: private hiring of labor, private transport of produce, and private ownership of the means of production other than land. Thus privatization might be thought of as the most concentrated and compelling instance of the snowballing tendency of reform in state socialism. One initial privatizing reform brings a second, then it is discovered that the second reform cannot work without a third, and so on, in an accelerating logical progression that quickly outstrips the reformers' control.

Beyond demonstrating this logic of privatization at work, China's reform also reveals the deeper, noneconomic motivations that state-socialist leaders have for embracing privatization. It is not as if Deng unwittingly opened some Pandora's box of privatization, which economic necessity then kept him from shutting. Rather, the evidence suggests that privatization may be a normal part of socialist development in a poor peasant country. The reason for this latent link between privatization and socialist development lies in the state's *political* motives for promoting privatization.

Politically, privatization represents a change in the way the state exercises power in the countryside, not necessarily an overall reduction in state power. On the contrary, moving away from collective organization at the optimal point in a state's evolution may enhance its political strength. To see this we must place privatization in its historical context.

Privatization in socialist agriculture is mostly an undoing of collective farming. The lineage of privatization therefore traces back to the initial act of collectivizing the farm sector—an act with political origins. For it is a mistake to think that a young revolutionary state collectivizes agriculture purely for economic reasons. Under the conditions of the early People's Republic—that is, in a poverty-stricken, technologically backward countryside, under a state with a covetous attitude toward the farm product—collectivization of agriculture gives mixed economic results at best. From the viewpoint of politics and central finance, however, collectivization serves the state extremely well: it asserts control over the agricultural product and over the bane of all governments, the peasantry. Through collective administration the state commands the production process and gains direct access to the harvest for compulsory procurements of farm output. Thus Chinese collectivization, over the period of a generation, consolidated political suzerainty over the peasantry.

Once collectivization has consolidated political control, the state can permit the rural economy to evolve more freely without endangering centralized state power. Privatization is not the necessary outcome of this evolution, but it is a likely possibility. For in addition to favoring economic development (especially if the government has bungled the collectivist experiment), privatization offers the state new means to control peasants. Some of these new control mechanisms are obvious: tax levers, credit incentives, and monetary policy. And even though reducing collective supervision over peasant life may loosen the state's direct grip, it also removes the only buffer between the peasant community and naked state power. The state can therefore opt for privatization without risking a severe diminution of its power.

The political element in privatization is more subtle than this, however. State-socialist leaders do not merely acquiesce to privatization, accepting its economic advantages because it is neutral with respect to state power. They go further: the leaders actively promote privatization, for as it proceeds, they learn, it *increases* their power by strengthening the state's uncertain political base. Privatization offers the socialist state the potential constituency in society it often lacks, and which it needs to be more effective in governing. The heavy-handed rule of state socialism has usually created weak societies (that is, weak in alternative norms and organizations). Any society weak in organizations—or possessing only dummy organizations set up by the state—presents little resistance to state initiatives. But it offers no muscle to back the state, either. The state can thus have a breathtaking autonomy that masks a barren poverty of social support. This problem is especially acute for state socialism. The most astounding truth that sprang from the collapse of state socialism in Eastern Europe in the late 1980s was that the governments of East Germany, Czechoslovakia, Poland, and Rumania had virtually no support in society. Granted, this hidden weakness was at its most severe in the imposed socialism of Eastern Europe, and therefore might seem irrelevant to China, Vietnam, and other systems with indigenous peasant origins. But in fact it is a more generalized problem that plagues any new state possessing the autonomy to act without consulting society. As Stepan has pointed out:

> The phrase "relative autonomy of the state" implies that the state elite is not *constrained* by class fractions and has a significant degree of freedom to impose its design on society. "Autonomy" is therefore often interpreted to mean strength. However, while autonomy may be a source of strength in the installation phase, in the institutionalization phase relative autonomy may be a source of weakness because a state elite is not *sustained* by constituencies in civil society and therefore is almost exclusively dependent upon its own internal unity and coercive powers. The other side of the coin of autonomy is thus isolation and fragility.[23]

The case of China suggests that privatization can give the state-socialist system a way out of this dilemma. Rural privatization breaks up the relatively homogeneous relationship of peasants to the state. By cutting new cleavages of occupation, income, and status through the peasantry, privatization stratifies rural society more finely than collective farming does. The peasants who have gained disproportionately from the new economy suddenly have a much greater stake in the preservation of state policies and in support of the state itself. For its part, the state has the policy tools to enhance this new tie to the more entrepreneurial peasants. With new tax, credit, and commercial policies it can further encourage and enrich the emerging rural elites, and it can use the propaganda machinery to drive home the point that their benefactor is none other than the state. In forging this alliance with a class fraction of the peasantry, privatization can therefore mend one of the basic weaknesses of state socialism: it can provide the state with a political base in society.

In China all the pieces of this sequence were present in the reform

---

23. Stepan, *State and Society*, pp. 301–02. Emphasis in the original.

period, without a public alliance between state and rural entrepreneurs ever quite coming to pass. The evidence presented here will show that state leaders were aware of this potential alliance from an early date. Their preferential treatment of economically successful peasants was conspicuous throughout the reforms. The interest that this "advanced" fraction of the peasantry had in supporting the state was also unmistakable. And, late in the reform period, the entrepreneurial local cadres emerged as a key transitional group for the transfer of political power from a collective administration to a commercial elite. What was missing was a positive pronouncement from the central leaders embracing this new alliance of private and state power. But the point here is not how far this process went in China, or where it stopped short. The point is that the Chinese case yields an insight into the theoretical development of state socialism. It shows that privatization is not an anomaly or even such a remarkable irony in state socialism. Indeed, it may be the most natural evolutionary course for socialism in a poor agrarian country, a course eased and finally hurried on its way because it serves the basic political needs of the state.

Chapter Three

The Creation of
Family Farms

Deng Xiaoping came to power determined to transform the Chinese countryside. Through the rural reform program, he aimed to swell China's farm product and boost agricultural support for an expensive modernization scheme. But Deng and his reform-minded allies soon discovered that maverick peasants were a step ahead of them. In the rural policy confusion of the late 1970s, peasants had already taken things into their own hands, trying out new forms of productive organization to improve their poverty-stricken lives. Peasants' spontaneous experiments rapidly moved rural China toward family farming and commercialization of agriculture. The peasants set such a fast pace of change that the views of Deng's coalition on a given reform barely had the chance to coalesce before peasants pushed ahead with the next innovation. This lag created a peculiar pattern of politics, in which state policy continually chased after what peasants had already done.

Although the pattern of peasants leading the state prevailed in all the pivotal areas of rural reform, it was most pronounced in the one truly radical change: the creation of family farms. The move toward family farming was the reform period's outstanding example of peasant efficacy under a strong state. This is not to say that all peasants favored the return to family farms. Because of their geographical settings or historical successes with collective farming, some communities resisted the dismantling of the communes. But across vast areas of China where peasants had fared poorly under the rigidly uniform policy of collectivism, family farming had overwhelming appeal. In some provinces, peasants deliberately misinterpreted the first mild reforms, pushing them in the more radical direction of family farming. In others, more daring peasants plunged wholeheartedly into illegal family farming, producing surpluses that convinced some provincial leaders that small farms could better serve the state than collectives. Multiplied by thousands upon thousands of cases, these small acts by peasants gathered a force that dragged state policy behind it.

Eventually the central leadership acquiesced in family farming. Like the peasants' other pioneering departures that the state would later accept, individual farms appeared to raise production, fueling the leaders' cherished modernization program. But by acquiescing, the state ceded the initiative for charting the course of rural reform. Reform thus carried China in a direction the leaders never planned, creating more radical policy changes than they anticipated at the Third Plenum.

Ironically, when the state at last endorsed family farming in the early 1980s, it pressed the new policy with the same insensitivity to local conditions with which it had once enforced collective farming—this time over the resistance of those communities that genuinely preferred the collectives. Yet on the whole—and certainly in its genesis—family farming was a local initiative, and one that would prove immensely popular across the nation. It is presented here as a case study in how peasants in a weak society can influence policy under a strong state.

The State Confronts the Threat
from the Countryside

When Deng Xiaoping assumed power in 1978, nothing posed a greater danger to his domestic policy than stagnation in agriculture. The centerpiece of that policy was the economic program popularly known as the Four Modernizations. Deng's reform coalition yearned to achieve the Four Modernizations by the turn of the century. The major obstacle to realizing this goal was China's weak farm sector. If the state could reinvigorate agriculture, then it could requisition a richer supply of rural goods and capital to provision and finance the modernization scheme. If not, the

Four Modernizations would only be another installment in the government's long history of grand but empty talk.

The Price of Modernization

Although Deng's Four Modernizations were scaled down from the grandiose version pushed by Mao Zedong's immediate successor, Hua Guofeng, the program still promised to be fabulously expensive. Perhaps inadvertently, Deng set towering goals for the Four Modernizations when he happened to speculate publicly in 1980 that per capita national income might *fan liang fan*, or quadruple, by the year 2000.[1] *"Fan liang fan"* soon became a catch phrase meaning to "quadruple the economy" by the end of the century. This notion of quadrupling caught on in leadership circles, and by September 1982 the Twelfth Party Congress had endorsed it as official policy. The precise goal was to quadruple the gross value of industrial and agricultural output (GVIAO)[2] from 710 billion yuan in 1980 to 2.8 trillion yuan in 2000. The average annual increase of 7.2 percent necessary to reach that goal appeared to be a staggering rate.[3] Few nations have ever sustained such growth. The Soviet Union achieved 7.1 percent average real growth for the years 1960–70; and Japan had exceeded that with 10.4 percent annual growth in its spectacular quadrupling of real gross national product from 1956 to 1970.[4] Thus Deng picked out an economic target at the farthest horizon of what seemed possible. While the effort needed to reach his goal was awesome, getting there was

1. *Far Eastern Economic Review*, Apr. 28, 1983, p. 44.

2. China preferred to use GVIAO as a standard measure of output, rather than gross national product or gross domestic product, because of the small size of the country's service sector.

3. Enthusiasts behind the quadrupling policy were actually hedging their bets with inflation. After all, only the value of output was to quadruple, not real output. At the time the *fan liang fan* policy was formulated, China claimed an official inflation rate of about 2 percent. With that level of inflation, a real average growth rate of just 4 to 5 percent could quadruple nominal output by 2000 (as opposed to over 7 percent without inflation). See *Far Eastern Economic Review*, Dec. 10, 1982, p. 60. In the actual event, of course, inflation soared before the 1980s were half gone, and China completed its first doubling of GVIAO in 1987, three years ahead of schedule. See *Beijing Review*, Jan. 1–7, 1990, p. 7.

4. *Far Eastern Economic Review*, Dec. 10, 1982, p. 60; *Beijing Review*, Feb. 28, 1983, p. 14.

not completely inconceivable. If the economy could indeed quadruple, Deng later claimed, China's total output would "rank it among the advanced countries in the world," and China's people would have "a comfortable life."[5]

The key question for the genesis of China's rural reform was what sort of burden this ambitious economic expansion would place on agriculture. In other words, what were Deng and his allies compelled to demand from farmers? In the late 1970s, when the reformers were sorting out their plans, China's backward farm sector contributed only about 30 percent of GVIAO,[6] though it accounted for the lion's share of the country's population. The reformers knew that to reach their goal of quadrupled GVIAO they would have to rely mainly on industry, expanding it faster than the overall target of 7.2 percent annual growth. The plan nonetheless saddled agriculture with a fearsome task: 5.0 to 5.5 percent annual growth.[7]

Agriculture instantly became the tightest bottleneck in the reformers' scheme. China's rural areas had never been able to sustain growth rates exceeding 5 percent. Gross value of farm output had topped 5 percent growth only for short stretches of a few years, and these bursts were restricted to periods of recovery from such economic disasters as the Great Leap or the Revolution itself.[8] Total agricultural output value for the period from 1953 to 1980 averaged an annual increase of only 3.4 percent.[9] Thus Deng's coalition was asking peasants to raise output at rates unknown in the history of the People's Republic.

The situation in Hubei Province typified the reformers' dilemma.[10] On the industrial side, a quick jolt of growth did seem pos-

5. Deng Xiaoping, *Fundamental Issues in Present-Day China* (Beijing: Foreign Languages Press, 1987), p. 74; from a speech in 1984. Deng of course omitted that in per-capita terms China would remain poor.

6. *Statistical Yearbook of China [1986]* (Hong Kong: Economic Information and Agency, 1986), p. 31.

7. *Beijing Review,* Feb. 28, 1983, p. 20.

8. For examples see *Statistical Yearbook of China [1985]* (Hong Kong: Economic Information and Agency, 1985), pp. 27–28.

9. Ibid., p. 20.

10. Once the state drew up its blueprint for quadrupling the national economy, the provinces scrambled to draft plans showing they too could achieve their own *fan liang fan.* Hubei Provincial Party Secretary Huang Zhizhen gamely an-

sible. As in most of China's interior provinces, industry in Hubei operated well below its potential in the late 1970s. The province already had a substantial industrial plant—with fixed assets about equal to those of Shanghai—while its output lagged far behind.[11] Optimistic provincial leaders claimed this shortfall proved that industry had the capacity for dramatic progress without stupendous investment.[12] But agriculture was another story. Although Hubei's farm sector was healthier than the norm for Chinese provinces,[13] the chances for any dramatic surge in production seemed slim. Hubei leaders pinned their hopes on the varied ecological system of the province, which could enable peasants to diversify production. Yet the potential was limited. Hubei's surpluses of grain, cotton, and edible oils were too important to the national economy to be displaced by other crops. These three basic crops took up 85 percent of the sown area,[14] so with cultivated land in critically short supply (only 0.08 hectare per person) there was little room for new crops.

In light of these constraints, implementing the quadrupling (*fan liang fan*) policy was bound to put heavy demands on peasants in Hubei as well as other provinces. In Hubei, which suffers a natural

nounced preliminary calculations for quadrupling his province's economy at the end of 1982. See Huang Zhizhen, "Zhenfen geming jingshen, nuli kaichuang xin jumian" (Inspire revolutionary spirit and energetically open a new phase), *Dangyuan shenghuo [Hubei]* 1983: 1, p. 6.

11. Ibid., p. 8.

12. Ke Qing, "Wuhan diqu lilun jie guanyu 'shi lingdao xian' tizhi gaige wenti de chubu taolun" (Initial discussions of reform for a system of 'the cities leading the counties' in Wuhan district theoretical circles), *Shehui kexue dongtai [Hubei]* 1983: 12 (Apr. 20), pp. 12–14.

13. Hubei's per capita gross value of agricultural output generally ran some 20 percent above the national average. *Far Eastern Economic Review*, Sept. 25, 1981, p. 59; based on a World Bank report.

14. Ma Junxian, "Cong Hubei tong Jiangsu de duibi zhong kan wo sheng nongye cunzai de wenti he qianli" (Problems and potential in our province's agriculture as seen through a comparison between Hubei and Jiangsu), *Shehui kexue dongtai [Hubei]* 1983: 28 (Oct. 1), p. 21. At that time about 70 percent of the sown area was sown to grain, 8 percent to cotton, and 7 percent to oil. Cutting back on any of these, especially grain or cotton, would have hurt the national supply. As the second biggest cotton producer in the nation, after Jiangsu, Hubei annually exported about 200,000 tons of cotton to other provinces. See Zhang Mingxiu et al., "Tantan Hubei sheng de nongye youshi wenti" (The problem of agricultural superiority in Hubei Province), *Nongye jingji congkan* 1981: 2, pp. 12–16.

disaster (usually from flooding of the Han and Yangtze rivers) about once every three years, unprecedented rural growth would require extraordinary efforts from peasants in good years. Therefore farmers who heard the propaganda about quadrupling the economy viewed the state's intentions with anxiety and distrust. As peasants in Xianning County in Hubei said, "We're afraid it will be like 1958 when we had the Great Leap Forward. That was pushed to the point where there was no food to eat."[15] Why did the reform coalition feel it was necessary to demand so much from peasants? The answer lay in the Chinese leaders' vision of modernization and the peculiar part agriculture played in it.

The Need for Higher Agricultural Production

It was not agriculture but industry that stood at the center of China's vision of modernization in the late 1970s. This pride of place for industry was expressed in the most incongruous ways. Industry added the modern touch to the bucolic scenes on postage stamps and calendars, where landscape paintings depicted smokestacks nestled amid the pastoral splendor. The metaphors of daily life also expressed the superiority of factory over farm, often in odd ironies. The polyester fabric produced by the petrochemical industry, for example, though harshly uncomfortable in China's southern climes, was the chic fabric of choice there, over the cotton that came from the farm. In government this devotion to industrial development as the embodiment of the modern vision was expressed in the immense power of the heavy industrial ministries. For decades these ministries' clout had assured the priority of factory over farm, and on the eve of reform in 1978 they had seen their most extravagant industrial dreams incorporated in Hua Guofeng's Ten Year Plan.[16]

Yet in spite of this habitual infatuation with industry, the new

15. Xianning xian Fushan gongshe dangwei (Fushan Commune Party Committee, Xianning County), "Jianchi 'san bao san jiang' de fangfa" (Support the 'three tasks three talks' method), *Dangyuan shenghuo [Hubei]* 1983: 1, p. 20.

16. Announced in early 1978 at the first session of the Fifth National People's Congress, the Ten Year Plan set the steel-production target for 1985 at more than 250 percent of the 1977 output. Nicholas R. Lardy and Kenneth Lieberthal, eds., *Chen Yun's Strategy for China's Development: A Non-Maoist Alternative* (Armonk, N.Y.: M. E. Sharpe, 1983), p. xxxv.

reform coalition devoted its first modernizing efforts to the weak farm sector. This was not because the reformers had reversed the entrenched preferential ranking of industry over agriculture. Indeed, typical reform-period statements of the relation between farming and industry continued to emphasize the subservience of agriculture. Consider this formulation from China's most prestigious economic journal: "The development of industrialization under socialism demands that agriculture supply industry with ever-increasing quantities of commodity grain and industrial raw materials, and that it accumulate funds for construction and provide an expanding market."[17] This standard line on agriculture's supporting role for industry could have come from the script for any Chinese development scheme since 1949. But Deng's reformers interpreted such a statement in a special way. The reformers recognized (with some alarm) that such a formula for agriculture's service to industry could be read the other way around: that is, as industry's abject dependence on agriculture.

Industry's reliance on agriculture in the domestic economy was inescapable. In the first place, with heavy industry concentrated in urban centers like Shanghai and Tianjin, the work force had to subsist on grain requisitioned from the countryside. Every year the state compelled massive grain deliveries from farmers, averaging about 50 million metric tons (milled) in the late 1970s. Roughly half of this grain was needed to feed the urban work force alone.[18] The reformers believed that such grain procurements were not nearly large enough to sustain rapid modernization. Unless grain deliveries increased, the huge numbers of people expected to switch from farm to nonfarm labor under the Four Modernizations could never be fed. Second, in addition to feeding the workers, agriculture had to feed industry itself. Textiles, fibers, clothing, foodstuffs, beer, and cigarettes were all

17. Wang Songpei and Zhu Tiezhen, "Lun woguo nongye jitihua de guanghui daolu" (The glorious path of our nation's collectivization of agriculture), *Jingji yanjiu* 1981: 6, p. 45.

18. About 70 percent of state domestic grain sales went to the nonagricultural (*fei nongye*) population. Of these sales to nonfarm people, about 70 percent in turn (hence half the total of state grain sales) went to the urban (*chengzhen*) population. Wang Zongji and Ji Cuilan, "Woguo de liangshi shengchan yu jingying qingkuang" (Our nation's grain production and management situation), *Jingji yanjiu ziliao* 1983: 11, p. 34.

mainstays in China's light industry, and all had to be nourished with such farm goods as cotton, silk, hemp, grain, and tobacco. Altogether some 70 percent of the raw materials used in light industry came from agriculture.[19] Third, the main market for the products of light industry lay in the countryside, causing still further worry for the reformers. Reform leaders like Chen Yun reckoned that the buying power of the farm sector was too weak to sustain expansion in light industry. And finally, because China had always used agriculture as its source for capital accumulation, the reformers feared strangulation of industry if agriculture could not be squeezed any further to support industrial growth. All of these intimate connections between agriculture and industry were long familiar to the reformers in 1978. Indeed, some twenty years earlier Mao Zedong had concluded that the dependence of factory upon farm was so great that "we may say that in a sense agriculture is itself industry."[20]

Less familiar to the reformers, however, and all the more disturbing, were the ways in which agriculture held the key to the foreign technology needed to modernize China. The People's Republic still had but slim experience with world trade when the reform coalition came to power. A few years earlier, when the diplomatic coups of the early 1970s had reopened the lanes to Western trade, China had gone on a foreign shopping binge with an almost empty wallet. The target was foreign industrial technology. Under Zhou Enlai and Deng Xiaoping (in a previous political incarnation), the government negotiated equipment and whole plant acquisitions with Japanese, European, and American companies, causing a balance-of-payments crisis by 1974 and cancellations of contracts by 1975.[21] But the craving for

19. This figure also includes raw materials from forestry, which is included in the Chinese definition of the agricultural sector. Wang Fenglin, "Guanyu nongye ye yao shixing jihua jingji wei zhu, shichang tiaojie wei fu de taolun" (Discussion on giving first place to the planned economy and making market adjustment supplementary in agriculture too), *Jingji yanjiu cankao ziliao* 1982: 125 (Aug. 16), p. 42.

20. Mao Zedong, "Talks at a Conference of Secretaries of Provincial, Municipal and Autonomous Region Party Committees," *Selected Works of Mao Tsetung*, vol. 5 (Beijing: Foreign Languages Press, 1977), p. 381.

21. Carl Riskin, *China's Political Economy* (Oxford: Oxford University Press, 1987), pp. 193, 259.

advanced technology had been aroused. The subsequent ascendancy of Deng's reformers coincided with a second burst of foreign technology purchases averaging unprecedented totals of U.S. $3 billion a year for 1978–80.[22] The total value of foreign trade had doubled once in the 1970s, and now it was doubling again under the combined influence of the Ten Year Plan and the reformers' ambitions. Hired Japanese consultants were estimating at the time that the Ten Year Plan would require over U.S. $70 billion in plant and technology imports (a sum equalling all of China's export earnings for the entire period since the Revolution).[23] Although Deng's coalition would scrap the Ten Year Plan itself, huge technology imports pressed ahead in the late 1970s, in tandem with a breathtaking expansion of imports generally.

The atmosphere in which the reformers drafted their plans for China was therefore one of giddy excitement over the modernizing promise of imports and anxiety over how to pay for them. The leaders hoped that growing oil exports would relieve some of the pressure (and later they did). But no matter what miracles occurred in the oil industry, the reform leaders knew the main exports for earning foreign exchange would have to come from agriculture. Chinese estimates have historically identified agriculture as the ultimate source of well over half the nation's foreign exchange earnings.[24] Data gathered by the U.S. Central Intelligence Agency (CIA) fully corroborate these estimates. CIA figures show that in the mid- and late 1970s—when the reform coalition was formulating the new economic strategy—agriculture accounted for nearly two-thirds of China's foreign exchange earnings. In the reformers' triumphant year of 1978, for example, agricultural products and the manufactures based on them made up 62 percent of the value of all exports.[25] Clearly, more foreign

22. *Beijing Review,* Mar. 10, 1986, pp. 23, 24.

23. Riskin, *China's Political Economy,* p. 319.

24. Wang Fenglin, "Guanyu nongye," p. 42; Qiu Xiaohua et al., "The Relationship Between Agriculture and Foreign Trade in China," translated in JPRS-CAR-88-040 (July 26, 1988), p. 21, originally in *Jingji yanjiu* 1988: 5.

25. This estimate is based on CIA figures for the value (in U.S. dollars) of Chinese exports by Standard International Trade Classification (SITC) category. To arrive at the total export value represented by agriculture (including manufactures based on agricultural raw materials), I have summed the values in the following

technology for modernization could only be purchased with the fruits of a dramatic revival in Chinese farming. Still more worrisome was the fact that China's weak agricultural performance also ate up foreign exchange by failing to meet domestic demand for farm goods. China had been a moderate net importer of grain since 1961, which helped to free grain land for such economic crops as cotton, hemp, and jute.[26] But the deficits in foreign grain trade set new records every year from 1977 through 1982.[27] (Nearly all these enlarged grain imports were needed to feed the urban population.)[28] In 1978, the year the reformers took power, agricultural *imports* topped U.S. $2.5 billion, swallowing up a quarter of that year's foreign exchange earnings.[29]

For all these reasons, Deng's Four Modernizations were vulnerable to threats from the Chinese countryside. Poor agricultural performance could wreck the program by undermining both industry and foreign trade. Thus even though the Chinese vision of modernization focused on industry and advanced technology, Deng's coalition

SITC categories: 0, 1, 2 (excluding items 27 and 28), 4, 55, 61–65, and 84–85. These categories represent food and live animals, beverages and tobacco, crude materials of agriculture (and some forestry), animal and vegetable oils and fats, essential oils and perfume materials, manufactured goods from agricultural materials, clothing, and footwear. For the raw data, see Central Intelligence Agency, Directorate of Intelligence, *China: International Trade Annual Statistical Supplement [1981]* (Washington, D.C.: Central Intelligence Agency, 1981), EA 82–10015 (Feb. 1982). The absolute size of agricultural (and agriculture-based) exports soared throughout the 1970s. However, the proportion of export value ultimately based on agriculture declined over the decade, from 74.1 percent in 1970, to 63.0 percent in 1975, to 52.4 percent in 1980. The biggest declines in agriculture's share of export value came because of the spectacular increase in the share represented by oil.

26. On the rationality of grain imports (as well as the argument for limiting them) see Wang and Ji, "Woguo de liangshi shengchan yu jingying qingkuang," pp. 29–38. See also Nicholas R. Lardy, *Agriculture in China's Modern Economic Development* (Cambridge: Cambridge University Press, 1983), pp. 28–29.

27. In the grain trade, China's main export was rice while the predominant import was wheat. This made matters worse, for world wheat prices rose faster than rice prices through the 1970s. The deficits after 1977 were not brought under control until the mid–1980s, and then only temporarily. The deficits cited here for 1977–82 are calculated from *Statistical Yearbook of China [1983]* (Hong Kong: Economic Information and Agency, 1983), pp. 422, 438.

28. Lardy, *Agriculture*, pp. 194, 247 n. 7.

29. Ibid., p. 88.

was forced to turn its attention to agriculture as soon as it consolidated power in 1978.

Farm conditions presented the coalition with a crisis. The Third Plenum declared that "agriculture, the foundation of the national economy, has been seriously damaged in recent years."[30] This was not just rhetorical hyperbole. The farm sector that Deng inherited from the deposed leftist leadership was stagnant. The Left, which had dominated rural policy since 1966, had insisted that farmers pour their energy into grain production. Yet from 1966 to 1977, grain output posted average annual increases only a hair above 2.5 percent. Economic crops, neglected by the Left, had not fared well. Tobacco output slumped badly, recovering only at the very end of this period. Edible oil production (from crops like peanuts, rapeseed, and sesame) was nearly flat except for a peak in 1975. Cotton, essential to China's light industry, had the most alarming performance of all: average annual output for 1966–77 was actually below the 1966 level.[31]

Agriculture's overall weakness was bad enough, but even worse was the fact that state control over the agricultural product was slipping. The Four Modernizations required not just bigger harvests, but bigger harvests the state leadership could get its hands on. The mechanism by which the state customarily seized control over the agricultural product was the procurement system. Begun on a modest scale in 1953, state procurement had grown into a huge, complex system covering nearly all types of farm products, which peasants were compelled to sell to the state at depressed prices. After ousting the Left, Deng and his allies had to confront a decline in the proportion of total farm output taken by state procurement. In the case of grain—the main crop for which the procurement system had been devised in 1953—the portion of the harvest that peasants yielded to the state was lower in the 1970s than in either the 1960s or the 1950s.[32] In other

30. "Communique of the Third Plenary Session of the Eleventh Central Committee of the Communist Party of China," *Beijing Review* 21 (Dec. 29, 1978), p. 12.

31. All of these growth trends are calculated from output figures in *Statistical Yearbook of China [1984]* (Hong Kong: Economic Information and Agency, 1984), pp. 141–43.

32. This measure is net of resales back to the countryside. In 1953–59 net marketing of grain averaged 20 percent of the crop; in the 1960s, 18 percent; and

words, the state's share of the harvest was shrinking. Meanwhile, the state's need for grain had grown faster than either grain production or grain procurement. In 1978 the net take of grain from the peasantry was 19 percent bigger than it had been in 1953; but the urban population this grain had to support had increased by 120 percent.[33] The state's ability to procure grain and other crops simply had not kept up with its need for them.

The reformers had to reverse this deteriorating situation or to surrender their whole domestic program. The weakened farm sector threatened everything it touched: industry, foreign trade, the procurement system, and the welfare of the city populace and of the state itself. Rural China's debility endangered the whole economy and, with it, the reformers' fondest policy hopes. Thus the agricultural crisis of the late 1970s threatened to destroy Deng's cherished modernization program before it even got off the ground. The unavoidable question hanging over the new reform leadership was, therefore, how to get more out of the peasants.

The State's Fear of the Peasants

One way to get more out of the peasants was through coercion. The commune and procurement systems together offered the state an immense coercive apparatus for squeezing the peasantry harder. Forced extraction of farm goods had worked well enough before—at horrible human cost—even in the desperate, grain-short years of the Great Leap Forward.[34] Now, however, the leaders rejected coercion. For

in 1970–78, 15 percent. See *Statistical Yearbook of China [1984]*, p. 370. Net marketing of grain is not a perfect measure of net state procurement, but it is very close, especially for the years before 1979, when procurement accounted for nearly all grain marketing.

33. Again, these are net marketing figures. *Statistical Yearbook of China [1984]*, p. 370; *Statistical Yearbook of China [1985]*, p. 185.

34. Grain procurements in the Great Leap years of 1958 and 1959 were about one-third larger than the average level in the First Five Year Plan (1953–57), in spite of the catastrophic drop in actual grain output. In the ensuing famine, China's death rate doubled within two years. Song Guoqing et al., *Guomin jingji de jiegou maodun yu jingji gaige. Di er bufen zhi yi: Cong chanpin tonggou dao dizu dishui* (Economic reform and contradictions in the structure of the national economy. A section of part 2: From unified purchase of products to land rent and land tax), printed by Zhongguo nongcun fazhan wenti yanjiu zu (Research Group on Prob-

one thing, even though force could succeed in wrenching more of the farm product away from peasants, it could do little to expand production, and would probably even damage it. Further, the leaders shied away from coercion because they believed it was politically dangerous. Years of abusing the peasantry had produced a deepening anxiety the leaders could no longer ignore. Their relationship with the rural population had changed: they were now a little afraid of the peasants.

By the new coalition's own account, peasants were exasperated by the end of the Cultural Revolution decade (1966–76). Their percapita income, among the world's lowest to begin with, had risen by only ten yuan over that whole period, for a miserable annual increase of less than sixty cents U.S.[35] The accumulated rural discontent aroused in the new leaders the same uneasiness that China's vanished dynasties had known. The Communist state had at last come of age, so to speak, inheriting the perennial fear of a restive peasantry that had haunted all previous Chinese governments. This anxiety crept into speeches by central leaders. At a conference on problems in the countryside, for instance, the head of the Party's propaganda department, Deng Liqun, warned his colleagues: "To look down on peasants, to ignore peasants, to exclude peasants from one's thoughts— these are the unhealthy sentiments of a few people, especially some intellectuals. Since they look down on peasants like this, the peasants also have the right to forget about them, to desert them! This is a common occurrence in history: the peasants bear in mind those who show real concern for them and serve them; but whoever forgets about the peasants and does not serve them, the peasants will cast aside."[36]

Deng Liqun's ominous tone infected other leaders as well, notably Du Runsheng, a top agricultural expert. In a rambling speech on

lems of Chinese Rural Development), April 1983, vol. 2, p. 32; Yang Jianbai and Hu Weilüe, "Renkou fazhan yu jingji fazhan de guanxi wenti shitan" (Exploration of the problem of the relationship between population growth and economic development), *Jingji yanjiu cankao ziliao* 1982: 68 (May 3), pp. 9–10.

35. *Beijing Review,* Jan. 24, 1983, p. 14.

36. Deng Liqun, "Zai Zhongguo nongcun fazhan wenti yanjiu zu taolunhui shang de jianghua" (Speech at the conference of the Research Group on Problems of Chinese Rural Development), *Nongye jingji congkan* 1981: 3, p. 5.

farm economics, Du linked peasant dissatisfaction over a weak rural economy with the specter of peasant revolts from the past:

> In Chinese history it is the rural situation that determines everything. If the situation in the countryside is good, then the whole nation is at peace; otherwise there is turmoil and upheaval. Many feudal dynasties met destruction because of peasant revolutions that burst out when the rural economy reached the verge of collapse. . . . The greatest problem in socialist transformation is also the transformation of agriculture. Socialist construction is still based on agriculture. Since the founding of the nation the health of the economy has been inseparable from the rural situation.[37]

Du's allusion to peasant revolution was not meant to be taken literally—neither he nor Deng Liqun was suggesting that the Communist state was about to "meet destruction" at the hands of the peasants. What these speeches did signify, however, was that central leaders felt suddenly vulnerable to a recalcitrant and belligerent peasantry, just when they needed to get more out of the countryside. With their modernization program so dependent upon agriculture, the leaders were particularly sensitive to traditional forms of peasant resistance—lying, falsifying production reports, foot-dragging, and conniving locally against outside officials. Although peasants were hardly plotting to overthrow the state, the leaders feared that even passive resistance could choke the flow of farm goods, bringing down their whole modernization program.

These misgivings led the central leaders to an ambivalent attitude toward the peasantry. Peasants were not exactly the state's adversaries, yet they posed a threat; and though they were not trusted allies either, their contribution would make or break the state's whole domestic program. In the eyes of the leaders, the peasantry was an unreliable force to which the state found itself wedded. For better or worse, the futures of state and peasant were bound uneasily together. Du Run-

37. Du Runsheng, "Du Runsheng tongzhi zai quanguo nongye jingji yanjiu gongzuo zuotanhui shang de jianghua" (Comrade Du Runsheng's speech at the national conference on research work on agricultural economics), *Nongye jingji congkan* 1981: 4, p. 1. At the time of this speech, Du was a vice-minister of the State Agricultural Commission. The next year he was promoted to head of the State Commission on Rural Policy Research.

sheng expressed this fatalism: "If the peasants do not prosper, China will not prosper. If life is hard for the peasants, it will be hard for China. If the peasants' way of life remains antiquated, then China cannot modernize! It is the peasants who determine everything under heaven."[38]

Bowing to this threat from the peasantry, the Third Plenum made a crucial decision to stress the positive side of the ambiguous relationship between state and peasant. The antagonistic element in state-peasant relations would surface again and again in the reform years, but at least at the outset the state center was determined to make common cause with peasants as far as possible. The state would try to obtain greater efforts and more farm goods from peasants not by coercion (or at least not only by coercion), but by winning their grudging cooperation. The Third Plenum decided, therefore, that the first task of modernization was to "release the socialist enthusiasm" of peasants, that is, to "pay full attention to their material well-being."[39]

This pronouncement, highlighted in the Third Plenum's communique, was quoted endlessly in the provinces. At an academic symposium in Hubei it was decided that this task was the key to modernizing agriculture: "If you depart from definite material interests then it is impossible to arouse the enthusiasm of any class. Therefore at the initial stage we want to give peasants a chance to recuperate, let them increase both production and income so they have warm clothes and plenty to eat. . . . Only in this way will peasants have the interest or the strength to push ahead with the modernization of agriculture.[40]

This appeal to peasants' material well-being was the starting point of the official reform effort. The reforms were meant to induce peasants to produce more and to part willingly with more of harvest. By

38. Du Runsheng, "Zai Zhongguo nongcun fazhan wenti yanjiu zu taolunhui shang de jianghua" (Speech at the conference of the Research Group on Problems of Chinese Rural Development), *Nongye jingji congkan* 1981: 3, p. 2.

39. "Communique," p. 12.

40. Tang Xiaolin and Li Weiwu, "Hubei sheng nongye xiandaihua xueshu taolunhui guandian zongshu" (Summary of viewpoints at the Hubei provincial academic conference on agricultural modernization), *Shehui kexue dongtai* 1981: 4, p. 31.

offering peasants higher income, the state would encourage greater production, so there would be more farm goods for the state to procure. It was not altruism or sympathy for the peasants' plight that drove the reformers—only the state's interests. Chen Yun put the point plainly: "If the peasants' income is raised, the *state* stands to benefit the most."[41]

Although this effort at winning peasants over was primarily intended to revive the rural economy and bring in bigger procurements, it reached far beyond reform of the procurement system alone. Because the basic appeal was a general improvement in peasant life, a series of broader and more profound reforms emerged that touched nearly every aspect of rural society. The reforms swept cadres and Party members down a road they never expected to travel, and many opposed the direction they believed the leadership had chosen haphazardly. This opposition—along with the general uncertainty about what was happening in rural policy—increased the farther down the administrative ladder one was from Beijing. The lowest Party morale and the greatest confusion occurred at the local level. This combination of uncertainty and flexibility that prevailed in the reform years gave peasants their opening to take a creative hand in the making of rural policy.

Peasants Invent Rural Policy

Peasant innovation succeeded in leading the way of reform for two reasons. First, key provincial and central figures in the reform coalition adopted a benign, wait-and-see attitude toward local experiments. Second, even though the state opened the way for reform, the central leadership lost control over much of the creative process from the beginning. Fighting the last skirmishes against factional adversaries after the Third Plenum, the leaders around Deng Xiaoping were still not settled in their rural policy at the end of the 1970s. Peasants seized the initiative, making up

41. Chen Yun, "Chen Yun's Speech at the CCP Central Committee Work Conference," translated in *Issues and Studies* 16 (April 1980), p. 95. Emphasis added.

new ways of doing things and reinventing old ones. The rural cadres' perpetual predicament in the no-man's-land between village and state was worse than ever: they were caught between a peasantry suddenly challenging their authority and a state sending them incomprehensible instructions. Cadres either were left behind or joined peasants in improvising rural policy, while the state followed in the wake of changes it did not command.

Deng's coalition expressed its original intentions for rural reform in what became known as the "two documents on agriculture," approved at the Third Plenum.[42] The Party circulated these documents to rural cadres nationwide beginning in January 1979. The original reforms outlined in these documents fell roughly into three categories, all operating within the existing commune system. First were material incentives to peasants. These included higher procurement prices for goods sold to the state; a small expansion of private plots within the dominant collective land system; a new incentive scheme based on the principle of more pay for more work; and the "responsibility system," which guaranteed peasants certain levels of remuneration for the delivery of procurement quotas to the state. The second category of reforms aimed to make agriculture somewhat more commercial by encouraging small family sideline production, greater diversification of agriculture, and greater tolerance for free markets. The third category comprised structural changes to make the communes less top-heavy. The lowest of the commune's three administrative levels—the production team—had virtually no power or independence. To elicit more local initiative, the Third Plenum's program gave more autonomy to the team and created a smaller, more manageable unit below it called the work group, which usually comprised a few families.

What is striking about this initial reform program is how little it

42. The Third Plenum's "two documents on agriculture" were: "Zhonggong zhongyang guanyu jiakuai nongye fazhan ruogan wenti de jueding (cao'an)" (Resolution of the Chinese Communist Party Central Committee on certain problems in the acceleration of agricultural development [draft]), reprinted in *Zhonggong yanjiu* 13: 5 (May 1979), pp. 149–62; and "Regulations Governing Rural Commune Work (Draft)," translated in *China Report: Agriculture*, no. 55 (Oct. 4, 1979), JPRS 74309, pp. 4–28.

anticipated the more radical changes it set in motion. The "two documents" contained no hint that the Third Plenum reformers had any idea how far commercialization would go in the next few years, nor to what degree the newly commercialized economy would be operated by private individuals and companies rather than public collectives. In fact, the state initially outlawed what were to become the most important reform measures. Foremost among these was the most fundamental change of all, family farming, which the Third Plenum specifically banned.[43] The original program also prohibited practices that later were at the core of the privatized rural economy: privately hiring labor, renting land, running private credit operations, privately owning large-scale productive goods, and practicing commerce as a full-time profession. Similarly, the early reform documents reaffirmed central support for the commune system, although the state would dismantle the communes only a few years later.

The central leaders' opposition to radical change in the early years of reform shows how little foresight and control they had over where their program was leading. Taken together, the later radical reforms represent an abrupt change in the direction of rural development in China. Yet the state arrived at the eventual set of reform policies almost passively and unconsciously, behaving in a mode more of acquiescence than leadership. To approve the final reforms, Deng's coalition had to reverse its announced positions on one rural policy after another. Policy and politics in the reform period came to follow a distinctive pattern: One year the state would discover peasants pursuing some deviation and issue proclamations to ban it. Then a year later the same practice would be pronounced tolerable under "special circumstances." By the time another year passed, the very same activity would be declared official policy to be followed uniformly throughout the nation. Thus the rural reforms were an extreme instance of a strange but recurring variety of policy-making under Chinese Communism, in which the state belatedly embraces what the peasants have already done.

The most revealing example of this peculiar pattern of policy-

43. "Zhonggong zhongyang guanyu jiakuai nongye fazhan," p. 154; cf. "Regulations," p. 18.

making is the case of family farming, which the state vehemently opposed at the outset of reform.

The system of family farming the reforms brought to China evolved from an early reform known as the "responsibility system" (*zeren zhi*). The responsibility system was originally a contractual relation between collective and state. Groups of farmers were given land to work, and their responsibility was to sell a certain quota of output to the state. In return they received a guaranteed payment and sometimes the chance to dispose of the surplus however they chose. The "responsibility field" (*zeren tian*) was taken on in this way by one of the lower-level units of the commune organization, such as a production team or a newly established work group. Thus the responsibility system was supposed to operate collectively, within the commune structure.

But what quickly evolved from the responsibility system was something else entirely: family farming. Under the system that came to dominate Chinese farming in the 1980s, individual families displaced the collective units in the contract, each getting a share of the village's cultivated land. The land that a family contracted for was rarely a single plot. To distribute good and bad land fairly, most villages gave each family scattered, tiny parcels of land of varying qualities and uses. (Thus the picture that the term *family farm* may conjure up is misleading.) In return for the use of the land, the family guaranteed that it would sell a fixed quota of the output to state procurement agencies at the depressed official prices. After fulfilling this procurement duty, the family was free to consume the balance of its output or to sell it, either to the state or on the free market. Countless variations on this system generated a bewildering array of names.[44]

44. Some of the most common variations included *bao chan dao hu* ("contracting output to households"), *bao gan dao hu* ("contracting work to households"), *shuang bao* ("the two contracts"—shorthand for the two variations above), and *da bao gan* ("long-term contract work"). Each of these systems had its own peculiarities and refinements. Hundreds of articles appeared in the Chinese press differentiating and analyzing these and many other responsibility systems. For example, see "Jizhong nongye fenpei banfa jianjie" (A brief introduction to several methods of distribution in agriculture), *Jingji guanli* 1979: 4, pp. 31–34; and Liu Xumao, "Woguo nongcun xianxing de jizhong zhuyao shengchan zeren zhi" (A brief introduction to the main responsibility systems practiced in the countryside), *Jingji guanli* 1981: 9, pp. 12–14.

When family farming was the most controversial question on the rural scene, in the late 1970s, one of its most common forms was *bao chan dao hu* ("contracting output to households"), or the household contract system. For the sake of simplicity, I will use *household contracting* as a generic name to represent all the variations of family farming in which peasants occupied land and promised to fulfill a quota of sales to the state.

The state's stance on household contracting is an excellent example of the irresolute policy-making that characterized the reform years. At first household contracting was banned outright. The Third Plenum documents of December 1978 said: "It is forbidden to practice the household contract system (*bao chan dao hu*)."[45] The state's next major document on agriculture, "Several Questions on Strengthening and Perfecting the Production Responsibility System in Agriculture" (issued in September 1980), signaled a shift in the state's position. It declared that in poor, remote, mountainous, and backward districts, where "the masses have lost faith in the collective," household contracting "is permitted" and is "nothing to be afraid of." The majority of districts, however, were told to uphold the collective economy; for them "it is not desirable to practice the household contract system."[46] Yet only a year later the state reversed itself and gave full approval to household contracting. Central Document Number 1 for 1982, entitled "Summary of the National Conference on Agricultural Work," included the household contract system in a list of state-approved "responsibility systems of the socialist collective economy."[47]

Thus between December 1978 and January 1982, household contracting in the eyes of the state went from being "forbidden," to "not

45. "Zhonggong zhongyang guanyu jiakuai nongye fazhan," p. 154; cf. "Regulations," p. 18.

46. "Guanyu jinyibu jiaqiang he wanshan nongye shengchan zeren zhi de jige wenti" (Several questions on strengthening and perfecting the production responsibility system in agriculture), reprinted in *Zhonggong yanjiu* 15: 3 (Mar. 1981), pp. 115–16.

47. "Zhonggong zhongyang zhuanfa 'quanguo nongcun gongzuo huiyi jiyao'" ("Summary of the national conference on rural work," circulated by the Central Committee of the Chinese Communist Party), reprinted in *Zhongguo nongye nianjian 1982* (1982 Chinese agriculture yearbook) (Beijing: Nongye chubanshe, 1982), p. 1.

desirable," to "permitted" in backward areas, to enshrinement as part of "the socialist collective economy." What Deng's coalition condemned at the Third Plenum became national policy only three years later. Household contracting, in its several variations, became the predominant form of rural social organization. Virtually the whole countryside was divided into family farms as the result of a movement that first flourished without the blessing of the state.

Agitation for family farming was not uniform among peasants. To trace the birth and early development of family farming, however, it is necessary to concentrate on the peasants who invented and popularized it. Family farming took root under the care of peasants generally following one of two patterns. Where provincial leaders were more open to innovation, the transition to family farming came earlier than elsewhere. In these provinces, maverick peasants experimenting with family farming could take advantage of conflicting orders from above and occasional provincial-level support. Provinces following this pattern included the two famous pacesetters, Anhui and Sichuan, and, to a lesser extent, Gansu and Shaanxi. A second pattern prevailed where provincial leaders were more cautious, conservative, or committed to the advantages of collectivism. Here the changeover to family farming was slower and was carried out with greater secrecy and more conflict. In these provinces family farming also appeared spontaneously before it was officially approved, and peasants actively manipulated policy to inject elements of family farming where they could. But wide-scale adoption of individual farms did not occur until the central government finally acquiesced to what the innovators were doing. In much of China, including Hubei, Hunan, Jilin, Zhejiang, Jiangsu, and Liaoning provinces, this was the more common pattern. The example of Anhui can be used to demonstrate the first pattern; Hubei typifies the second.

Anhui

The earliest instance of people going back to family farming in Anhui Province was in Guzhen County in 1977, during the first spring planting after Mao's death. Spontaneous attempts at family farming soon broke out in other counties in the north (Fengyang), center (Feixi), and east (Lai'an, Dangtu, and Wuhu) of Anhui.[48]

48. Qin Qiming, "Bao chan dao hu de yuanqi, zhenglun, he fazhan" (The

In Feixi, for example, family farming began as it did everywhere: as an improvisation. In 1978 Anhui suffered its worst drought in one hundred years. Fearing the loss of the autumn rice harvest, the province ordered everyone to plant "life-saving wheat" as a winter crop. Collective planting of winter wheat for the emergency progressed slowly. In many parts of Anhui it was never planted at all. But in Feixi County, production teams in Shannan Commune tried an innovation to ensure that the winter wheat would be sown. Instead of planting the wheat collectively, they allotted each able-bodied adult 0.1 hectare of land plus three yuan to help cover production costs. In return, the peasants promised to turn over 100 kilograms of wheat to the collective after the harvest. This improvisation was, of course, a form of *bao chan dao hu,* or household contracting. But peasants did not dare to call it openly by that name, so team members and local cadres agreed on phony names to use for the system when talking to outsiders.[49]

Both the spontaneous start of this venture and the secrecy to which villagers agreed were typical of the first attempts at unsanctioned family farming. The same fear of discovery that impelled the Feixi peasants to invent a fake name for their household contracting system drove peasants in Wuhu County to agree to a clandestine pact. In Wuhu's Huangchi Commune, peasants and cadres drew up a list of twenty-one points to protect themselves when they divided the fields among households. One point was that everyone would keep the system secret. Another was that if the people taking the lead (*daitou de ren*) in family farming were imprisoned, everyone else would share the responsibility of taking care of their families.[50]

In spite of the attempt at secrecy in Shannan Commune, the news about individual wheat fields was impossible to contain. The practice quickly spread to some eight hundred teams in Feixi County. At this point a second feature of politics in the reform period came into play: disagreement among cadres high and low over what policy was supposed to be. After the news of Feixi's household contracting came out late in the autumn of 1978, indignant cadres began writing letters to

origins and development of the household contracting system and the debate regarding it), *Nongye jingji congkan* 1981: 4, pp. 37–38.

   49. Ibid., p. 37.
   50. Ibid.

the Anhui Provincial Party Committee, asking, "Where is this leading the peasants?" The Provincial Party Committee, under the innovative leadership of First Secretary Wan Li, reacted by approving of experiments with household contracting by a few Feixi County teams.[51]

At this juncture the county government in Feixi, emboldened by the province's call for experimentation with family farming, announced its support for the innovation. But the county quickly reversed itself because of chilling signals from Beijing. In March 1979 a letter prominently displayed on the front page of the *People's Daily* made a big stir by criticizing responsibility systems that signed contracts with work groups (that is, subdivisions of production teams). "This is just the first step," the letter's author warned. "The next step will be to allocate land to individual households in a household contracting system." No doubt the Feixi officials took note here, for this fatal "next step" is exactly what had already happened in their county. The letter went on ominously: "This practice would . . . create confusion in the minds of cadres and people, dampen enthusiasm, hamper production, and adversely affect agricultural mechanization."[52]

The letter was accompanied by an editorial note pointing out that this danger of family farming had already materialized in Anhui. Upon reading this omen, Feixi County officials became alarmed that they might be in trouble. Their fears proved right. By July Feixi was under criticism for encouraging the household contract system. Now on the defensive, county officials issued a document rectifying the error and called meetings urging the peasants to "turn around." Then, at the instigation of some local cadres, the provincial government intervened with instructions to the contrary, telling Feixi County officials, "Don't do an about face"—in other words, keep up the experiment with family farming.[53]

By this time the confusion for local cadres and peasants was get-

51. Ibid., pp. 37–38. The province also approved experiments with family farming in Guzhen County, Chuxian Prefecture, and other places.

52. This letter, published in *Renmin ribao*, Mar. 15, 1979, p. 1, was written by a Gansu official named Zhang Hao, who had observed the work-group responsibility system in Henan. A partial translation of the letter is available in British Broadcasting Company (BBC), *Summary of World Broadcasts*, FE 6071 (Mar. 20, 1979), B II, p. 2. My quotations are from the BBC version.

53. Qin, "Bao chan dao hu de yuanqi, zhenglun, he fazhan," p. 38.

ting out of hand. Three sets of contradictory orders were coming from above. The top leadership in Beijing was against the experiment in family farming. The Anhui provincial leaders were for it. The county officials kept vacillating—they were for it, then against it, then reluctantly for it again. With total confusion in the message they were getting from above, the local cadres could no longer tell what policy was. Many middle-level cadres (county and commune officials) who had opposed family farming from the beginning did their best to disrupt it, even in the teams designated by the provincial government for further experiments. These conservative cadres cut off supplies of production materials to villages with family farms, withheld credit, and called meetings of Party members to criticize the experiments. Lined up against these hard-line officials were the hundreds of village cadres who had colluded with peasants in secretly dividing the land. Conflict between the cadres over family farming became bitter: "Some [cadres] said they weren't even afraid of losing their official positions for it. If they had to go back home and sell sweet potatoes for a living they would still practice the household contract system. Others said household contracting amounted to the 'restoration of the old order'—it ruined twenty years of gains under collectivization. Some cadres said you could cut their heads off and they still wouldn't practice it."[54]

In the meantime, the "two documents on agriculture" had arrived in Feixi County. Here another pattern of behavior typical of the reform years emerged: deliberate misinterpretation of central documents at the local level. Even though the Third Plenum documents explicitly banned family farming, some local cadres and peasants interpreted the documents in a way that would support what they wanted to do—to continue dividing up the collective land. In Feixi the documents were brought down by propaganda teams to mobilize the masses for discussions on how to speed up agricultural development. Peasants at Shannan Commune only wanted to talk about family farming. They told the propaganda team this: if you want to speed up agriculture, try household contracting.[55] The central documents

54. Ibid.
55. Ibid., p. 37.

also failed to clarify policy in other Anhui counties, again because of peasants' insistence on interpreting them according to their own lights. For example, Anhui Provincial Radio reported that "the wind of dismantling the production teams blew very rapidly" in Dangtu County, where "people gained a one-sided understanding of the spirit of the documents" and tried to split up more than fifty production teams in a single commune.[56] All across the province this movement for family farming spread quickly, to 10 percent of teams in Anhui by the end of 1979, and to half by October 1980.[57]

Anhui became famous in China as the maverick province that made itself the vanguard of family farming (with Sichuan as a close second). Outsiders have often assumed that Anhui and Sichuan led the way because their Party first secretaries, Wan Li and Zhao Ziyang, forged ahead—both through their own boldness and on instructions from Deng Xiaoping. But the evidence shows a much more complex situation. While Wan's forbearance gave peasants and village cadres more room to maneuver, the impulse for change was local and massive rather than directed from above. Support for family farming experiments from Wan's provincial administration did give peasants and adventurous local cadres an edge in resisting their superiors. But the peasants still outstripped the pace of change sanctioned by the province and turned to household contracting in numbers far greater than the province approved for its cautious experiments.[58] Peasants divided up the land spontaneously and secretly, with or without official permission. Officials in Beijing, in the provincial capital in Hefei, and in the counties were all in conflict. Rather than coordinating a concerted new policy departure, they all sent contradictory messages to the beleaguered village cadres, who often faced the choice of conspiring with the peasants or being cast aside by them. The state apparatus was no longer drafting policy and implementing it. The real creativity and energy in making family farms in Anhui came from the peasants.

56. Anhui Provincial Radio (Mar. 16, 1979), translated in BBC, *Summary of World Broadcasts*, FE 6071 (Mar. 20, 1979), B II, p. 3.

57. Qin "Bao chan dao hu de yuanqi, zhenglun, he fazhan," p. 47.

58. For one example of peasants going beyond what was sanctioned, in an experiment in Anhui's Fengyang County, see Katsuhiko Hama, "China's Agricultural Production Responsibility System," *China Newsletter*, 40 (September-October 1982), p. 7.

Hubei

In Hubei peasants also pressed toward family farming but made much slower headway in the face of the provincial leadership's caution and intransigence. Official Hubei policy strictly followed whatever was sent down from Beijing, from the first hint of reform through the 1980s. The provincial leadership thus remained unrenowned but stable during the reform era. Two provincial Party first secretaries, Chen Pixian and Guan Guanfu, dominated the period. Chen led the province from 1978 until he was promoted in 1982 to a succession of posts in Beijing, where he did not distinguish himself for good or ill. Chen's promotion was not like those of Wan Li or Zhao Ziyang, whose achievements with rural reform as provincial leaders in Anhui and Sichuan won them entry to the highest circles of power in Beijing. Nor was Guan, who led Hubei from 1983 to the end of the decade, remarkable in any way. Guan had come up through the ranks of Hubei's provincial administration (particularly in finance) and was a competent bureaucrat. Led by such conservative officials, Hubei stayed safely to the rear of the maverick reform provinces. But the prudent leaders of Hubei also avoided emulating their counterparts in provinces like Hebei, which later suffered Beijing's ire for its determined resistance to reform.

Hubei's leadership was scrupulous about not taking chances or conducting experiments. Thus from 1977 through 1980, while Anhui, Guizhou, Gansu, and Sichuan moved decisively toward household contracting, Hubei remained committed to collective responsibility systems. Only in the middle of 1980, following cues from Beijing, did Hubei approve the giving of land contracts to a few households.[59] Even at that, the *Hubei Daily* cautioned, "these methods should be used only under certain specific conditions."[60] The examples the paper offered of "specific conditions" included a contract for land too remote from a production team to be worked collectively and a contract for a family of disabled people living on a mountain who could not get down to their team's collective fields. Obviously the paper's editors did not intend for family farming to take Hubei by storm.

59. The most important of these cues was the *Renmin ribao* article of April 9, 1980, giving limited support to the idea of family farming.
60. *Hubei ribao*, July 20, 1980, p. 1.

Nor did the provincial government. As late as 1981, Governor Han
Ningfu said, "Starting from the real conditions in our province, we
affirm the principle of generally *not* practicing the household contract
system."[61]

In spite of this unfavorable setting, family farming grew spontaneously in Hubei. In isolated parts of the province peasants gave up
on collective farming altogether and turned to household contracting.
This occurred as early as 1979 in Lichuan County.[62] For the most
part, however, wholesale adoption of family farming was more rare
in Hubei than Anhui. It was limited to counties like Lichuan, which
abuts the Qiyue Mountain Range—a poor, sparsely populated area
where both government vigilance and collective organization were
weak. Peasants in the more populous parts of Hubei, such as the
Jianghan Plain, had to be more cautious and frequently more devious.
The general pattern in the genesis of family farming in Hubei was for
peasants to push the limits of accepted policy in the direction of family farming, if they could not get away with dividing the land outright. In other words, given the chance, peasants injected a family or
lineage element into a policy, undermining its collective aspects. An
example of this is the way that Hubei peasants manipulated one of the
earliest reforms, the creation of work groups.

Work groups, the new subdivisions of the collective production
teams, included several households each. Their smaller scale was intended to make them more efficient than the cumbersome teams,
which included roughly one hundred to two hundred people. As soon
as work groups appeared in Hubei, so did the peasants' tendency to
push new policy in the direction of family farming and away from
collective organization. Peasants saw the work group as an excuse to
dismantle the production team, and they were happy to justify this
centrifugal impulse with arguments borrowed from the Third
Plenum. For example, peasants and cadres in one commune pushed
the official line on the advantage of smaller scale one step further.

61. Han Ningfu, "Zai Hubei sheng wu jie renda san ci huiyi shang guanyu
zhengfu gongzuo de baogao" (Government work report at the Third Meeting of
the Fifth Hubei Provincial People's Congress), *Hubei ribao*, Mar. 4, 1981, p. 3.
Emphasis added.

62. Zhang et al., "Tantan Hubei sheng de nongye youshi wenti," p. 16.

They decided: "The smaller the production team, the better can production be done. Dividing the production team into work groups is not as good as straightforward disbandment."[63] Armed with this logic, a number of the commune's teams wrote reports explaining why they should break up and requested permission to do so.

Usually this change was not so open and ingenuous, however. From the beginning of the work-group policy, the *Hubei Daily* reported that all over the province teams were splitting up secretly. Peasants used work groups as a pretext (and a disguise) for cannibalizing the teams:

> Right now the practice of unchecked team-splitting has broken out in some places. Teams that should not be broken up are loudly demanding that they be divided too. Some teams have claimed that they are merely dividing into work groups, but in fact they are taking fixed assets and other means of production and giving them over to work-group ownership. The work groups run their own finances entirely independently, changing team accounting into work-group accounting, which is a very serious error.[64]

The work groups were also subject to the peasants' impulse to rearrange policy along family lines. Peasants bent on family farming saw work groups as a pointless halfway measure. When cadres in Hefeng County divided villages into work groups, the peasants asked, "As long as you're letting us divide into work groups, why not just leave everything to us?"[65] If the cadres prevented them from dissolving the collective all the way down to individual families, peasants often did the next best thing: they made work groups into family and lineage organizations. Reports from all over China told of "father-and-son" work groups, "Huang clan" groups, or "Wu family groups."[66] Division by lineage threatened not only the collectives but the social peace, for it turned cadres with one surname against cadres and peasants with other surnames. One report on this phenomenon

63. BBC, *Summary of World Broadcasts*, FE 6067 (Mar. 20, 1979) B II, p. 13.

64. *Hubei ribao*, Mar. 19, 1979, p. 1.

65. *Hubei ribao*, July 18, 1980, p. 2.

66. *Far Eastern Economic Review*, Apr. 6, 1979, p. 15; Jürgen Domes, "New Policies in the Communes: Notes on Rural Societal Structures in China, 1976–1981," *Journal of Asian Studies* 41 (February 1982), p. 257.

in Hubei's heavily populated Xiaogan Prefecture said: "When some places start clamoring to split up the teams, then contradictions between surnames and disputes between lineages flare up. Relations between cadres and commune members are wrecked."[67]

Peasants in Hubei also attempted to break down collective organization by manipulating central documents. As in Anhui, they willfully misinterpreted official pronouncements in ways that would support family farming. In one among many such instances, peasants in Sui County divided their production team's land, machinery, tools, and animals. Then, having appropriated this collective property, they took a stance of high-minded innocence and claimed, "To act in this way is in conformity with the spirit of instructions from higher authority!"[68] In Dangyang, Yichang, and other counties, peasants were even more meticulous in pursuing deviation. They actively searched the Third Plenum documents for passages they could cite to support their attempts to break up the production teams.[69]

As a result of these centrifugal impulses, rural Hubei drifted into a muddle. Some local cadres colluded with peasants; others, feeling betrayed by the slide into work groups, said that all their years of labor to build the collectives amounted to "whistling in the wind."[70] In the confusion, family farming emerged in the form of household contracting. Although family farming did not sweep the province as it did neighboring Anhui, Hubei's leaders felt that their control over the countryside was slipping. The provincial establishment, which so carefully toed the line from Beijing, placed blame squarely on local leaders for innovating without permission. According to a complaint in the *Hubei Daily,* "The household contract system has come about only because the chaotic (*hunluan*) situation in production management has failed to put a stop to it."[71] In places where peasants went to extremes (such as Hefeng County), they literally dismantled the collectives: they not only divided the collective land, tools, machines

67. *Hubei ribao,* Apr. 5, 1979, p. 3.

68. Hubei Provincial Radio (Mar. 14, 1979), translated in BBC, *Summary of World Broadcasts,* FE 6071 (Mar. 20, 1979), B II, p. 4.

69. *Hubei ribao,* Mar. 19, 1979, p. 1.

70. *Hubei ribao,* July 18, 1980, p. 2.

71. *Hubei ribao,* Mar. 14, 1980, p. 1.

and animals, but also split up the pigsties, chopped down the trees for fuel, dug up the collective tea bushes, and took apart the collective buildings brick by brick and walked home with them.[72]

The contrast between the creation of family farming in Anhui and that in Hubei shows that peasant influence was clearly limited by the determination of the state to assert its power. In Anhui, where the tolerant attitude of the provincial government partly contravened orders from Beijing, peasant innovation progressed more quickly and on a wider scale. In Hubei, where provincial leaders insisted on the central line of the moment, peasants had to be more cautious. They did not succeed in wholesale change to family farming as Anhui peasants did, but acted in a more manipulative way, twisting policy in the direction of family farms. This contrast shows that the state's coercive response could (as in Hubei) still restrict peasant actions. But the similarities between Anhui and Hubei offer some additional insights. First, given the very narrow range of available forms for political action, peasants in both provinces were most effective with similar tactics: deliberately misconstruing orders, secretly experimenting, disguising family farming so as to have the effect if not the appearance of what they wanted, and engaging local officials in conspiracies to defy the state. Second, despite the limits on their actions, peasants managed to exceed what the government would countenance. In Anhui peasants went far beyond the limited experiments that the province sanctioned. Even in Hubei the provincial government was angry at peasant unruliness and felt betrayed by the connivance of local officials in peasant innovations. Third, and most important, in both provinces peasants demonstrated the capacity to create possibilities and choices that the state center might eventually find more attractive than its own policy program. However circumscribed peasant power may have been, it was still the peasants' creation, not the program of the strong state, that finally became policy.

72. *Hubei ribao*, Nov. 9, 1981, p. 1.

Chapter Four

The Pattern of Politics in the Reform Era

Although family farming was the most conspicuous show of peasant power, it was not an anomaly. It was only one example of peasants innovating while the state followed behind. This same revealing pattern occurred with private land rental, hiring of labor, private credit, private commerce, and other core elements of eventual reform that state policy explicitly rejected into the early 1980s. In each case peasants led and the state scrambled to keep up. The actions of the three main parties in the struggle over family farming—the state, the cadres, and the peasants—explain this recurrent pattern of politics in the reform years.

The State

The ancient Daoist principle of good government was *wuwei,* or "taking no action." The Chinese state during Deng Xiaoping's rural reform at times seemed to be following the Daoist maxim. Although the state saw some of its primary rural goals accomplished in the end, it did not assert active leadership over the process of reform. The movement of change was from the bottom up, with the state center approving changes rather than commanding them. Command on a large scale came only at the end, when the state forced reluctant localities to adopt reforms created in other localities. Thus the state controlled the final word on reform, but not its creative spark or evolution.

Deriving policy from local experiment is a common theme in the

history of the People's Republic of China. But to see the state so reluctant and uncertain in such a massive policy change as Deng's rural
reform was unprecedented. The only rural changes that could match
the epochal magnitude of Deng's reforms were Land Reform, farm
collectivization, and the Great Leap Forward. Each of these involved
full mobilization of the Communist Party apparatus, all-embracing
onslaughts of propaganda, and mass campaigns directed by the state
center. The contrast with the rural reforms under Deng could not be
more stark. New ideas sprang from ordinary peasants and local cadres
with no official blessing; the state's vast policy-making machinery got
involved belatedly in every instance. Timid and indecisive, the state
repeatedly adopted positions that were clearly out of touch with the
current situation in the countryside.

The state took this uncertain approach to rural policy because it
operated under too many constraints to press forthrightly for radical
reform from the top down. Instead of trying to overcome these constraints, reform leaders chose a strategy of waiting and acquiescing,
putting the state's weight behind changes that coincided with general
policy goals. Internal limitations and a fear of alienating the peasantry
forced the leadership to adopt this strategy. In following it, the state
ceded control over the direction of reform to people at the bottom of
the rural hierarchy.

Cracks in the Coalition

The first constraint on state action was internal disagreement. Nearly
every rural policy question created conflicts within the leadership—
in Deng's coterie, in the Secretariat, in the ministries, and among provincial leaders. Questions about family farming divided conferences
of Party theoreticians (in Beijing, in 1979) and economists (in Miyun,
in 1979), as well as meetings of the State Agricultural Commission
(for example, in January 1980).[1] Intense debate over the responsibility
system split the September 1980 meeting of the Secretariat with the
provincial first secretaries.[2] Arguments over private land rental and

1. Qin Qiming, "Bao chan dao hu de yuanqi, zhenglun, he fazhan" (The
origins and development of the household contracting system and the debate regarding it), *Nongye jingji congkan* 1981: 4, p. 39.
2. *Renmin ribao*, May 20, 1981, p. 4.

hired labor were particularly acrimonious, and disagreements over procurement prices pitted the top agriculture officials against the industrial ministers.

These were not merely squabbles over the minutiae of policy. Rather, they were divisions that reflected deep factional and bureaucratic rivalries, as well as conflict over the most basic choices of development strategy. Remnants of Hua Guofeng's leftist "whatever" faction, which remained entrenched in the Party in the early reform period, openly opposed rural change. Taking their nickname from the principle that whatever Mao said was correct and whatever decisions he made should be upheld, members of this faction scorned the reforms as reactionary and ludicrous. To them, favoring agriculture was backward in the first place, and the small-scale farm production that reform promoted was laughable. Ji Dengkui, a principal within the leftists' formidable "little gang of four,"[3] captured the whatever faction's sentiments in his acid ridicule of reform farm policy. "Your papers," he said, "are daily talking about private plots and household sideline production. Is it possible that chickens, ducks, fish, and rabbits can build socialism?"[4]

Although Ji was driven from power along with the rest of the little gang of four in early 1980, many of his objections were echoed even within the reform coalition itself. Conflict over rural policy followed bureaucratic rivalries, riddling the state apparatus with pockets of recalcitrance against reform. Consider, for example, the effect of the fight between the coalition's economic chief, Chen Yun, and the so-called petroleum faction.[5] Like other members of the reform coalition, petroleum faction leader Yu Qiuli shared Chen's belief that

3. Along with Ji, "little gang" members Wang Dongxing, Wu De, and Chen Xilian were ousted from the Politburo at the Fifth Plenum of the Eleventh Central Committee in February 1980. Hua Guofeng lingered on as titular Party chairman until mid-1981, a humiliating symbol of the emptiness of leftist power at the top.

4. Attributed to Ji Dengkui by *Far Eastern Economic Review*, Sept. 25, 1981, p. 49.

5. The petroleum faction was a group of technocrats and economists who enjoyed Zhou Enlai's support and ran the Chinese economy from the late 1960s until they came into conflict with Chen Yun in 1979. They favored heavy industry, high rates of growth and capital accumulation, and involvement in the world economy. See Parris H. Chang, "Chinese Politics: Deng's Turbulent Quest," *Problems of Communism* 30 (January-February 1981), pp. 1–21.

the agricultural crisis imperiled China's modernization. But that did not mean he was prepared to see his own bureaucratic ox gored to save farming. As head of the State Planning Commission, Yu had long favored the heavy industrial ministries like the Ministry of Metallurgy, which were run by his petroleum faction partners. Yu, like Ji, was determined not to see the most modernized sector of the economy yield priority to the backward farm sector. This bureaucratic loyalty drove him to attack the "readjustment" Chen started pushing in March 1979.[6] As the chief advocate of balanced growth, Chen called for a readjustment of resources and priorities away from heavy industry in favor of agriculture and light industry. Chen targeted the Ministry of Metallurgy specifically, saying its steel production goal should be cut by one-fourth. Yu fought back to defend heavy industry and his factional constituency, but lost. Chen then succeeded in having Yu replaced at the State Planning Commission with his own long-time protégé, Yao Yilin; and he saw the Ministry of Metallurgy chastised for its promotion of massive steel projects (particularly the troubled Baoshan plant in Shanghai). Yet Chen's nemesis Yu Qiuli was not finished. Yu immediately secured a position in the newly created State Energy Commission, where he regained his old bureaucratic rank and continued to represent his factional constituency.

Hence even though Chen won one battle for agriculture, his failure to achieve complete victory meant continuing disagreement at the top over the rural question. The reformers consistently had trouble mobilizing constituencies within the state apparatus strong enough to launch bold agricultural policy departures from the state center. To succeed, a major policy change ordinarily required a broad alliance backing it in the massive bureaucracy.[7] Deals had to be made; support of various ministries, provinces, and commissions had to be lined up.

6. Nicholas R. Lardy and Kenneth Lieberthal, *Chen Yun's Strategy for China's Development: A Non-Maoist Alternative* (Armonk, N.Y.: M. E. Sharpe, 1983), pp. xxxvi–xxxvii.

7. On the importance of bureaucratic politics inside the state apparatus, see Kenneth Lieberthal and Michel Oksenberg, *Policy Making in China: Leaders, Structures, and Process* (Princeton: Princeton University Press, 1988).

The Third Plenum's initial rural reform package could muster this kind of wide support only because it was so mild. After all, the initial reforms altered the organization of farm work without touching the collective system and raised procurement prices without challenging state planning. The much more radical reforms that followed—family farming, free markets, and privatization—alienated too many bureaucratic constituencies to collect a ready alliance. And just as Chen was frustrated by the recalcitrance of the petroleum faction, more aggressive reformers in the market-oriented liberal group regarded Chen as the obstacle to progress. Thus the reform coalition never agreed on a single coherent vision of rural change and development.

Another division on rural policy that beduled the coalition came from the military. During his long campaign to regain power in the 1970s, Deng courted no institution as assiduously as the military. Once he seized control, however, he wanted to modernize the army along with the rest of China. Modernization meant enhancing the army's professionalism and technological capability while eliminating the vestiges of its guerrilla heritage. With these goals, Deng sought a smaller, tighter, more expert military machine. Throughout the 1980s he attempted a huge demobilization with an aim of cutting one million troops. Demobilization was to be achieved both by attrition through retirement (an unwelcome event for nearly all officers, who would lose pay, perquisites, and status) and by recruitment of fewer but more technologically sophisticated soldiers. Modern weapons and professionalism may have pleased the army, but demobilization made the army leadership restive and somewhat threatening to the reform coalition. As a bureaucratic institution, the military resented the effort to tamper with its size and recruitment practices.

The issue of army size and recruitment directly connected the military leaders' dissatisfaction to rural reform. The People's Liberation Army recruited almost exclusively from the countryside. While urban men scorned the army, generally preferring even unemployment to enlistment, peasant men saw the military as one of their only avenues for escape from the village and a rise in status.[8] Peasant

---

8. Sulamith Heins Potter, "The Position of Peasants in Modern China's Social Order," *Modern China* 9 (October 1983), pp. 465–99.

women likewise preferred to marry army recruits over ordinary peasants. As a result, no other part of the central state had so vital a connection with the peasantry as did the military.

Rural reform threatened this connection. As peasant income rose and village life became more attractive, the army grew alarmed about its recruitment prospects. The decline in the relative appeal of army life poisoned the military's response to rural reform. The military certainly did not applaud rural poverty, and one would expect that an institution with such an intimate relation to the peasantry would favor the dramatic rise in rural living standards brought by reform. Yet the military read the decline in rural poverty that accompanied reform as a decline in its own fortunes. In the 1980s peasant men who could make far handsomer livings in the village saw little reason to submit to the hardships of army life. Peasant women turned up their noses at prospective mates from the military in favor of prosperous farmers and rural businessmen.

Consequently the reform coalition had to beware the army's skepticism, resentment, and even outright opposition to rural reform. Because the military was one of the pillars of the Chinese state—and certainly of Deng's political base—its unenthusiastic stance toward rural reform intensified the state's caution and indecisiveness on rural policy.[9]

Added to the factional rivalries in the government and the Party, the military's position made it all the more difficult for the state to mount a bold program. Together these bureaucratic divisions prevented the state from seizing a unified vision of rural reform and made it more likely that any radical changes would have to originate outside the state bureaucracy.

The Language of Political Discourse

The nature of political discourse in China also constrained the state from leading radical reform. Political discussion used a specialized vocabulary formed during decades of influence from the left wing of the

---

9. On demobilization, see June Teufel Dreyer, "The Demobilization of PLA Servicemen," in June Teufel Dreyer, ed., *Chinese Defense and Foreign Policy* (New York: Paragon House, 1989), pp. 297–330.

Communist Party. By the time of Deng's reforms, the language and imagery of public debate bore a strong imprint from the Left, especially in such policy areas as agriculture, which had been the terrain of prolonged Left-Right conflict. The concepts used in the discussion of rural policy were all charged. Even the words that signified radical reform choices in agriculture carried a negative stigma.

For example, family farming and related practices had been vilified for so long and in such vitriolic terms that it was risky for any political leader to be associated with them. Everyone in the late 1970s remembered that the charges against the highest-ranking victims of the Cultural Revolution had included the promotion of family farming. Liu Shaoqi had confessed that he had encouraged "the working of land by individual rural households" after the Great Leap disaster. Deng Xiaoping and Deng Zihui (then head of the Central Committee's Village Work Department) were also accused of promoting family farming in the guise of "responsibility fields" during the post-Leap famine. Zhao Ziyang, too, had been castigated for committing the same offense while leader of Guangdong Province.[10] The terms used to discuss policies related to family farming (*bao chan dao hu, san zi yi bao,*[11] *zeren tian,* etc.) had been steeped in contempt. They all had a noxious flavor. But radical reformers had no other vocabulary with which to advocate the various forms of family farming. Bringing up these policy options therefore opened the speaker of the tainted words to easy attack.

That the Cultural Revolution had been discredited did not eliminate the danger that its rhetoric could destroy the reformers. The influence of the Left continued to dominate the language of political discourse after its leadership was politically dead. Even the most powerful leaders of Deng's coalition could not risk an open call for family farming or other radical changes that had been reviled in public for

10. Laszlo Ladany, *The Communist Party of China and Marxism, 1921–1985* (Stanford: Hoover Institution Press, 1988), p. 286; David L. Shambaugh, *The Making of a Premier: Zhao Ziyang's Provincial Career* (Boulder: Westview Press, 1984), pp. 56–57; *Far Eastern Economic Review,* Jan. 29, 1987, pp. 10–11.

11. "Three freedoms and one contract," the name given to a form of family farming practiced in the early 1960s, referred to private plots, private sideline enterprises, free markets, and household contracts for grain production.

years. A political vocabulary had been built up to denounce family farming, and it was ready for manipulation by any opponent hoping to destroy the reformers. For this reason, the public statements of the reformers always had a defensive tone, suggesting that while everything was changing for the better in the countryside, deep down everything was staying the same: the socialist system had not been tampered with. Hindered by the lack of a new political vocabulary to champion their cause, advocates of radical reform were perpetually forced to mute or disguise their message, even within their own circles of power.

Deliberate Acquiescence

The state failed to assert any clear will during some of the most radical changes of the early reform period. Leaders at all levels agreed that agricultural change was crucial to China's modernization. But when officials spoke of this monumental task, they wavered. As the Hubei Provincial Party Committee said, "There is no question that because of our long years of pushing political movements, our ideological methods are inappropriate for building modernization. . . . When it comes to this we are short of knowledge and have little experience."[12] Although claiming ignorance and inexperience was a ritualized formula in Chinese politics, in this case the Hubei Party Committee was simply stating the truth.

In another sense, however, the state's inaction had a positive, deliberate side. Given the lack of consensus on how to deal with agriculture, and considering the political danger inherent in promoting radical change, reformers at all levels chose to be prudent. Prudence meant watching rather than acting, allowing ground-level changes to grow on their own. The central leadership intentionally refrained from interfering with rural changes that deviated from official policy and waited to see whether illegal innovations would work.

This wait-and-see attitude had its most productive antecedent in Sichuan Province. Beginning in 1977, Sichuan had pioneered a series of rural reforms that won its first party secretary, Zhao Ziyang, promotion to premier in 1980, where he survived until the political

12. *Hubei ribao*, Jan. 31, 1979, p. 2.

crisis of 1989. Early reforms in Sichuan paralleled the radical changes in Anhui, including household contracting and liberalized marketing. Indeed, even more than Wan Li in Anhui, Zhao was willing to countenance extreme free-market measures that dismayed older reformers like Chen Yun. The genesis of radical reform in Sichuan is difficult to trace. Specifically, it is hard to say how much of the change Zhao actually ordered and how much was the spontaneous creation of villagers. At the beginning of Zhao's tenure in Sichuan (1975–80) the peasants of the province lived in nightmarish conditions. One report said Sichuan's situation in 1975 and 1976 was so desperate that peasants were selling their children, and neighboring provinces were flooded with Sichuan beggars.[13] Under similar conditions after the Great Leap in the early 1960s, peasants across China had abandoned the communes and split the fields into family farms. Sichuan's plight in the late 1970s may well have sparked the same spontaneous attempt at radical change. There are, however, historical reasons to believe that Zhao favored radical reform and may have had a strong hand in pushing it. Earlier in his career, when Zhao had responsibility for agriculture as a high official in Guangdong Province, Guangdong had been among the first to try freer markets and household contracting after the Great Leap disaster.[14] His lasting sympathies apparently stayed with these radical reform policies. Some analysts have credited Zhao personally with the innovations in Sichuan in the 1970s. An early biography of Zhao states that he (along with Deng) championed the Sichuan experiments, but concludes that change came through a "collective effort" heavily influenced by people at the local level.[15]

Assuming that Zhao did favor radical reform as a solution to Sichuan's crisis of the 1970s, we see that he faced a special dilemma, which he solved in a way that set the pattern for state behavior in the reform era. From his own bitter experience in the Cultural Revolution, Zhao was mindful of the perils of advocating radical change too conspicuously. His leadership therefore took the form

13. Cited in Shambaugh, *Making of a Premier*, p. 107 n. 5.

14. These changes were in the form of *san zi yi bao*, which contracted output quotas directly with the household. Shambaugh, *Making of a Premier*, pp. 22–23.

15. Ibid., pp. 105–06.

of easing restraints, permitting change to occur on its own. Zhao's method was to let peasants and local cadres work out their own arrangements for rural life and then to approve whatever raised production and income, as long as the state's share of the harvest was guaranteed. This hands-off method meant tolerating many practices that were illegal at the time, including hiring labor and dividing the fields among households. Zhao said the correct way to treat these unauthorized innovations was the "four don'ts" (*si bu*): don't publicize them (*bu xuanchuan*), don't oppose them (*bu fandui*), don't support them (*bu zhichi*), and don't stop them (*bu zhizhi*).[16] Zhao chose this deliberately ambiguous course for two reasons. First, open support for radical reform would only alert the opponents of change, giving them a chance to block the experiments and to attack Zhao for sponsoring them. Second, letting many different creations develop freely meant that only an innovation capable of succeeding by its own tenacious merit would survive. Once a successful innovation became a fact of rural life, it would be too late for opponents to stop it.

Zhao Ziyang's four don'ts soon spread to the rest of China (though they were boiled down to two in Hubei—don't support, don't oppose).[17] As Zhao's tactic of benignly ignoring unsanctioned innovation spread, so did appreciation for the wider-ranging possibilities it nurtured. Summing up his openness to new possibilities, Zhao said, "We should feel free to adopt all those structures, systems, policies, and measures which can promote the development of production, and not bind ourselves as silkworms do within cocoons."[18] Deng Xiaoping himself encouraged this open-minded stance, saying, "We should let every family and every household think up its own methods of doing things, and let them find more ways to raise production and increase income."[19] To gather information about rural innovations (that is, "to better understand the

16. Interview with a Secretariat official, 1984. According to my informant's memory, Zhao made this remark in 1979. The idea caught on in reformist circles, capturing the spirit of their political strategy.

17. *Hubei ribao*, Nov. 2, 1980, p. 1.

18. Quoted in Shambaugh, *Making of a Premier,* p. 122.

19. Quoted in *Renmin ribao*, May 20, 1981, p. 4.

creations and opinions of the cadres and the masses"[20]), Central Committee members went to rural areas across the nation in the spring and summer of 1980. They were struck by the great variety of commercial, productive, and organizational experiments underway. In a break from past Communist practice, the leaders decided to preserve this diversity. Deng's coalition, consciously diverging from the path of its leftist predecessors, wanted flexible policy. One of the core reform documents (written in 1980) said: "In different places, in different communes and teams, even within the same production team, we should start from real needs and real conditions and permit a variety of forms of management, many kinds of labor organization, and many types of remuneration methods to exist simultaneously."[21]

This willingness to be flexible made the state's behavior unusually acquiescent. The Third Plenum adopted a simple and passive criterion for judging policy: "We have only to see whether or not a given policy can arouse the laborer's enthusiasm for production."[22] With this formula, proponents of reform high in the state apparatus made room for radical change while distancing themselves personally from controversial policy positions. As a result, the reform era evolved more freely, while the state tacitly countenanced whatever might bring about its goals of rural revival and higher production. The state was divided, timid, and irresolute in this period, ideologically paralyzed and intermittently afraid of the peasants. But its fitful behavior and its failure actually to make policy were also partly deliberate, the result of a measured willingness to see what improvisations might work. In fear and respect for the crucial role agriculture and the peasantry would play in their modernization drive, the leaders left peasants room to act.

20. Ibid.
21. "Guanyu jinyibu jiaqiang he wanshan nongye shengchan zeren zhi de jige wenti" (Several problems in strengthening and perfecting the production responsibility system in agriculture) (Central Document no. 75 for 1980), reprinted in *Zhonggong yanjiu* 15: 3 (March 1981), p. 114.
22. "Zhonggong zhongyang guanyu jiakuai nongye fazhan ruogan wenti de jueding (cao'an)" (Resolution of the Central Committee of the Chinese Communist Party on certain problems in the acceleration of agricultural development [draft]), reprinted in *Zhonggong yanjiu* 13: 5 (May 1979), p. 154.

The Rural Cadres

After the state, the second player in the genesis of reform was rural officialdom. By the mid-1980s, rural cadres learned that the entrepreneurial thrust of reform made their skills lucrative. Networks of connections, lines on market information, access to telephones, and inside knowledge of rural industry gave cadres an unbeatable edge in new commercial competition. But it was only later in the reform period that astute cadres realized what a gold mine reform could be for them—the first face that reform presented to cadres was ugly and threatening to their status. They were largely suspicious and resentful of reform through the process of its birth and growth. To understand the genesis of reform, therefore, it is necessary to see how the cadres' recalcitrance affected their behavior in the 1970s and early 1980s.

The local officials who had to deal with reform included the county and commune cadres, who handled mainly administrative work, and the brigade and team cadres, who oversaw day-to-day work in the villages. These officials occupied an ambiguous political niche. On the one hand, cadres represented the state. They were the lowest officials in the state apparatus that reached all the way up to Beijing. While cadres had no say in making state policy, their first duty was to enforce it far from the state center. On the other hand, as community leaders, they represented local interests against the state—a shadowy function they could carry out only in subtle, often surreptitious ways. Cadres suffered from great tensions in their ambiguous dual role, and many cadres felt that reform made this already difficult position untenable.

Cadres' reactions to reform depended partly on their position in the rural hierarchy. County cadres suffered little loss of power under the new policies. Reform changed the nature of their work, but never threatened their positions. Further down, the brigade cadres, at the second of the three ranks of the commune structure, often enjoyed some security as well. With nonfarm collective enterprise concentrated in the brigades, many cadres at that level could be sure their expertise would still be needed even if the enterprises were decollectivized. But at the top and bottom tiers of the commune—among the commune cadres and the team cadres—decollectivization held special perils. In the first mild reforms, commune-level cadres instantly scented a trend that would eventually (in 1984) break their monopoly on political, economic, and social control. And team cadres, who organized and directed the collective labor of the villages, could see that decollectivization would slash their power—if their jobs survived at all.

At this most local level where the team leaders presided, many villages were untouched by the turbulence of the reform years. Cadre and peasant together weathered the successive policy lurches and reversals as smoothly as they could. In other villages, reform was a period of high excitement for those cadres who colluded with peasants in innovations beyond the state's wishes. But most cadres were neither as lucky as those who coped smoothly nor as adventurous as the radical innovators. Most were caught in the period's distinctive pattern of local turmoil with the state anxiously watching the outcome. With peasants challenging their authority and the state failing to back them up, cadres felt they were the losers in the first wave of reform. Worse still, when the state did assert itself, it was with reform policies that many cadres opposed. Some reacted by conspiring with the peasants, defying or hoodwinking their own superiors. More bullheaded or fearful cadres held out against new policies, trying to block change. Others, at wit's end, just abandoned their authority. As a result, the rural cadres played a strikingly small, ineffective part in the events of the reform years.

Most cadres forfeited control because they were hampered by one of three problems: they were opposed policy, they were paralyzed by fear of making mistakes, or they were baffled as to what policy was supposed to be.

Opposition to Policy

Cadres' opposition to change had two sources. The first was practical: reform threatened the cadres' personal power and comfort. For example, one early reform gave more autonomy to the production teams. This provoked the commune cadres, who were quick to charge that "everybody just wants autonomy, nobody wants leadership."[23] But team cadres suffered an even greater loss of power,

23. *Hubei ribao*, Apr. 12, 1979, p. 3.

for their main bailiwick was collective farm labor, which virtually disappeared in many villages. Contracting work out to individual households eliminated many of the administrative tasks connected with collective labor. The job of recording each team member's labor in collective work became obsolete. The duties of accountants were threatened with drastic reductions. Peasants running family farms didn't need bosses. Before the reforms, these tasks cushioned cadres from manual labor. As one rural survey put it, "The long period of incessant political movements in the countryside and the use of administrative leadership methods in farm production, with the endless flow of meetings, inspections, investigations, and work-point appraisals, made it so that some cadres participated less and less in collective productive labor. Some of them developed the ideology of 'love ease and hate work.'"[24] Rather abruptly, the reforms presented team cadres with the unpleasant prospect of going back to labor in the fields.

The other source of cadre opposition to central policy was ideological. Ideological resistance was a constant part of reform politics, and it was enormously frustrating to the central leaders. Even five years after reform started, Party propaganda chief Deng Liqun complained that cadres would still not give in: "Among the cadres there are lots of ideological problems concerning implementation of rural policy, and this cannot drag on any longer."[25] Deng excoriated rural cadres who "scoff at [the reform program] and find fault, who come out and say, 'It's got the same defects as all your old rightist stuff,' and then propose going back down the old road."[26] Still, to Deng—who was, after all, in charge of propaganda—there must have been little mystery to the cadres' ideological doubts. Years of propaganda had taught them that capitalism was synonymous with such reform measures as private plots, family sidelines, free markets, and the principle

24. This finding is from a rural survey in the Xiaogan Prefecture of Hubei, carried out by the Propaganda Department of the Provincial Party Committee. *Hubei ribao*, Nov. 4, 1980, p. 2.

25. Deng Liqun, "Jiaqiang he gaijin nongcun sixiang zhengzhi gongzuo de jidian yijian" (Some opinions on strengthening and improving rural ideological and political work), *Jingji yanjiu cankao ziliao* 1983: 1 (Jan. 1), p. 14.

26. Ibid., p. 15.

of more pay for more work. However, collectives, the larger the better, were associated with socialism, and now the reforms were dismantling them. It is not surprising that cadres, as the *Hubei Daily* reported, "have doubts and resentment against the policies formulated by the Center (*zhongyang*), to the point where they suppress the wishes of the peasants."[27]

In spite of the official portrayal of cadre opposition as contrary to peasant wishes, in many cases ideological resistance to reform expressed heartfelt local sentiment. Peasants who were not the least doctrinaire had genuine fears that reform would polarize villages into rich and poor. Taking apart the collectives sharpened this peril for the poorest, who depended on meager welfare offerings from collective funds. Richer villages that had done well with collectivized agriculture also had reason to fear that reform could harm their interests. This was especially true in the northern plains where the terrain favored mechanization of farming. Both large-scale tilling and expensive machine purchases were more feasible under the collective system. The idea that collectives were better was not merely ideological reflex in such areas. The Chinese press claimed that cadres were ideologically blinded to the advantages of reform, but this criticism was often too sweeping, concealing these regional differences and genuine concerns.[28]

Fear of Change

Ideology also played a part in the second disability that incapacitated cadres: fear. Rural cadres had suffered searing ideological attacks before, and now their fear that it might happen again paralyzed them. At different times in the 1950s and 1960s cadres had followed some of the very policies now being promoted in the reform package. Each time this had led to personal disaster for cadres when the ideological current swung back to the left. By the 1970s, cadres were shell-shocked from too many political campaigns and drastic swings in policy. Consequently, according to the *People's Daily*, many of them

27. *Hubei ribao*, June 7, 1979, p. 1.
28. For a compilation of these objections to reform from rural people, see David Zweig, "Opposition to Change in Rural China," *Asian Survey* 23 (July 1983), pp. 879–900.

suffered from a "fear-the-right disease."[29] Cadres with this ailment automatically shrank from any policy associated with the right wing. When called upon to implement the reforms, they froze. In Hubei's Sui County, cadres' ideological reflexes against the new policies were automatic: "Some comrades still have a lingering dread. As soon as you say we are going to put our main energy into building production and revolutionary technology, they fear it means 'going back on the road of retrogression.' If you talk about acting in accordance with economic laws and using economic methods to run agriculture, they're afraid it means 'denying politics in command.' If you bring up respecting the autonomy of the production team, they are scared it will weaken Party leadership."[30]

Because of ideological pitfalls, any change in policy put the cadres at risk. And the constant reverses of the reform years goaded cadres to new heights of anxiety. In response to the 1980 slogan, "Liberate thinking and loosen policy," one cadre nervously asked, "Right now policy is loose enough as it is. If we relax policy any further, won't we be making a deviation?"[31] The *Hubei Daily* complained that this slogan to relax policy made little headway among fearful cadres. "This is not because policy has already been loosened," the paper said, "nor because the masses have not demanded it. Rather, the reason is that in some places the leading comrades haven't had the guts to take control."[32] Some cadres, however, responded to repeated policy reversals not with fear but with anger. Near the end of 1980 one exasperated cadre said, "We're fed up with the losses we've suffered in the past few years because of too many changes in policy. The policies of the last two years are barely in place. Why do we have to change again?"[33] Each successive reform only increased the danger of being criticized, for cadres were convinced that leftist policy would have a vengeful return. So they dug in their heels and resisted any change at all. Consequently policy

29. *Renmin ribao,* Jan. 26, 1979, p. 1.
30. *Hubei ribao,* Jan. 13, 1979, p. 1.
31. *Hubei ribao,* Sept. 20, 1980, p. 1.
32. *Hubei ribao,* Aug. 24, 1980, p. 2.
33. *Hubei ribao,* Sept. 20, 1980, p. 1.

"got stuck" (*qiake*),[34] and the state was frustrated by the immobility of its own cadres.

Confusion over Policy

The third disability that hampered rural cadres was confusion and disagreement over policy. Often cadres could not tell what policy was supposed to be, as shown in the discussion of Anhui in chapter 3. In some provinces confusion reached the point where contiguous counties had opposite policies.[35] Conflicting orders from above made things worse, and even central documents from Beijing failed to help, for they were subject to different interpretations. The leadership in Beijing complained that its documents were not even reaching parts of the countryside. More than six months after Central Document Number 75 for 1980 was issued to settle questions about the responsibility system, many rural cadres were following its guidelines solely on the basis of hearsay: they had never seen the document.[36] When documents did reach the local level, the state charged that cadres either read them heedlessly or, worse, leapt at absurd interpretations to justify disobeying their instructions:

> Often it is just that they [the cadres] have never read the Party documents, or they have not read them carefully. And since they don't understand what the relevant documents really say—neither the spirit nor the substance of their contents—they have no basis for distinguishing right from wrong. When they run into someone who criticizes certain policies and principles in Party documents in a one-sided way for no good reason, then they start parroting them. They can't help being led around by the nose under the influence of absurd arguments.[37]

Hence the state laid the blame for confusion and disagreement over policy at the cadres' doors.

These three disabilities among rural cadres—opposition to reform, fear, and confusion—damaged the cadres' competence and au-

34. *Hubei ribao*, May 22, 1979, p. 1.
35. Qin, "Bao chan dao hu de yuanqi, zhenglun, he fazhan," p. 38.
36. *Renmin ribao*, Mar. 2, 1981.
37. *Hubei ribao*, Nov. 30, 1980, p. 1.

thority. A rural-affairs journal reported: "Some basic-level cadres do not draw the line clearly. They are afraid of making mistakes. They don't dare to take control, don't dare to manage. They don't dare to promote [political] education boldly and forcefully, to conduct propaganda for the socialist system, or to attack evil winds and noxious influences. They just let things take their course, and this produces chaos."[38] Cadres abdicated their own authority rather than swallow policies they feared or detested. In Hubei, for example, beginning in late 1980, "wavering ideology among rural cadres in Shishou County became serious. Some demanded new elections [so they could be replaced], others asked to be relieved, and some just stayed in bed and gave up their responsibilities altogether."[39] In some cases cadres repudiated their leadership positions in disgust. In other cases their unwillingness to assert their authority was calculated and deliberate, amounting to passive resistance against reform. Defiant cadres used the rhetoric of the reforms to hinder administrative work. Seizing on the propaganda for production-team autonomy, Hubei cadres allegedly reasoned: "When the team has autonomy, then the peasants can plant the fields and the cadres can take it easy."[40] The state condemned this kind of passive resistance as "the bureaucratic work style that uses respect for team autonomy as an excuse for not going down to the villages, not visiting the teams, hanging around the office all day, depending on the telephone and filling out statistical reports, and making no real effort to do anything."[41]

Active resistance to central reform policy sometimes surfaced as sabotage. For example, in Laifeng County, Hubei, cadres secretly opposed the peasants' independent family sidelines, such as raising poultry. Investigators found "there are few open restrictions against commune members' family sidelines today—or at least you can't see them. But closer examination turns up a lot of problems."[42] What

38. Zhao Yong, "Huifu sixiang zhengzhi gongzuo de chuantong" (Restore the tradition of ideological and political work), *Nongcun gongzuo tongxun* 1981: 2, p. 26.

39. *Hubei ribao,* Mar. 17, 1981, p. 2.

40. *Hubei ribao,* Apr. 12, 1979, p. 3.

41. Ibid.

42. *Hubei ribao,* May 22, 1979, p. 1.

turned up was that cadres publicly supporting the sidelines policy by day were poisoning the peasants' chickens and ducks at night. Tensions were worst in villages where cadres openly opposed reform. A study conducted in Yunnan, Guizhou, Hubei, and Anhui provinces showed that public opposition by cadres led to peasant-cadre conflicts of such proportions that rural organization broke down altogether. The study reported that when cadres resisted family farming, "the cadres and masses lock horns, for the cadres are determined to block the household contract system. Later, when they can no longer withstand the mass pressure, they just give up and refuse to have anything more to do with it. The masses then rush headlong into action. Nobody drafts any contracts, and the result is that the state procurement quotas all go unmet."[43]

In the end, many cadres were left out of the picture. The changes of the reform period went on despite them, toward results over which they had little influence. Every time the press complained about disorder, confusion, weakened authority, and policy chaos in the villages, it traced these problems to the cadres.[44] Meanwhile, cadres who felt betrayed by reform believed they could no longer rely on state backing. Neither the state nor the cadres could grasp real control over the rural situation. Each blamed the other to a large extent for its own diminution of power. But whoever was to blame, it left the stage to the peasants.

The Peasants

The independent actions of peasants were more effective and influential in the reform years than in any other period since Liberation. Peasants had no organized movement, yet their actions followed surprisingly similar patterns in different places in China. One reason was that peasants shared certain

43. "Lian chan ziren zhi keyi shixing nongye jihua guanli" (The linked production responsibility system can be used with planned agricultural management), *Shehui kexue yanjiu cankao ziliao* 1982: 33 (Nov. 21), p. 23.

44. Part of this was scapegoating, of course. The state habitually blamed local cadres for rural troubles throughout the era of the People's Republic, especially after the Great Leap Forward.

motivations: the need to alter the stagnant conditions of rural life, an impulse toward entrepreneurship, a desire to test the authority of rural cadres, and a perennial tendency toward family farming.

The Peasant Condition

In 1978, state leaders publicly made a startling admission: China's rural poverty was so severe that 100 million peasants did not even have enough grain to eat.[45] This relentless poverty governed peasant political action in the reform years. Peasants' enduring motivation was to escape their economic plight. The great variety of local invention that followed upon Mao's death burst forth because peasants everywhere were scrambling to raise living standards any way they could.

The reform period came at the end of twenty years with almost no improvement in quality of life for peasants. Their income in the years 1957–77 was virtually flat: annual increases came to 1 percent or less.[46] Education, health care, and other forms of collective consumption improved slightly, but all such services represented a tiny fraction of real income in the countryside. Food consumption—the most critical measure of all—actually *fell* in the years 1957–77. The per capita food supply never quite recovered from the famine after the Great Leap. By 1977 the Chinese diet still did not quite equal the 1957 level of 2000–2100 calories a day, a level of subsistence which itself fell

---

45. "Zhonggong zhongyang guanyu jiakuai nongye fazhan," p. 151.

46. This estimate is based on several sources. Yang Chengxun, in the standard journal *Economic Research*, said peasant income in the eighteen years 1959–76 had an annual increase of less than 1 percent. "Lun nongcun shichang dui woguo xiandaihua jianshe de cujin zuoyong" (The function of the rural market in advancing the construction of modernization), *Jingji yanjiu* 1982: 3, p. 21. An official of the Ministry of Agriculture told an American scholar in 1981 that the total annual per capita income from collective distribution increased only eight yuan from 1957 to 1977. Even with the addition of noncollective income, the annual rate of increase would be well under one percent. See Victor Lippit, "The People's Communes and China's New Development Strategy," *Bulletin of Concerned Asian Scholars* 13 (July-September 1981), p. 22. An estimate from the other end of the scale comes from China's National Statistical Bureau, which said that from 1956 to 1976 per capita peasant income increased each year by two yuan (still a pitiful amount). However, the National Statistical Bureau's figures have been criticized even within China for being inflated by some 15 to 20 percent. See Zhang Liuzheng, "Woguo nongmin shouru he xiaofei de jiankuang" (Peasant income and consumption in our country), *Nongye jingji congkan* 1981: 4, pp. 43–47.

below the food requirement for Chinese estimated by the United Nations Food and Agricultural Organization.[47]

At first glance this stagnation in peasant welfare seems impossible, given the growth in total output and per-hectare yields that Chinese agriculture had achieved since the 1950s. Several factors explain this apparent discrepancy. First is rising population. Per capita agricultural output, the first determinant of peasant income, barely rose from 1957 to 1977 because production increases failed to outdistance population growth. Second, rising costs and high rates of accumulation snatched the benefits of bigger harvests out of peasant hands. The Chinese called this phenomenon "increasing production without increasing income" (zeng chan bu zeng shou). Output from a given piece of land can increase with more of such inputs as chemical fertilizer, but this boosts production costs. Per-hectare yields can therefore swell dramatically without any benefit to peasants. For this reason, peasants ran into the frustrating problem of adopting improved technology that raised per-hectare yields while per-hectare income actually declined.[48]

Still more maddening to peasants was that, after the mid-1960s, even if a production team succeeded in raising both output and income, peasants were often prevented from realizing this achievement as higher consumption. The state instead insisted on high rates of accumulation—that is, the gains had to be reinvested, not consumed. The most explicit and unpopular way of enforcing this high accumulation policy was through caps on income. Peasants received collective income in both cash and kind, and teams that achieved high produc-

47. Nicholas R. Lardy, "Food Consumption in the People's Republic of China," in Randolph Barker, Radha Sinha, and Beth Rose, eds., *The Chinese Agricultural Economy* (Boulder: Westview Press, 1982), pp. 147–62. See also Nicholas R. Lardy, "Economic Development in China: A Thirty Year Perspective" (paper presented at the Maxwell Summer Lecture Series, China Today, Syracuse University, 1979), p. 20.

48. For an example of this phenomenon in Jiangsu, see Li Kegang, "Dangqian nongcun renmin gongshe jiti jingji fazhan de jige wenti" (Several problems in the current development of the collective economy of rural people's communes), *Jingji kexue* 1981: 3, pp. 72–77. For an analysis of another instance, in Heilongjiang, see Bi Jingquan, "Nongye zeng zhi bu zeng shou de yuanyin hezai?" (Why does agriculture have higher expenses without higher income?), *Jingji kexue* 1981: 3, pp. 77–81.

tion had to set a cap on the share that individual peasants could receive. This practice was widespread in Hubei in the 1970s. Prosperous teams were not allowed to give each member more than 150 yuan per year, nor grain rations exceeding 300 kilograms (or in some cases as little as 210 kilograms), nor more than 3 kilograms of edible oil.[49] One commune in Zhongxiong County that enforced such limits reported (perhaps with some exaggeration): "With this restriction, even though Shengli Brigade year in and year out increased production, increased income, increased the contribution to the state, and increased accumulation, and the whole brigade's accumulation fund swelled to over two million yuan and collective savings reached over one million yuan, still commune members' distributed income could not go up and there could be no improvement in their lives."[50] Although such accumulation funds were frequently squandered in ill-conceived, unproductive investments, heavy accumulation could also benefit peasants by spreading rural industry. Even productive use of accumulation funds aroused peasant resentment, however, for reinvestment often took place outside a team's control. A team that worked well was always subject to raids on its resources by higher-level administrators. Peasants in a given village could unwillingly have their output piled up in an accumulation fund, only to see it taken away for an outside project that did them no good at all.[51]

By the time the reform period opened, peasants of all strata were ready to take advantage of the new political climate to improve their lot. In the more prosperous villages, they were enraged with frustration at the limits on their income. For families in the poorer regions, the need for change was all the more urgent.

Entrepreneurship

The peasants' desire to change their poor circumstances was not born out of the blue after Mao died. It was there all along. But until Mao's death many routes to improving income were cut off. Cadres and

49. For citations of a few instances, see *Hubei ribao*, Jan. 12, 1979, p. 1; Feb. 22, 1979, p. 2; and Feb. 27, 1979, p. 1.

50. *Hubei ribao*, Jan. 12, 1979, p. 1.

51. Criticism of this raiding upon the resources of the lower levels of commune administration was a constant theme in reformist journalism of the period.

peasants alike were held in check by ideology that condemned entre-preneurial activities as capitalism and saw attempts to prosper as the sign of bourgeois aspirations. And although the commune system cre-ated economies of scale in Chinese agriculture, it also produced dis-economies when it forbade any production outside its collective structure. A great deal of diversified production went undone because it was too small to be carried out by the collective. Leftist ideology scorned the idea of such small-scale production as springing from the latent "small peasant mentality," which allegedly inclined peasants to-ward small-scale capitalism.

Loosed from these constraints in the late 1970s, peasants launched enterprises of every imaginable sort. Individuals tried rais-ing ducks, keeping bees, putting on theatricals, and teaching neigh-bors how to use new rice strains; they made bird cages, bean curd, bamboo flutes, and bicycle spokes; they spun wheels of fortune in the street to profit from the seemingly universal urge to gamble and they brought televisions into their courtyards, inviting crowds in to watch for a small fee—altogether a bewildering array of entrepreneurial ac-tivity, ranging from the inspired to the pathetic. The variety of pur-suits also took a variety of forms, from simple family operations to companies of shareholders receiving dividends. All these activities contributed to the characteristic pattern of policy and politics in the reform years: they were spontaneous innovations widely dispersed over the country; the state watched their growth warily, often con-demning or suppressing it along the way; and in the end encourage-ment for this peasant entrepreneurship, which the state first opposed, became state policy, for ultimately it coincided with state goals.

Just as support for reform did not necessarily correspond to in-come level, so the impetus behind entrepreneurship had no clear class character. It was not the case that only the rich backed individual entrepreneurship while the poor remained loyal to the collectives. The array of entrepreneurial activities came from peasants of all strata trying to improve their standard of living. Indeed it was often the poorest peasants for whom some alternative source of income could make the biggest difference. Consider Zhang Lixue, a peasant of northwest Hubei whose story was reported in the local papers. Zhang had three small children, and his wife was too sick to work. With only Zhang to take part in collective labor, the family's income was too small to buy medical care for his wife or to pay for his children to go to elementary school. Therefore he began rising before dawn and gathering firewood to sell from a shoulder pole. This was precisely the sort of small production that the Left specialized in ferreting out. As an example of an "upstart trying to get rich quick," Zhang was "marked as the archetype of the small producer. He was criticized at big meetings and struggled (*dou*) at small meetings, and his suffering was beyond words."[52]

Even if Zhang's case was romanticized and exaggerated by the reformist press, it still typified the dilemma of poor people in the 1960s and 1970s who had no way out except through entrepreneurship. The rural poor were stuck in a political system that denied self-help and offered little in its place. No less than richer households who used the reform atmosphere to launch lucrative businesses, the poor jumped at the chance to increase income through small business and commerce.

Testing the Limits of Authority

The third motive behind peasant actions in the reform period was the impulse to test the authority of the local cadres and administrative structure. The authority of the collective structure was nearly always narrow and confining, and it gave local cadres extensive control over people's daily lives. Peasants' feelings toward local authority therefore depended upon the qualities of the individual cadres in question. Cadres who worked hard and showed great stamina in physical labor won respect, and those who were well organized and managed the village economy successfully were the ones peasants wanted to keep in office. Bullies were bad in peasants' eyes; incompetents were worse.[53]

Successful cadres continued to enjoy peasant respect in the reform years, especially if they were sensitive to the fast-changing economic opportunities and helped their villages take advantage of them.

52. *Hubei ribao*, Jan. 2, 1979, p. 2.
53. For a subtle account of peasant-cadre relations, see Anita Chan, Richard Madsen, and Jonathan Unger, *Chen Village: The Recent History of a Peasant Community in Mao's China* (Berkeley: University of California Press, 1984).

But for cadres whom villagers despised, the reform period was precarious. With the balance of local power subtly shifting almost from
day to day, peasants pushed until they found the limits of the power
of unpopular cadres. Particularly vulnerable were cadres who had
bullied peasants in the heyday of the Left and shut off opportunities
to raise peasant income. The central leadership after 1976 made some
effort to steer anger at such cadres toward the leftist Gang of Four
instead, and discouraged peasants from settling old scores.[54] The
propaganda aimed at redirecting peasant fury had a reasonable premise, for the Left's policies against private plots and "capitalist tails"
like family sideline production were clearly antipeasant. Yet this propaganda failed to deflect peasant rage at local authorities who had implemented those policies. Propaganda chief Deng Liqun confirmed
that peasants were indifferent to propaganda condemning the Gang
of Four. What crimes Mao's wife Jiang Qing and her alleged collab-
orator Lin Biao had committed were beyond the direct experience of
peasants. As Deng Liqun put it, "Of course before the Third Plenum
there was destruction by the Lin Biao–Jiang Qing counterrevolution-
ary clique. . . . But most of the cadres and the masses have never seen
the Lin Biao–Jiang Qing gang. They only know this cadre or that
cadre, this activist or that activist. [They remember:] You subjected
me to rectification once; he criticized me; that guy confiscated my
private plot; and that one led a raid on my house and ransacked it."[55]
The only villains that mattered to peasants were the local ones, usually
cadres who had failed to uphold peasant interests.

Animosity toward these unpopular cadres came into the open
during the reform era, when peasants pressed to see how far they
could go in ignoring or defying them. The press commonly condemned the peasants' indifference to authority as an "excess of democracy," and the cadres said peasants were "hard to control."[56] While

54. *Gang of Four,* an epithet supposedly coined by Mao Zedong and used by
the group's political enemies, referred to Jiang Qing (Mao's wife), Zhang Chun-
qiao, Yao Wenyuan, and Wang Hongwen. At the far left wing of the Communist
Party, all four achieved prominence in the Cultural Revolution and became especially powerful in the last few years of Mao's life.

55. Deng, "Jiaqiang he gaijin," p. 17.

56. *Hubei ribao,* Mar. 17, 1981, p. 1. Cf. *Hubei ribao,* June 7, 1979, pp. 1–
2.

this defiant attitude alarmed state leaders, even more disturbing was how often cadres gave in to peasants. "What is frightening," the Hubei press reported, "is that we have some leading comrades who have lost definite views of their own on this problem and have lost the courage to handle problems boldly. Completely helpless, they treat problems lightly, or even sit back and blame the Center, claiming, 'The central documents are too far to the right!' "[57]

A good illustration of this attitude of capitulation prevalent among cadres is the story of a commune Party official in Wufeng County, Hubei. The leader was returning home one day along the accustomed path when he encountered a peasant family building a new house in the middle of a collective rice terrace. He knew that his duty was to put a stop to this plundering of collective property, but he thought better of it and altered his route to go around that particular field. Ever afterward, whenever he was going that way, he took a detour so he would not have to confront the family.[58] This story is a small indication of a subtle shift in power relations that both cadres and peasants intuitively recognized in many communities. Peasants either felt a change or prompted one, pressing against the outer edges of authority after Mao's death, seeing how far their inchoate autonomy could be pushed. Cadres, for their part, sensed a new confidence, even belligerence, in peasants, which they preferred not to test in the changed, uncertain circumstances. This reluctance to confront their challenges enhanced peasants' strength in each instance, giving them a cumulative power that was harder to resist in each subsequent challenge to authority.

Moving toward Family Farming

The fourth motive for peasant action in the reform period was the desire for family farming. This desire combined a negative impulse to escape the collectives with a positive attraction to the family farm.

Chinese sources emphasize only the negative impulse. In its single-minded drive to discredit former leftist policies, the Chinese press of the 1980s portrayed peasant enthusiasm for household con-

57. *Hubei ribao,* Apr. 12, 1979, p. 3.
58. *Hubei ribao,* Mar. 17, 1981, p. 1.

tracting as a repudiation of the old commune system. This explanation of the peasants' prompt abandonment of the collectives is too simple, but it does have some validity. Western and Chinese critics of the collectives usually concentrate on the problems of incentives in collective labor.[59] Even at a time when Hubei supported collectivism as the only correct path for agriculture, the *Hubei Daily* published a complaint about the "sluggish wind" (*tuola feng*) in collective labor—that is, a slow, dilatory work style.[60] Individual peasants saw their extra efforts in collective labor dissipated by the sloth of others; their own laziness didn't seem to hurt them personally, for someone else would pick up the slack. Hubei peasants put the matter this way: "You've got Brother Zhang and you've got Brother Li—if one works more and the other works less, it all comes out about the same."[61] But dissatisfaction with the poor performance of collective labor was only part of the problem, and perhaps the smaller part. The mass of evidence from south-central China suggests that the greatest objection to collectives was that they suppressed the small production separating bare subsistence from life with a slim margin of comfort. All manner of modest efforts—such as raising piglets on table scraps or planting a few extra vegetables—could best be carried out privately in the off-moments of the collective workday. In the leftist phases of policy swings, the collective system repeatedly suppressed such activities as capitalist deviations, thereby making life a little bit poorer. As a result, peasants were painfully conscious of the collectives' inefficient use of resources, especially in the many opportunities for household production foregone because of their small scale.

Yet dissatisfaction with the collectives only partly explains peasant desire for individual farms, for collective farming was not a failure everywhere. As one farmer said, peasants did not have uniform feelings about the collective system. "If it runs well, they like it; if it runs poorly, they don't."[62] And in many places it ran well enough, organizing work adequately and producing a livelihood for peasants. Merely to say that peasants wanted out of the communes, then, is not

59. For example, see Steven W. Mosher, *Broken Earth: The Rural Chinese* (New York: Free Press, 1983), pp. 36–41.

60. *Hubei ribao*, Feb. 11, 1979, p. 2.

61. *Hubei ribao*, Jan. 5, 1981, p. 2.

62. Interview, Hubei, April 1983.

enough. What this explanation overlooks is the positive attraction Chinese peasants felt for family farming. This attraction was a powerful undercurrent in rural politics that state policy since Liberation had not stanched. Rumors in late 1980 of permission to split collectives into family farms even tempted Hubei peasants in factory jobs to go back to the land. The pull of the independent farm had to be extraordinarily strong to tempt these people, for usually the fondest dream of Chinese peasants—especially young peasants—was to find a way out of agriculture and into an urban factory job. Yet letters from home with rumors about an imminent wholesale division of the land were enough to make workers of peasant origin think of packing for home. As one factory manager said, "A lot of workers in our factory have their families in the countryside. They all hear that their families are going to divide up the fields, and they're all agitated about it. There's not much I can do to keep control here."[63]

The appeal of family farming was partly false and partly backward, but it had so many strands that it was hard to dislodge from peasants' imaginations. Ownership of land was the traditional mark of security and status. As an economic venture, private farming ostensibly offered a family independence and control over their own labor.[64] The family farm was also the realm of the patriarchy. Male dominance still thrived in the collectives, of course, but men as individuals felt they could strengthen their supremacy over women and their self-esteem by ruling the domain of a traditional farm. The cultural and religious symbolism of the family farm also remained a deep if obscure attraction. For all of these reasons, family farming was an idea that never quite disappeared. "Dividing the fields," as General-Secretary Hu Yaobang observed, "is a habitual idea among the peasants."[65]

63. *Hubei ribao*, Nov. 3, 1980, p. 2. Similarly, in nineteenth-century England, industrial workers of rural origins maintained the ideal of the independent family farm long after they had left the countryside. See E. P. Thompson, *The Making of the English Working Class* (New York: Vintage Books, 1966), pp. 229–30.

64. For an economic analysis of peasant preferences for family farms, see Victor Nee, "Peasant Household Individualism," in William L. Parish, ed., *Chinese Rural Development: The Great Transformation* (Armonk, N.Y.: M. E. Sharpe, 1985), pp. 164–90.

65. "Zhongyang shujichu tongzhi tingqu nongcun gongzuo huiyi huibao de

The curiosity is how this "habitual idea" could have survived for so long in the People's Republic. Peasants of the reform period took to family farming as if it were the most natural thing in the world, even though they had passed two and a half decades in a collective farm system. A whole generation grew up in collectives but still leapt at the chance for family-run farms. Why did this spontaneous reversion to family farming happen so suddenly a quarter-century after collectivization? The answer is that it was not really sudden. The return to the family farm—or at least to the nearest facsimile possible under China's economic system—was not a bold new departure pioneered in the reform period.[66] In fact the reform period marked the third time in the history of the People's Republic that household contracting occurred openly and on a wide scale.

The first time was when cooperatives were set up nationwide. The cooperatives were organized with extraordinary speed in 1955 and 1956. The majority were erected virtually overnight with little preparation, and many got off to an uncertain start. Cadres and peasants, unsure of how the collective organizations were supposed to operate, invented the household contract system. This system essentially took landlord-tenant relations with which peasants were familiar and adapted them to the new collective setup. By mid-1956 this blend of a familiar arrangement with the Party's concept of collectivization had become a common solution for structuring cooperatives.[67] This instance of household contracting survived until late 1957, when a spate of articles appeared in the *Peoples' Daily* criticizing it.[68]

---

chahua" (Remarks by comrades of the Central Committee Secretariat while listening to the report from the conference on rural work), reprinted in *Zhonggong yanjiu* 16: 4 (April 1982), p. 107.

66. Frederick W. Crook has gone so far as to argue that for the ten years from collectivization up to the Cultural Revolution (i.e., 1956–65), the persistence of household contracting, often in disguised form, was responsible for the viability of the cooperatives and even the people's communes. See his "Chinese Communist Agricultural Incentive Systems and the Labor Productive Contracts to Households, 1956–1965," *Asian Survey* 13 (May 1973), pp. 470–81.

67. Gui Chen, "Guanyu 'bao chan dao hu' de ziliao" (Materials on "contracting output to households"), *Nongye jingji congkan* 1981: 3, p. 46.

68. For examples of criticism and debate over household contracting, see *Renmin ribao* issues of October 13, 1957; October 18, 1957; November 3, 1957; November 13, 1957; and November 20, 1957. These articles discuss the phenom-

The second widespread adoption of household contracting came during the "three hard years" of 1959–61. Initial reports of the resurgence of household contracting circulated in late 1959, when the extent of the disaster of the Great Leap Forward was just becoming apparent in Beijing.[69] As the calamity in the countryside grew, so did household contracting. Peasants and local cadres used household contracting to keep production going in spite of the crushing state procurements of crops during this period. To meet the procurement burden, they parceled land out to families with agreements on how much of the produce would go to meet state quotas. The state later gave qualified support to this system, and it grew quickly, reaching, for example, 65 percent of Anhui's teams by the fall of 1961.[70]

When the third revival of household contracting, under Deng Xiaoping's reforms, is compared with the two previous instances (1956–57 and 1959–61), certain patterns emerge. Each resurgence occurred when rural policy was in confusion or when state control over the countryside suffered a partial breakdown. In the first instance (1956–57), after cooperativization, rural policy was in confusion: cadres were not sure how to run the new cooperatives and therefore improvised a solution along with the peasants. In the second instance (1959–61), not only was policy in confusion, but the catastrophe in the countryside caused a breakdown in state control that was nearly total in some places. The third instance (from 1977 into the reform era) also witnessed policy confusion and a loss of control over peasants by cadres and state. In all three of these periods peasants and maverick cadres acted independently of the state. Each time the state opposed household contracting, at least initially, and each time the peasants acted without organization, with no national movement or coordination of any kind. And yet, in all three instances, they reinvented the same system of family farming. Thus the impulse toward

enon in several provinces, including Shanxi, Guangdong, Jiangsu, Zhejiang, and Henan.

69. The reappearance of household contracting in Henan was criticized in *Renmin ribao* issues of November 1 and 2, 1959.

70. See Gui, "Guanyu 'bao chan dao hu' de ziliao," p. 50, for a description of this period. The figure of 65 percent comes from Katsuhiko Hama, "China's Agricultural Production Responsibility System," *China Newsletter* (September-October 1982), p. 7.

family farming in the reform years represents not an anomaly but a mainstay of politics in the Chinese countryside. What was anomalous under Deng was that family farming and other peasant-driven changes survived—as they had not in their earlier incarnations—and became national policy.

Between their poverty, their desire to prosper with new forms of production, their resistance to abusive authority, and their latent impulse toward family farming, peasants had powerful motives for change. The image of a docile peasantry grimly following whatever orders the state sent down does not fit with the evidence of the reform era. Obedience to dynamic leadership by Deng was not what made things happen in the countryside—peasants already had every reason to act. The circumstances of Deng's early rule finally gave them the *chance* to act, and they did—in a creative burst of energy.

Peasant initiative was the most creative part of the peculiar pattern of politics that marked the reform era. That pattern, with peasants leading and state policy following, resulted from complex interactions among state, cadre, and peasant. After separating the intertwined threads of motivation tugging at these three groups, we can summarize the contribution from each. The state was acquiescent, always a step behind the peasants, but willing to approve whatever might increase its supply of farm goods for the modernization program. The cadres, caught between state and peasant, helplessly watched their power fall into the chasm that separated the two sides. And the peasants seized the initiative—reshaping and sometimes creating the substance of policy, moving China toward family farming and a more commercialized rural economy.

The fundamental question remains: What gives peasants the influence to assert their will under conditions of a strong state and weak society? The case of China suggests two key ingredients: (1) a state whose first priority is balanced economic growth and (2) something to make peasant action cohesive in the absence of autonomous political organization.

The essential precondition was Deng's adoption of the Four Modernizations as his government's fundamental policy goal, committing the state to rapid, balanced economic growth. This was crucial in determining peasant power: it made state goals hostage to the peasantry's position in agriculture. Deng's government had no choice but to cooperate with peasants, for critical nonfarm targets in the modernization program proved one after another to be dependent on farmers increasing production. This dependence on agriculture cut the state off from resort to force as a means for subduing the peasantry. There is no question that the state had the power to wrench more output from peasants, but it could unleash that power only at the cost of destroying any chance for agricultural revival as peasants recoiled in uncooperative hostility.

Thus the state's need for better agricultural performance necessitated a milder approach to enlisting peasants in the modernization effort. This approach took the form of extreme caution in state policy. Divisions within the state—plus the unwanted strictures imposed by the habitual language of political discourse—only compounded this caution, at times turning prudence into timidity. The more nimble officials, such as Wan Li and Zhao Ziyang, raised this restraint in state authority to a new art of governance. They nurtured disobedient creativity on the farm, protecting it from publicity and criticism until it could walk on its own strength. In the hands of Wan and Zhao, deliberate acquiescence in the face of peasant action became positive statecraft; in the hands of some other officials, acquiescence merely made the state irresolute and ineffective. In either case, peasant initiative flourished.

But a second condition is still necessary if peasant action in a weak society is to have any real influence—cohesion. In a strong society rural communities might have cohesion in the form of organization, ideology, and communication, deriving from unions, cooperatives, kinship groups, political parties, ethnic identity, and so on. This is not to say that these organizations act in the interests of the majority of peasants. Obviously, in most countries they do not. But they nevertheless represent a societal counterforce to the state, which rural China lacked. Chinese peasants, however, had an unexpected source of cohesion that was not based on any active organization or system of beliefs. In China the structure of state socialism itself gave peasants cohesion. This was never the state's intention, of course. The collective structure had the primary effect of giving the People's Republic the ability to reach directly and immediately into the lowest level of society anywhere in the vast countryside—an intrusive power possessed by no other state in Chinese history. Yet the quiet, almost unnoticed, consequence of this structure was to lock peasants into a sameness of circumstance that could produce unconsciously uniform peasant action on an enormous scale.

Socialism does not require national uniformity. But the historical fact is that under the state-socialist systems that sprang up in Europe and Asia in the twentieth century, uniformity was habitual and rigid. In China it was an obsession. The government paid lavish lip service to the idea of "suiting policy to local conditions" (*yin di zhi yi*), but its real practice was ever the same: national models and national policies, universally enforced.

All four motives driving peasant initiative which I discussed in this chapter were reactions against the state's obsession with nationally uniform policy. I noted that poverty was the first spur to peasant action, but national policies enforcing high accumulation rates irritated rich and poor communities alike. Thus, while miserably low consumption drove poor regions to agitate for change, the rigid income caps aimed at limiting consumption drove richer districts to join them. Rigidity also stiffened the collective structure against peasant desires, and this exacerbated the movement toward family farming. For example, the private plots that provided at least a symbolic outlet for the deep cultural appeal of family farming came under attack by the Left as a deviation from collectivist practice. The state's insistence on a uniform collective structure regardless of ecological setting added to the desire for change, firing passions to destroy the production teams across south-central China. And even in the northern plains, where collective farming made more sense, peasants believed that the insistence on narrowly collective production harmed rural output, for it squeezed out the myriad minute-scale projects unfit for collective labor. The push for entrepreneurship was universal, infecting even the regions whose terrains were most conducive to successful collectivism. The bottled-up energy, potential, and resentment burst out everywhere at once against the limits on entrepreneurship. Similarly, the uniform administrative structure imposed on the countryside engendered the same types of corruption by cadres everywhere. Thus abusive cadre power also came under attack without regard to region. Altogether, peasants living in vastly different settings confronted a nearly identical face of state power.

Dealing with a state that appeared everywhere the same made peasants behave with a more singular identity than they actually possessed. This is the irony of state socialism. Although democratic socialist thinkers have always believed that socialism would do away with class, the obsessively uniform structures and policies of state socialism make class a more stringent and concrete category than ever. China's collective system locked rural people into an identity *as peasants* that became the first and last fact of their social existence. They lived a life of enforced separateness. Rural people were effectively tied to the land, with the army (mainly for men) and marriage (mainly for women) as the only likely avenues out. They were barred by law from residing in the cities by a system of household registration (*hukou*) that severely restricted internal migration (and continued to do so through the 1980s).[71] Leaving the collective to start a business was banned. Even moving to another collective was extremely rare. In effect state socialism in China created a structure in which ascriptive status was personal destiny, albeit in the guise of a "modern" social system. People were born into peasant status and most were bound to die with it. The practical circumstances to which that status tied them likewise delivered many millions of people into the clutches of the same troubles and offered them the same few choices. When a sense of loosened authority and uncertainty followed upon the death of Mao Zedong, therefore, it was little wonder that millions of people independently tested the same possibilities and paths for change. With a class identity that shaped their lives, peasants acted as if in concert, with an effect approaching the power they would have had if they had acted consciously as a class.

In this way China's state-socialist system imbued disparate peasant acts with the cohesion they needed to have cumulative force. This force was strong in experiments with entrepreneurship but greatest in

71. On the origins and effects of the household registration system, see Mark Selden, *The Political Economy of Chinese Socialism* (Armonk, N.Y.: M. E. Sharpe, 1988), pp. 165–68.

the movement for family farming. What peasants actually did in agitation for family farms was pedestrian. The political activity they engaged in was barely political. The evidence I have cited shows local conspiracies that came together spontaneously and without plan. Authority was challenged only at the level of the most humble officials; wherever possible, peasants defused even that small confrontation by engaging the local cadres in collusion. Secrecy abounded. Peasants made up names of bogus new organizational structures to disguise the dismantling of collectives. They entered pacts of mutual protection to insure a livelihood for families of arrested conspirators. They twisted policy intentions to get what they wanted and willfully misinterpreted orders. They played dumb. They lied. All of this was no more than the usual mundane activity of peasant politics. What made it important was that in this instance it occurred on a massive scale at a moment when the state was irresolute. What would ordinarily be construed as peasant resistance became more than resistance. It became a force with the power to shape and create policy.

The Final Irony

The movement of rural Chinese toward family farming reveals peasant power at its height under a strong state. State uncertainty and peasant cohesion came together in a critical combination lasting several years. But even if this combination brought peasant power to its zenith—raising family farming and other innovations to the status of national policy—it is important to note that this zenith lies low in the wider sky of politics in general. Peasant power under conditions of weak society and strong state is limited. The outcome of the story of family farming in China offers a sobering example.

Family farming was reborn inside China's collective structure after 1976 and grew as a protest against it. The energy and creativity for this radical change came from peasants and cadres at the bottom of society. Family farming grew with nourishment from local people, spreading spontaneously, often with a feeling of tremendous excitement; later it flourished with at least the tolerance of somewhat more distant officials. But as national policy after 1982, family farming was implemented with the government's habitual insensitivity to local concerns. Although family farming began as a peasant innovation, that did not mean all peasant communities wanted it. The innovating activists, though acting in great numbers in the late 1970s, fell far short of a majority of all peasants. The quiet push toward family farming in Hubei was more typical than the outright abandonment of collectives in Anhui. The actual preferences of China's hundreds of millions of peasants are impossible to tabulate. No one knows how many favored what variety of rural organization. My own sense is that a majority preferred family farming without ever becoming activists on its behalf, although there is no consensus among scholars on this point.[72] When official policy reversed and demanded that all communities take up family farming in the early 1980s, most peasants appeared to accept their share of the land with pleasure.

Yet without question a significant minority of communities opposed this division of the land, sometimes bitterly. For reasons of wealth, ideology, topography, farm mechanization, and market access, these communities had deep misgivings about family farming. They preferred the collectives but were helpless to resist family farming once the government mandated it. The government implemented the new policy quickly. By 1984 over 90 percent of China's production

72. Both the origin and popularity of family farming have been controversial among scholars. Andrew Watson's work suggests that family farming was very popular and that the movement of reform was from the bottom up, with state policy lagging behind events. See Andrew Watson, "Agriculture Looks for 'Shoes that Fit': The Production Responsibility System and Its Implications," *World Development* 11: 8 (1983), pp. 705–30; also "New Structures in the Organization of Chinese Agriculture: A Variable Model," *Pacific Affairs* 57 (Winter 1984–85), pp. 621–45. A quite different view emerges from the work of Jonathan Unger, whose surveys suggest that while peasants may have preferred family farming, its arrival in the countryside was from the top down, with peasants playing little part in its creation or its implementation. See Jonathan Unger, "The Decollectivization of the Chinese Countryside: A Survey of Twenty-eight Villages," *Pacific Affairs* 58 (Winter 1985–86), pp. 585–607. For a still more skeptical view of peasants' role in reform, see Kathleen Hartford, "Socialist Agriculture is Dead; Long Live Socialist Agriculture! Organizational Transformations in Rural China," in Elizabeth J. Perry and Christine Wong, eds., *The Political Economy of Reform in Post-Mao China* (Cambridge: Harvard University Press, 1985), pp. 31–61. I will return to a discussion of these different interpretations of the origins of reform in chapter 9 of this book.

teams had been split into family farms.[73] The speed of decollectivization was no doubt connected to the popularity of family farming among the majority. But the speed also meant that opposition to family farming received virtually no hearing from the government. Women who recognized that family farming would deepen their subordination to patriarchal authority had no recourse. Poor families dependent upon collective welfare were instantly imperiled. And the collectives had well-to-do defenders as well as poor ones. Prosperous Guangdong and Jiangsu collectives had little to gain from destroying a system that had enriched them. Furthermore, whole regions in Manchuria, on the North China Plain, and on adjacent plateaus only stood to lose their natural advantage in mechanized farming when consolidated fields were divided. In one of the most poignant scenes in Carma Hinton's film trilogy on the South Shanxi Plateau village of Long Bow, the brigade leader gestures hopelessly at the shed full of idle farm machinery too big for any individual farmer to use after the land was divided.[74] Similarly, Heilongjiang farmers were dismayed at the family farms they were awarded in decollectivization: single strips one furrow wide and hundreds of meters long, carved from what once had been huge fields efficiently plowed by collective effort.[75]

The final irony of family farming is that what began as an innovation by communities seeking more self-determination ended up being forced upon a minority of communities against their will. The state's original insistence upon uniform collectivism created a backlash of sufficient coherence to convince the reformers to permit change. Then the same reform leadership reverted to the habit of uniform policy implementation—"one cut of the knife" (*yi dao qie*), as the Chinese call it—and forced the communities that preferred the collectives to give them up. Passions for family farming had provided the peasantry with enough cohesion to sway the acquiescent government. But passions for the communes were too sparse to resist a government that had finally decided on family farming. State socialism's fixation on uniform national policy lived on unabated.

73. *Renmin ribao,* Jan. 18, 1984, p. 1.

74. "All Under Heaven," a film by Carma Hinton and Richard Gordon.

75. Personal communication, 1984, from Kevin O'Brien, then a resident of Heilongjiang. He reported that collectives continued to use work-point remuneration as late as 1984.

The first necessary element for peasant influence—the state's commitment to a basic project of balanced economic growth—held steady through the 1980s. The second element—peasant cohesion—remained intact as well, for the policy of splitting the collectives was enforced with the same national uniformity as were earlier, opposite policies. Peasants facing similar difficulties as newly independent small farmers had sufficient cohesion to press for changes in credit practices, private land transfers, hiring labor, and further expansion in entrepreneurship. The result in the later reform years was that peasants retained the ability to push hard and effectively in new policy areas against a reluctant state. But the irony of the state's insistence on family farming once it was officially sanctioned points to limits on how far peasants can carry policy in new directions.

The point of the tale of family farming is not that China had a quasi-pluralistic political system. It had nothing of the kind. State leaders were not trying to follow the popular will. The leaders were divided, with some set against radical reform and some quietly pressing for it. Peasant activists benefited from the restraint that radical reformers at the centers of power managed to impose upon the state. But no one in the high state apparatus was acting out of a democratic notion of obeying the people's desire. The reform coalition had the power to crush peasant resistance and confiscate peasant goods at will, as the government had done in the past. Nor did reform leaders lack the stomach for such ugly repression; they killed Tibetans throughout the 1980s and slaughtered Han Chinese beneath the world's most intense scrutiny in 1989. They realized, however, that violating peasant desires has a cost, and under some circumstances that cost is too great for the state to choose to pay. Such was the case in the reform period. That was what gave peasants power.

Chapter Five

Stealth and
Manipulation in
the Marketing War

The battle over family farming
was the most sweeping and dramatic conflict of China's rural re-
form. But while the stunning abandonment of the communes was
capturing world attention in the early 1980s, the Chinese government
and the rural populace squared off in a quieter, barely publicized
struggle. This was a reprise of the most ancient of all state-peasant
conflicts, one that had pitted the peasantry against each dynasty that
arose to govern China: the struggle over the harvest.

"Struggle over the harvest" brings to mind a vision of state agents
wrenching farm goods away from peasants, either by merciless taxation or outright confiscation. Under the People's Republic, however,
the struggle over the harvest took place in the act of buying and selling—that is, in markets. The objects of the struggle were prices for
farm goods and the quantities peasants were required to sell. The setting of the fight was the market in every guise: free markets, black
markets, and, above all, the state market known as the procurement
system. The procurement system was a specialized market for farm
goods, with only one buyer: the state. The state unilaterally decided
the supply of each farm good entering the system and fixed the price.
Peasants were assigned quotas—for either quantities to be delivered
or areas to be cropped—and then had to sell their quotas to the state
whether they liked the price or not. Through this monopsony, the
state could procure farm output at depressed prices and control both
peasant labor and peasant production decisions. The procurement
system dominated every aspect of farm-good marketing in the Peo-

ple's Republic. It was the central arena in the battle for control of the harvest.

Before Deng Xiaoping's final return to power, the state fought this battle ruthlessly, as in the Great Leap Forward, when state agents procured so much grain that millions of peasants starved to death. By the 1970s state procurement was less predatory, but it still crushed peasants' enthusiasm for farm production. The reformers wanted to combat this depressive effect on the flow of marketed farm goods. They hoped to induce farmers to sell to the state more willingly. Deng's new government therefore mounted two major procurement reforms: paying peasants higher prices for their output (from 1979 on), and freeing most crops from mandatory state procurement (in 1985).

These changes altered the nature of the state-peasant conflict over the harvest. With reform, the object of struggle switched from the harvest itself to how it was marketed—in particular, to the prices the state paid for the farm product. The old war of state coercion versus peasant resistance gave way to a more equal contest of manipulation. State and peasant both bent the freer marketing regime to their own ends. Peasant goals in this contest were simple: they wanted higher prices at dependable marketing outlets, plus the freedom to make their own cropping decisions. In their fight to reach these goals, peasants made great headway. For at least five years (1979–84) they shoved the average prices for farm goods above the modest price rises Deng's reformers had approved. Millions of peasants also successfully evaded the state plan, planting higher-priced economic crops instead of the low-priced grain that the government demanded.

Yet during the 1980s peasants did not succeed in remaking the marketing system as they wished. In fact, the large gains they achieved goaded the state into a backlash. By boosting prices and making their own cropping decisions, peasants threatened the conservative reformers' sense of state security. Conservatives believed peasant abuse of the price system endangered the state budget. Resistance to procurement also aroused fears of losing control of peasants, for domination over marketing gave the state control over peasants' output, cropping decisions, and labor. To fight back, the state in 1985 mounted a major procurement reform that created an entirely new price structure, putting an end to peasant manipulation of the procurement bill. To keep control over peasant marketing choices, the 1985 procurement reform also retained the compulsory nature of the system for the most important crops. Specifically, it helped the state to command peasants to plant unprofitable grain. The state publicized these 1985 changes on prices and control as another step forward in farm progress, but they were a thinly disguised step back. They might best be called the backlash reform of 1985.

Like peasants' successes of the reform years, their frustrated efforts to achieve control over marketing are instructive about peasant power. If the struggle over family farming demonstrates the conditions necessary for a small amount of peasant power to flourish, then the struggle over marketing reveals the limits on the peasantry's power when its goals threaten the security of a strong state.

The Procurement System

Deng pleased nearly everyone in rural China by reviving free markets. Each successive year of his rule, village fairs became more boisterous. But away from the eye-catching scene of the new free markets, the vast bulk of China's farm-good marketing continued to be transacted in the more sullen mode of state procurement. Twice each year peasants hauled in their major crops and joined endless lines at the procurement stations. The stations might be staffed by agents of the grain departments, the supply and marketing cooperatives, the cotton companies, or departments under the Ministry of Commerce—all buying up the harvest for the state.[1] Inside the courtyards of the procurement stations, towering dunes of grain attested the state's power to reach deep into the countryside to seize the harvest.

Outside the gates, peasants lined the roads, perched on every imaginable conveyance: makeshift arrangements of hand tractors

---

1. A smaller portion of goods was also procured by agents from the Forestry Ministry, the Foreign Trade Ministry, the Light Industry Ministry, the Aquatic Products Bureau, and the Bureau of Medicine. Ye Nong, *Nongcun jingji zhengce wushi ti* (Fifty topics in rural economic policy) (Suzhou: Jiangsu renmin chubanshe, 1982), pp. 93–94.

hitched to jerry-rigged wagons; carts harnessed with mules, horses, water buffalo or tiny donkeys; and the brutal two-wheeled carts drawn by human beings. On each cart were great heaps of burlap sacks holding the quota of goods the peasant was required to sell. In the summer, the bulk would be winter wheat in the north; in the south it would be the first rice or oil crop, such as rapeseed. In the fall procurement, peasants would haul in the major crops of each region: corn, soybeans, wheat, second rice, and cotton. At the peak of each procurement period, the lines of peasants along the roads outside the purchasing stations could be miles long with waits as long as three days. The mood in these lines of carts was seldom festive. Once inside the gate, peasants made little money on their sales to the state, and in the late 1980s they were often paid in unreliable promissory notes called "white slips" (*bai tiaozi*). Except for a short period in 1983 and 1984 when the harvests were huge and peasants had manipulated the price system to their advantage, prices were well below the free-market level. Despite the reforms, at the beginning of the 1990s the procurement system still operated through coercion.

The lines of peasants selling their goods to the state were the last step in a complex annual procurement process that began with a plan drafted in Beijing. Every year central planners estimated what quantities of farm goods the state would need to export, to supply industry, and to feed city-dwellers, soldiers, and farmers growing economic crops. To meet these needs, the state had to procure scores of different farm products. Until 1985 the plan divided these products into two categories subject to mandatory procurement by the state. The first category comprised goods considered essential to the national economy: grain, edible oil, and cotton.[2] The state strictly controlled the distribution of these goods. In most periods before 1979, peasants were not permitted to sell them to anyone except the state, a prohibition that held for cotton even after the reforms. The second category consisted of other important products, including foodstuffs (such as fish, live pigs, eggs, and honey), industrial raw materials (like

---

2. Lumber was also included in the first category, though I am ignoring it because the main concern of this book is agriculture. Chinese documents on agricultural procurement do generally include lumber, and this is an artifact of China's fusion of agriculture and forestry in central administrative arrangements.

silk cocoons, hides, feathers, and hemp), and major exports (such as tea).[3] Although this second category covered over one hundred products in the early 1980s, it gradually shrank as reform freed more products from mandatory procurement, and it was eliminated entirely as a category after 1985, leaving only the major crops of grain, cotton, and oil subject to mandatory procurement.[4] (A third category of farm goods was a residual made up of minor local specialties that the state procured without mandatory quotas.[5]) For each of the farm goods in the first category and (until 1985) the second category, the plan fixed a quota to be procured from farmers.

After estimating the state's total needs, the planners divided the quotas among the provinces. A given province might be ecologically suited to produce about thirty to eighty major goods. Hubei, for instance, was assigned procurement quotas for about sixty products each year. The provinces further divided the quotas among their con-

3. First-category goods were purchased under *tonggou*, or "unified procurement." Second-category goods were purchased under *paigou*, or "assigned procurement." *Tonggou* was administered directly by the State Council, which set quotas for the entire nation. *Paigou* was administered by units subordinate to the State Council or by the provinces, which had some leeway to designate items for mandatory procurement and to set quotas. See Guo Jinwu, ed., *Jingji da cidian: shangye jingji juan* (Dictionary of economics: commercial economy volume) (Shanghai: Shanghai cishu chubanshe, 1986), p. 479.

4. Chinese sources give varying numbers of products from the second category as subject to procurement. At its height, mandatory procurement (that is, assigned procurement, or *paigou*) of second-category goods covered nearly all important farm goods other than grain, cotton, and oil. The most comprehensive list appears in a 1981 State Council document containing an addendum listing 128 specific products subject to *paigou*. Subtracting 53 medicinal herbs and 2 forestry products from this list still leaves 73 farm goods subject to procurement in addition to grain, cotton, and oil. For the complete list, see the State Council document, "Nong fu chanpin yigou yixiao jiage zanxing guanli banfa (cao'an)" (Provisional method for managing negotiated purchase and negotiated sale prices for agricultural and sideline products [draft]), in *Guanyu jiaqiang wujia guanli de jige wenjian* (Several documents on strengthening control over prices) (Shijiazhuang: Falü chubanshe, 1982), p. 38. Ye Nong (who was also writing in 1981) reproduces in *Nongcun jingji zhengce wushi ti* an identical list of 128 second-category goods.

5. Most of these were produced in small quantities and had short selling seasons. Authority to procure them was left to the provinces. Zhonggong Hunan shengwei xuanchuan bu bangongshi (Propaganda Department of the Hunan Provincial Party Committee), *Nongcun zhengce wenda* (Questions and answers on rural policy) (Changsha: Hunan renmin chubanshe, 1982), p. 119.

stituent prefectures, which in turn parceled quotas out to their counties, and so on down through the communes, brigades, and teams. With the advent of family farming, one last division assigned quotas to individual households. Ordinarily no one wanted a big quota, because the state paid depressed prices for farm goods. Even provincial leaders were known to squabble over their quotas, each trying to reduce his province's assignment.[6]

After all the bureaucratic divisions and redivisions of the procurement quotas, each peasant household got its individual assignment, based on how much land it held. The household then had to sign a contract specifying the quantity of goods it would sell to the state that year, the deadline for delivery, and the approximate prices (with variations for the quality of goods, which would be graded by state agents upon delivery). At harvest time peasants were responsible for bringing their quota of goods to local procurement stations, completing the procurement cycle. What began as a set of central planning decisions each year in Beijing ended with countless individual sales of farm goods in every far-flung village of China. The whole perennial process was a monument to the reach of the state.

From the vantage point of the reform period, the procurement system was an inheritance from an earlier period of dearth. The whole system was premised on the shortages of farm goods that plagued the People's Republic from the 1950s through the 1970s. Keeping the system alive in the reform years meant carrying on the legacy of deep distrust that had grown between peasant and state during those decades of dire rural poverty. Neither side trusted the other to handle the harvest with fairness or intelligence.

6. "Zhongyang shujichu tongzhi tingqu nongcun gongzuo huiyi huibao de chahua" (Remarks by comrades of the Central Committee Secretariat while listening to the report from the conference on rural work), reprinted in *Zhonggong yanjiu* 16: 4 (April 1982), p. 104. For earlier instances of provincial leaders struggling to cut down their provinces' burden of obligatory sales to the state, see Kenneth R. Walker, *Food Grain Procurement and Consumption in China* (Cambridge: Cambridge University Press, 1984), pp. 92–95. On the other hand, officials bucking for promotion were also known to volunteer to take on crushing procurement quotas. This practice was particularly rampant in the Great Leap Forward, with tragic results. See Thomas P. Bernstein, "Stalinism, Famine, and Chinese Peasants: Grain Procurements during the Great Leap Forward," *Theory and Society* 13 (May 1984), pp. 339–77.

The state instituted the compulsory procurement system soon after Liberation to take possession of the farm goods required for building the national economy. The state asserted a claim on any farm produce deemed important to the economy and announced a system of "planned purchase and planned supply," under which peasants could sell essential crops only to the state, at prices set by the state, and in quantities the state dictated.[7] The early Communist government asserted this claim modestly at first, beginning with grain and edible oil in 1953. But the state quickly expanded its claim to other goods, including cotton in 1954, live pigs in 1955, and scores of other items in 1956 and 1957, eventually reaching over one hundred farm goods subject to compulsory deliveries in the early 1980s. The extent of the state's claim on some goods varied over the years with the political climate. In periods when leftist factions were in ascendancy, the government declared that it alone could buy grain, while at other times (as in the reform years after 1979) it tolerated a limited free market in grain. Cotton, however, was never released to the legal free market. Even in the most liberal periods peasants were permitted to retain only one kilogram of ginned cotton for personal use, and any surplus could be sold only to the state. This restriction reflected the paramount importance of cotton in China's light industry: peasants were denied any control over its supply.[8]

7. Interpretations vary on why the state instituted compulsory procurement in agriculture. Audrey Donnithorne, in her pioneering work *China's Economic System* (New York: Praeger, 1967), sees agricultural procurement as part of the broad creation of central planning for the whole economy. Vivienne Shue, in chapter 5 of *Peasant China in Transition* (Berkeley: University of California Press, 1980), places procurement in the context of rural politics; highlighting the positive incentives for peasants to accept the procurement system as part of the transition to socialism, she argues that the goal of the new system was to restrain petty capitalism and destroy the marketing turf of independent entrepreneurs. Jean Oi, in *State and Peasant in Contemporary China* (Berkeley: University of California Press, 1989), takes a less benign view of the state, interpreting procurement as an aggressive attempt to impose both political and economic control over villages. Both Terry Sicular (in "Grain Pricing: A Key Link in Chinese Economic Policy," *Modern China* 14 [October 1988], pp. 451–86) and Kenneth R. Walker (in chapter 2 of *Food Grain Procurement*) emphasize the initiation of procurement as an answer to the state's need to capture grain and savings in anticipation of industrialization under the First Five Year Plan (1953–57).

8. Not only raw cotton, but any form of cotton that peasants were capable of processing at home, such as homespun and homemade yarn, was prohibited

As much as peasants may have resented the state's monopsony in marketing, the most frightful aspect of the procurement system was that the state reserved the power to determine how much of each peasant's output he or she had to sell. In a farm economy of shortage and poverty, this prerogative to define peasants' "surplus" led to terrible abuses. High quotas for some crops were a hardship; for grain they could be life-threatening. Right after the system was instituted, state agents exacted excessive grain procurements to make up for grain lost in the severe Yangtze River flooding of 1954. These forced sales of grain left many peasants without enough to eat by the spring of 1955.[9] The peasants' hunger made them into lasting adversaries of the state and its procurement system, giving state leaders, according to the influential economist Xue Muqiao, "a lesson we must never forget."[10] Yet this was merely a prelude to the massive starvation that followed the Great Leap Forward, when cruel zeal in grain procurement added horribly to the staggering rural death toll. Even though rural areas produced the food, the record grain procurements of 1958–61 took so much food away that the famine brought higher death rates to farm areas than to the cities (see table 2, on page 122). From 1959 on, per capita food-grain supplies for peasants fell behind urban supplies, and did not catch up until the 1980s.[11]

By 1978, when Deng's coalition began to contemplate real marketing reform, a legacy of distrust was already embedded in the procurement transaction. The new leaders publicly admitted that excessive procurements had indeed caused peasant hunger.[12] In addi-

from the free market. Zhonggong Hunan shengwei xuanchuan bu bangongshi, *Nongcun zhengce wenda,* p. 112.

9. Thomas P. Bernstein, "Cadre and Peasant Behavior Under Conditions of Insecurity and Deprivation: The Grain Supply Crisis of the Spring of 1955," in A. Doak Barnett, ed., *Chinese Communist Politics in Action* (Seattle: University of Washington Press, 1969), pp. 365–99; and Walker, *Food Grain Procurement,* pp. 59–60.

10. Xue Muqiao, *China's Socialist Economy* (Beijing: Foreign Languages Press, 1981), p. 276.

11. Carl Riskin, *China's Political Economy* (Oxford: Oxford University Press, 1987), pp. 136–38; Penny Kane, *Famine in China, 1959–61* (New York: St. Martin's Press, 1988). On the specific role of excessive procurements in the famine, see Bernstein, "Stalinism, Famine."

12. One of the most direct admissions came from Xue Muqiao. See Xue, *China's Socialist Economy,* p. 276.

tion, the monopsony in marketing had embittered peasants, who saw that the enforced low-priced sales to the state underwrote an urban prosperity they themselves were barred from sharing. And a quarter-century of farmers' attempted evasion of the procurement duty only confirmed for state leaders their somber assessment of the peasantry: peasants were too short-sighted to recognize the vital need for farm surpluses in building the economy and too self-serving to contribute the surpluses voluntarily. Like the peasants, therefore, the new reform leaders inherited the legacy of distrust that haunted agricultural marketing. Chen Pixian, Hubei's first party secretary during the most radical phase of reform, expressed the problem in a tone of paternalistic concern: "We want to enrich the countryside. But it should be done in a healthy way. Can we rely on the peasants to make free choices on ways of getting rich, in which they only look out for their own short-term interests? No, we can't. For that would strike at the state plan, infringe upon the interests of the whole nation, and thus harm the basic interests of the peasants as well."[13] Central propaganda retained the prereform characterization of procurement as a benign necessity that prevented prodigal rural folk from consuming all that the country needed for economic construction. As Chen Yun put it, "To eat is first, to construct is second. But if we eat everything, there will be no hope for our country."[14]

Yet with the inauguration of rural reform, a profound change did transform this unending battle over marketing. In the first twenty-five years of the procurement system, the fight for the harvest was stark and elemental.[15] The physical product—grain, above all—was the object. In those years of shortage and intermittent famine, state and peasant fought a crude, straightforward fight to control the harvested grain. Victories were measured in getting possession of more grain and denying the other side access to it. With reform, however,

13. Chen Pixian, "Jinyibu mingque dangqian nongcun gongzuo de zhidao sixiang" (Clarify the guiding ideology of current rural work), *Hongqi* 1982: 2, p. 6.
14. Chen Yun, quoted in Li Chengrui and Zhang Zhongji, "How to view the changes in people's livelihood over the past three years," *Hongqi* 1982: 8, translated in JPRS 81062 (June 16, 1982), p. 48.
15. On the struggle over the harvest before the reforms, see Oi, *State and Peasant*, chaps. 2–6.

the nature of the conflict changed. Although poverty remained relentless in many places, the dramatic national increase in agricultural production after 1979 brought much of rural China relief from the acute contest over grain. A modest but real surplus gave peasants room for wider desires. Demand went beyond food to basic consumer goods, bringing intensified desire for ready cash. In addition, family farming and liberal market reform gave peasants new leeway to press for more autonomy in farm work. With these new factors—peasant demand for cash plus the chance to pursue it with more independent cropping decisions—contention between state and peasant shifted from the control of the physical product of farming to control of the money that farm products earned.

The Contest to Manipulate Prices

Deng Xiaoping's reformers embraced price policy as fervidly as Mao's followers had embraced class struggle. The reformers extolled pricing as the key link to a rational, working future, the scientific instrument that enlightened leaders would wield to snap progressive policy into place. Hundreds of articles on prices flooded the economics journals during Deng's tenure, while scores of books on price theory lined the shelves of the best bookstores. New price incentives would smooth the way in agricultural marketing, which reformers saw as the conduit feeding richer farm output into the industrial modernization drive. The more liberal members of Deng's coalition regarded the old farm procurement system as archaic and crude. They believed they could revamp it with price incentives so that it would spur farmers to production increases and bring a larger, better mix of farm goods into the national marketing system.

With bold confidence in the efficacy of pricing, the new coalition made procurement reform its first domestic policy departure at the Third Plenum. The core functions of the procurement system were (1) to secure the peasants' surplus goods for the state, (2) to extract capital from the countryside, and (3) to control peasant cropping decisions. Before the reforms, the procurement system achieved these three goals mainly through coercion. The state simply dictated areas that farmers had to sow to each crop and then ordered the collectives to sell specific amounts of the harvest. This system achieved its goals—at least at a low, crude level—but at great cost to peasant morale and economic rationality. It was too rigid and centralized to allow independent cropping decisions finely adjusted to local conditions. The result was farm output well below China's capacity.

Deng's reforms attempted a dramatic improvement by switching from production planning to price planning. This initial marketing reform was embodied in the cumulative procurement price hikes of 1979–81. Simultaneously the reformers adjusted relative prices of farm products to promote the economic crops needed by industry. In the switch away from production planning, they also changed the way procurement orders were given. Instead of commanding what area was to be sown to each crop, the state relied more on price incentives after 1978.[16] This method granted farmers more leeway in production decisions, which was supposed to make better use of local agricultural strengths and to foster specialization. Altogether, the procurement reforms aimed to give the state more farm output, as well as a better mix of farm goods for supplying industry and exports, with as little open conflict with the peasants as possible.

Prices were the heart of the reformers' program. Their ideal was to set minimum procurement prices that would obtain maximum farm product, and to apply this formula without endangering growth in the farm sector or alienating peasants to the point where enforcement became too costly. The reformers believed price incentives could win peasant compliance with minimal resort to coercion.

This set of changes remade farm marketing in the years 1979–84 and elicited a response from peasants that, on the surface, could not have been more heartening for the reformers. But beneath the appearance of a textbook case for price responsiveness, peasants were launching a quiet, localized campaign to manipulate prices and boost the state's total procurement bill. Their initiative inflamed the lead-

16. For a detailed analysis of the change from production planning to price planning, see Nicholas R. Lardy, *Agriculture in China's Modern Economic Development* (Cambridge: Cambridge University Press, 1983), chap. 2.

ership's greatest fears—budgetary chaos and loss of control—and would eventually bring about the backlash reform of 1985.

The reform coalition opened this contest to manipulate prices with a price increase designed to reverse past damage to agriculture. Deng had come to power after a long period of stagnation in procurement prices for farm goods. The introduction of the procurement system in 1953 gave the state a way to pay farmers prices below the market rate and still compel delivery of their goods. State prices sank below market prices after 1953,[17] and by the time of the Great Leap Forward a burdensome depression in procurement prices had become a fixture of farm life.[18] Stagnation in state prices from the Great Leap to 1978 was interrupted by only two major price rises (in 1961 and 1966), and even these were partially offset by price reductions between 1961 and 1965.[19]

Price stagnation had its worst effects in the twelve years from 1966 to 1978.[20] Procurement prices remained virtually flat, while production costs soared because of efforts to modernize Chinese farming. With prices for farm output frozen at low levels, the cost of modern inputs swallowed up income from production gains, depriving peasants of the financial rewards for technological progress. For

17. Exactly how quickly procurement prices fell below market prices is a matter of controversy. Shue says that when the procurement system started, prices for compulsory deliveries of grain were keyed to local market prices. See her *Peasant China,* p. 221. Dwight Perkins, on the other hand, says that from the very outset of compulsory procurement, the state held prices below the market rate, with a gap of 20 to 30 percent in many areas. See Perkins, *Market Control and Planning in Communist China* (Cambridge: Harvard University Press, 1966), p. 50.

18. Song Guoqing et al., *Guomin jingji de jiegou maodun yu jingji gaige. Di er bufen zhi yi: cong chanpin tonggou dao dizu dishui* (Economic reform and contradictions in the structure of the national economy. A section of part 2: From unified purchase of products to land rent and land tax), printed by Zhongguo nongcun fazhan wenti yanjiu zu (Research Group on Problems of Chinese Rural Development), April 1983, vol. 2, pp. 31–32.

19. "Jianguo yilai nong chanpin shougou zhengce de yanbian" (The evolution of policies for procurement of agricultural products since the founding of the nation), *Jingji yanjiu ziliao* 1981: 1, p. 36.

20. This long price stagnation was interrupted only by minor rises. In 1971–72 prices of sugar and oilseeds were adjusted relative to grain. A small grain price increase in 1971 was offset by higher taxes and larger quotas. For details, see Sicular, "Grain Pricing," pp. 464–66.

example, in the 1960s and 1970s the rich Jiangsu counties near Shanghai increased the multiple cropping of grain, a technique requiring more irrigation equipment, electricity, chemical fertilizer, and other industrial inputs. As a result, grain output increased by nearly 100 percent. But production costs jumped by 250 percent.[21] Similarly, in Heilongjiang, with its low population density and high level of farm mechanization, peasants discovered that more purchases of machines, fuel, and fertilizer raised yields as expected, but left income stagnant.[22] In average and poor regions, the unchanging procurement prices of 1966–78 caused worse hardship. Production costs caught up with, and in some cases overtook, depressed procurement prices, with the result that peasants were forced to raise crops that cost more to produce than the state paid for them.[23]

Deng Xiaoping, Chen Yun, and others in the new reform leadership were convinced that the price stagnation of 1966–78 had undermined the state's procurement effort. The system had come to rely more and more on coercion as price incentives for peasants evaporated. But the coercive apparatus was not at its peak efficiency in the turmoil of the Cultural Revolution, and local officials were probably unwilling to go to the same lengths to confiscate crops that they had in the Great Leap. As a result, the whole system operated less effectively; the proportion of the harvest under state control declined. The state's dilemma is borne out by a comparison of the share of major farm goods the state was able to procure just before prices were frozen with procurements ten years later (table 1).

Table 1 compares state procurement in 1965, the last year before the price stagnation, with 1975. (Both 1965 and 1975 were strong years for agriculture.) The absolute size of procurements grew only slightly from 1965 to 1975, except in the case of pigs. For each crop, procurement size grew by 10 percent or less—painfully small gains when

21. Li Kegang, "Dangqian nongcun renmin gongshe jiti jingji fazhan de jige wenti" (Several problems in the current development of the collective economy of rural people's communes), *Jingji kexue* 1981: 3, pp. 72–77.

22. Bi Jingquan, "Nongye zeng zhi bu zeng shou de yuanyin hezai?" (Why does agriculture have higher costs without higher income?) *Jingji kexue* 1981: 3, pp. 77–81.

23. *Nongye jingjixue gailun* (An introduction to agricultural economics) (Shenyang: Liaoning renmin chubanshe, 1983), p. 253.

Table 1. The State's Share of the Harvest

	Total Output (millions of metric tons)	State Procurement (millions of metric tons)	Percentage of Output Procured
Edible oils			
1965	3.625	.958	26.4%
1975	4.521	.971	21.5%
Cotton			
1965	2.098	2.021	96.3%
1975	2.381	2.210	92.8%
Sugar			
1965	15.376	13.451	87.5%
1975	19.143	14.835	77.5%
Live pigs[a]			
1965	166.9	78.6	74.1%
1975	281.2	102.8	36.6%

Source: Nongye bu zhengce yanjiu shi (Ministry of Agriculture Policy Studies Office), *Zhongguo nongye jingji gaiyao* (Essentials of Chinese agricultural economics) (Beijing: Nongye chubanshe, 1982), pp. 43, 91–93.
[a]Live pigs in million head.

spread over ten years, especially since population shot up 27 percent in the same period. Equally disturbing to state leaders was the change indicated in the far right column of table 1: the state's share of all four major products declined from 1965 to 1975.

The marketing of the all-important grain crop reflected the same alarming trend, as shown in table 2. Consider the portion of the table up to the year 1978, when Deng took over. During this period free-market grain sales were banned, so state procurements accounted for nearly all the purchases in these figures. Deng and his colleagues had no desire to repeat the murderously excessive procurements of 1958–61, carried out during the Great Leap and the subsequent famine. But they were attracted to the moderately large procurements of the periods immediately before and after the Great Leap. Looking back to the years 1963–65—the time of the post-Leap recovery—Deng would have seen that peasants had been selling about one-quarter of the grain harvest. But after the price freeze in 1966, peasants had sold an ever smaller portion of their grain. By 1978, when Deng wanted to start

Table 2. Grain Marketed, 1957–1989

	Total Grain Marketed (millions of metric tons)	Percentage of Output Marketed	Remarks
1957	45.97	28.4	
1958	51.83	31.2	
1959	64.12	45.4	Great Leap Forward and
1960	46.54	39.1	famine
1961	36.55	29.9	
1962	32.42	24.4	
1963	37.00	26.2	Period of Recovery
1964	40.14	25.8	
1965	39.22	24.3	
1966	41.42	23.3	— Onset of procurement
1967	41.38	22.9	price stagnation
1968	40.41	23.3	
1969	38.45	22.0	
1970	46.49	23.3	
1971	43.83	21.1	
1972	38.54	19.3	
1973	48.41	22.0	
1974	46.89	20.5	
1975	52.62	22.3	
1976	49.15	20.7	
1977	47.67	20.3	
1978	50.73	20.1	
1979	60.10	21.8	— Major procurement price
1980	61.29	23.0	rise and legalization of
1981	68.46	25.4	free markets for grain
1982	78.06	26.5	
1983	102.49	31.9	
1984	117.25	34.7	
1985	107.63	34.2	
1986	115.16	35.4	
1987	120.92	36.2	
1988	119.95	36.7	
1989	121.38	35.9	

Sources: *Zhongguo tongji nianjian [1990]* (Statistical Yearbook of China [1990]) (Beijing: Zhongguo tongji chubanshe, 1990), p. 618 for marketing figures and p. 363 for production figures used to calculate second column; *Statistical Yearbook of China [1984]* (Hong Kong: Economic Information and Agency, 1984), p. 366.

Note: This series includes state procurements and market sales. Nearly all of the totals before 1979 represent state procurements, because free marketing of grain was illegal. For 1979 and subsequent years, when grain markets were restored, the proportions of market sales and procurements represented in these totals cannot be estimated because China has not released a complete series on state procurements alone.

The figures are for calendar year, at trade weight. Production figures measure grain in unprocessed form, while marketing figures measure processed trade weight; to calculate the percentage of output marketed I therefore converted production figures to trade weight at a ratio of 0.83. That is, for the entire mix of grains, the processed form is assumed to weigh 83 percent as much as the original grain.

his modernization scheme, the portion of grain peasants sold each year had fallen to one-fifth. Worse still, the absolute amount of marketed grain in the last few years before 1978 hovered near 50 million tons annually. This was not even a 10 percent rise in the two decades since 1957, the last year before the Great Leap sent agriculture into decline. [24]

In every sector of agriculture—grain, economic crops, and animal products—Deng's modernizers were gathering far less product than they needed to develop the economy. To save the state's shrinking share of the harvest, they decisively raised procurement prices (table 3). Deng's group, which took full control only at the end of 1978, followed up that year's modest price rise (a 4 percent increase that did not include most grains) with the big 1979 increases, the first major rises since 1966. The reformers raised the average prices of eighteen farm products by 22 percent in 1979 and continued to raise prices every year thereafter.[25] Of these increases, those with the most telling effect on rural reform were the series from 1979 through 1981, which cumulatively boosted procurement prices by 38.5 percent over 1978 levels. Although ostensibly larger price increases would come at the end of the 1980s, these were offset by inflation and by the elimination of premiums for peasants overfulfilling their quotas. The truly big increase for peasants was Deng's major price reform in 1979–81.

Although the 1979–81 price reform still left procurement prices substantially below free market prices, state leaders hoped the increase would stimulate greater production and make peasants more willing to sell to the state. The price reform succeeded in this aim to

24. Jean Oi (in *State and Peasant*, chapter 4) points out that from 1956 to 1978 the state established local grain reserves as a second strategy for controlling grain. By commanding the collectives to set aside large amounts of grain as reserves, the state asserted control over grain that it could not procure. Therefore the declining procurements I am addressing here may exaggerate the extent to which grain was slipping from state hands (since what was not procured was partly trapped in the reserve system). Nevertheless, in the late 1970s the reform leaders regarded the amount of grain being removed from the countryside to urban centers as sorely inadequate for their modernization plans.

25. Some sources put the 1979 price rise at 24.8 percent. For a detailed list of the specific 1979 increases, see Nongye bu zhengce yanjiu shi (Ministry of Agriculture Policy Studies Office), *Zhongguo nongye jingji gaiyao* (Essentials of Chinese agricultural economics) (Beijing: Nongye chubanshe, 1982), pp. 187–89.

Table 3. Farm-Good Procurement Price Rises versus
Inflation, 1978–1989

	Average Rise in Procurement Prices (%)	General Inflation[a] (%)	Remarks
1978	3.9	0.7	
1979	22.1	2.0	Deng Xiaoping's major procurement price reform
1980	7.1	6.0	
1981	5.9	2.4	
1982	2.2	1.9	
1983	4.4	1.5	
1984	4.0	2.8	
1985	8.6	8.8	Procurement prices rises offset by inflation and elimination of premium prices for extra-quota sales
1986	6.4	6.0	
1987	12.0	7.3	
1988	23.0	18.5	
1989	15.0	17.8	

Source: *Zhongguo tongji nianjian [1990]* (Statistical Yearbook of China [1990])
(Beijing; Zhongguo tongji chubanshe, 1990), p. 249.
[a]Inflation figures are from the overall retail price index.

an impressive extent. In the case of grain, for example, a dramatic reversal is shown in table 2. Price reform—plus the reopening of free
markets—brought massive increases in grain sales from 1979 on. Yet
the price reform also carried China's leaders into an unexpected nightmare that would disturb both their sleep and their policy designs for
the rest of the reform era: a budgetary nightmare. Paying farmers
more for their goods—even below the market rate—took more out
of the central budget. After the jolt of the 1979–81 increases, the leaders had terrible qualms about further procurement price rises. At least
by their own account at the time, the state could not afford to pay
any more. The 1979 price rise alone cost the state an extra 10.8 billion
yuan in increased procurement payments,[26] and by 1981 the extra central outlay to cover the higher prices reached about 12 billion yuan
every year. The entire state budget in those years was only about 100
billion yuan. Shaken by this shock to the budget, Premier Zhao Ziyang took a firm stance: "The price rise costs us 12 billion yuan. We

26. Ibid., p. 189.

don't regret adjusting the prices, but we can't go on eating this [kind of loss] year after year. Going on that way the state would collapse, industrial production could not develop, and there would be no increase in accumulation. . . . If the peasants want to get rich today they will have to rely mainly on growth in production. They can't depend on us to raise the prices."[27]

In spite of this declaration that the state would hold the line against further increases, procurement prices were not wholly within state control. For peasants themselves, in league with rural cadres, had discovered ways of manipulating the price system to their own advantage. The game was on.

At first glance it is hard to see how peasants could affect procurement prices. The state set prices by fiat. Peasants had no say in the matter, and there were no negotiations. The key to peasant manipulation of prices lay in the peculiar fact that there was not just one state-set price for a given farm product, but several. Over the years, the procurement system had operated on and off with three different types of prices. For some crops, one or two of these prices applied. Other crops were procured at all three prices. The first price was the list price paid for the basic quota of goods. Next was a premium price paid for extra-quota goods, which peasants were also required to sell to the state. Third was a floating price (suspended under the Left), which the state paid for voluntary sales beyond the mandatory basic quota and extra quota.

Deng's procurement reform of 1979 changed all three of these prices. The government first raised the list price paid for the basic quotas, then raised the premium prices on grain and oil crops that peasants were required to sell beyond their basic quotas. Previously the state had paid 30 percent above the list price for these extra-quota sales of grain and oil; now it would pay 50 percent above the list price. A new premium price, 30 percent above the list price, was added for extra-quota cotton. The state also revived "negotiated procurements" (yigou) in which peasants who had fulfilled all their quotas had the option of selling surpluses to the state at higher floating prices.

What did this reformed system look like to peasants in 1979? In

27. "Zhongyang shujichu," p. 104.

the case of second-category goods (pigs, hemp, fish, honey, etc.), the system was simple. Each family (or each collective, before family farming) had a quota it had to sell to the state, called "assigned procurement" (*paigou*). The price for this quota was the low list price (*paijia*). After meeting this quota, the family had the option of selling more to the state at the floating "negotiated price" (*yijia*). Or, if the family chose, it could take any surplus to the free market.

For the first-category crops that accounted for the lion's share of state procurement—grain, cotton, and edible oil—the system had an extra twist. Instead of having just one quota (called *tonggou*, or "unified procurement"), peasants also had to meet a second mandatory quota, called the extra quota (*chaogou*). The extra quota fetched the premium price (*jiajia*), set 50 percent above the list price for grain and oil, or 30 percent above the list price for cotton. After fulfilling this second quota, peasants could sell any leftover either on the free market[28] or to the state at the floating negotiated price.[29]

This multi-tiered price system gave peasants an opening to fight back and raise their income. Their main tactic was to twist the multiple price categories to defraud the state. So important was this maneuvering over the types of price and quota that the essentials of the system are worth a quick recapitulation. Thus: the list price was the lowest price, and it applied to the mandatory basic quota. The premium price applied to the extra quota, which was also mandatory for grain, cotton, and oil. The negotiated price applied to any surplus peasants sold to the state beyond the two quotas. Thus for the very same product (a certain grade of rice, for example), there were as

28. Grain and edible oils were permitted on the free market after 1979. Cotton, however, remained banned from the free market until 1985.

29. The negotiated price theoretically lay above the premium extra-quota price but below the market price. In practice the negotiated price was often identical to the premium price, and sometimes even below it. In fact, officials I interviewed at Huashan Commune (Wuhan Municipality, Hubei) in September 1983 could not distinguish between the premium price and the negotiated price at all, and insisted they were the same thing. The confusion is hardly surprising, for the State Council rules on negotiated prices were ambiguous, saying that sometimes negotiated prices could be above the premium price, sometimes below it, and sometimes equal to it. In other words, negotiated prices were intended to float, so that the state could use negotiated prices to influence free market prices. See "Nong fu chanpin yigou yixiao jiage."

Table 4. Procurement Price System, 1979–1984

Price	Categories of Farm Goods		
	First (grain, cotton, edible oils)	Second (other major goods—pigs, tea, hemp, etc.)	Third (minor farm goods)
List (*paijia*)	Basic quota (*tonggou*)	Basic quota (*paigou*)	—
Premium (*jiajia*)	Extra-quota (*chaogou*)	—	—
Negotiated (*yijia*)	Voluntary sales (*yigou*), after meeting basic quota and extra-quota	Voluntary sales (*yigou*), after meeting basic quota	All third-category sales (*yigou*)

many as three different prices for sales to the state. All three state prices were separate from free market and black market prices, and were nearly always lower than market prices. (The procurement price system is summarized in table 4.)

Given that the state decided the list price, the premium price, and even the negotiated price, how could peasants have any effect on prices? They could raise the *average* price by altering the proportions of the harvest that they sold to the state at each of the set prices. If peasants sold the whole harvest in the basic quota at list price, their income would be smallest. But if they sold a greater proportion at the higher premium price and the still-higher negotiated price, the total bill for the same crop would be higher. By shifting their goods into the two higher price categories, peasants achieved a higher average price for the whole procurement.

The legitimate way to accomplish this price shift was to raise production. The state encouraged peasants to do so by fixing the basic procurement quota for five years at a time, while permitting the extra quota at the premium price to be renegotiated every year. Once a family's basic quota for a crop was set, the family could expand production knowing that the increase would all be sold at the premium price, thus raising the average price of the whole crop. For example, peasants in Nanchang County of Jiangsu Province increased the value of their rice by expanding production after 1982. Because their basic quota for rice was fixed, they sold all of their extra output at premium and negotiated prices, raising the average procurement price by one-third.[30]

Peasants also quickly discovered illegitimate ways to boost prices. Some farmers would simply fail to plant all the crops assigned by the state plan, instead devoting all their land to a single crop in order to raise its average procurement price. This happened on a grand scale when the state raised cotton procurement prices four years in a row, 1978–81. The peasants of Shandong Province went on a furious binge of cotton planting, reneging on their quotas for other crops in the state plan. Many districts, especially in the northwest of Shandong, doubled or tripled their cotton output in defiance of the state plan, while their basic quotas for cotton remained frozen. Their deviance from the state plan paid off: at a time when the rest of the nation's farmers were having only one-third of their cotton procured at the premium price, Shandong peasants amassed so much cotton beyond their basic quota that fully 80 percent of it fell into the premium price category.[31] The champion at this artifice was a commune in Guan County, Shandong, which increased its cotton area tenfold in 1979–81, while its basic cotton quota stayed the same. The commune sold practically its whole cotton crop at the premium price.[32] This was not an isolated example. Nationwide, cotton procurement increased 270 percent between 1979 and 1982, but the portion procured at the premium price jumped by 630 percent.[33] This prompted Liu Zhuofu, then director of the State Bureau for Commodity Prices, to complain, "The higher income from the premium prices gives the peasants an incentive to expand cultivation blindly, at the expense of the area sown to grain. This makes a shambles of the cultivation plan."[34]

30. *Renmin ribao*, May 19, 1983, p. 5.

31. Liu Zhuofu, "Wujia fangmian de jige wenti" (Several problems regarding prices), *Jingji yanjiu cankao ziliao* 1982: 174 (Nov. 11), p. 9.

32. Xu Daohe and Gong Qiao, "Shandong, Henan yi xie diqu nongye jihua qingkuang de diaocha" (An investigation of agricultural planning in a few districts of Shandong and Henan), *Jingji yanjiu cankao ziliao* 1982: 134 (Aug. 31), p. 35.

33. Ji Cai and Jia Fang, "Gaige jiage butie de shexiang" (Tentative plans for reforming price subsidies), *Jihua jingji yanjiu* 1983: 21 (July 25), p. 15.

34. Liu, "Wujia fangmian de jige wenti," p. 8.

Individual families found their own ways of converting their harvest from quota to extra-quota sales and obtaining the premium price. For crops that stored well, such as corn, they deliberately fell short of their basic quota for a few years in a row, claiming they had suffered crop failures but actually hiding their output. Then they took this accumulated surplus and sold it in a single year as extra-quota corn at the premium price. Another ruse for swelling premium-price sales to the state involved collusion between units. One unit—say, Team A—would declare that some production problem had nearly ruined its crop. The team would claim that its yield was so poor that it could not even meet its basic quota. But in fact Team A had enjoyed a lovely harvest, which it gave to Team B. Team B would add A's harvest to its own, easily fulfilling its basic quota, with an enormous surplus that it would sell to the state at the premium price. Thus B took A's basic quota, which should have been sold at the list price, and sold it at the premium price instead. A and B would split the extra income.[35]

This same ruse worked through conspiracies between households, teams, brigades, and sometimes whole communes. Above the household level, this trick obviously required collusion by local cadres. Such collusion—never rare in rural China—became rampant after reform made profit the measure of success for rural officials.

Another scheme that required collusion by cadres was the manipulation of "reward sales" (*jiangshou*). Reward sales involved commodities that the state sold *to* peasants at low prices to reward them for selling their output to state procurement agents. This program, begun late in the Great Leap Forward and widely expanded in the reform years, made scarce goods available to households and larger units that cooperated with the procurement system. In the early 1960s basic consumer goods formed the backbone of reward sales. For example, selling farm goods to the state made peasants eligible to buy cheap grain and cotton cloth. This was a powerful incentive, for in those days such necessities were hard to find at any price, let alone at the low state price. In the more prosperous reform period, scarce

---

35. Ibid., p. 8; Song Guoqing et al., *Guomin jingji* (2 vols.), vol. 2, p. 42; Xu and Gong, "Shandong, Henan yi xie diqu nongye jihua qingkuang de diaocha," p. 33.

producer goods became the main incentive offered in reward sales: peasants gained the right to purchase chemical fertilizers and diesel fuel when they fulfilled their procurement duty.[36] Economic-crop farmers had to buy grain for their own subsistence, so the state also offered them grain in reward sales in exchange for selling their economic crops to procurement agents. It was this feature of reward sales—offering one farm good to peasants as a reward for selling another farm good to the state—that opened the system to fraud perpetrated by peasants on a massive scale.

To understand how this fraud worked, suppose that the state procured cotton from a given county, making the county eligible to buy reward-sale grain at the list price or lower. And suppose that the county also happened to sell grain to the state every year through the procurement system—a very common situation. If the county chose to cheat, it would use its own grain harvest to fulfill the basic grain procurement quota. Then, in addition, it would sell back to the state the grain it originally bought *from* the state as a reward sale. Because the county had already fulfilled its basic grain quota, it could sell this extra grain at the premium price. Thus the county bought reward grain from the state at the list price, then turned around and sold the very same grain back to the state at the premium price. Central officials estimated that of 12.5 million metric tons of grain devoted to reward sales in 1982, fully one-third was sold back to the state at a higher price by peasants involved in this sort of scam.[37]

In addition to using these various dodges to expand higher-price sales, peasants practiced sheer defiance: they refused to sell at the list price. This refusal was most common in the case of second-category goods, and it put state procurement agents in a difficult position. Forcing obstinate peasants to sell took time, and procurement agents had deadlines to meet. Furthermore, refusal to abide by the official

36. Reward sales varied from province to province. For some of the basic national guidelines, see "Jianguo yilai nong chanpin shougou zhengce de yanbian," pp. 38, 40.

37. Ji and Jia, "Gaige jiage butie de shexiang" p. 16. See also Zheng Yiwen, "Guanyu gaige woguo nong chanpin shougou zhidu de ruogan wenti" (Several problems regarding reform of our country's farm goods procurement system), *Jingji yanjiu cankao ziliao* 1983: 136 (Sept. 3), p. 18.

price was more likely to be the stance of whole communities or even prefectures than of one easily-handled individual. For example, in large areas of Hubei, the prices of items in short supply (including tung oil, black fungus, and tea) regularly rose out of control when their procurement season came around.[38] Rather than fight whole districts and miss their deadlines, procurement agents were likely to surrender, agreeing to forget the list prices and to buy everything at negotiated prices. Strictly speaking this was against the rules, but some agents found it easier to juggle accounts and take on debt to cover up the extra expenditure than to handle a host of angry peasants. [39]

Widespread peasant success in shifting procurement to the higher price categories laid a heavy financial burden on the state. For the state's local agents this burden was painful. And the cumulative cost for the central budget was, to state leaders, simply unacceptable.

Paying higher procurement prices created a special quandary for local procurement agents, for they had no flexibility concerning the prices at which they resold the goods they procured from peasants. When a procurement agency sold procured farm goods (to other commercial departments, to state enterprises and factories, or to other counties, prefectures, and provinces), the prices it could charge were set by state regulations. Most selling prices were fixed near the level of the low list price, even though the procurement agency may have bought the goods in question at the higher premium or negotiated price. If the harvest was particularly good, then the procurement agency's losses multiplied. Every time the agency bought more from peasants beyond their basic quotas, it had to pay premium and negotiated prices. Consequently the agency's average buying price went up, while its selling price remained fixed at the list price. Every additional purchase from peasants only lost more money, so eventually procurement agents refused to buy any more, regardless of what the peasants' contracts might say and regardless of the size of the harvest.

What bedeviled procurement agents here was the local manifestation of the fundamental irrationality plaguing the whole system: a

38. *Hubei ribao,* Aug. 28, 1981, p. 2.
39. Xu and Gong, "Shandong, Henan yi xie diqu nongye jihua qingkuang de diaocha," p. 34. Also see *Hubei ribao,* Dec. 9, 1980, p. 2; Dec. 14, 1980, p. 1; Dec. 19, 1980, p. 1; and Dec. 24, 1980, p. 1.

perverse effect of supply and demand on price. The original procurement system had been built to command control of scarce farm goods in a national economy of shortage. Its incentives were fixed accordingly, paying peasants extra for any little bit of their small harvest they would be willing to part with. But in conditions of more abundance these same incentives went haywire. State agents had the least incentive to buy when peasants had the greatest incentive to sell, and vice versa. After a bad harvest, the proportion of the crop that peasants could sell in extra-quota and negotiated sales was smaller, hence the average price was lower. When the harvest was good, they had more to sell beyond the basic quota, so the average price was higher. Thus China's procurement system turned the ordinary relation of price to supply and demand upside-down: when supplies were low, the price was low too; when supplies grew, the price went up.

This irrationality played havoc with the state budget during the farm boom that accompanied the reforms in the early 1980s. With production soaring and peasants bringing more and more extra-quota and negotiated-price goods to procurement stations, the per-unit cost of farm goods to the state steadily mounted. And to make matters all the worse, peasants had proven their sophistication at artificially exacerbating this natural trend with their schemes for surreptitiously shifting still more goods into the higher price categories.

This devious shifting of price categories by peasants became evident almost from the outset of the procurement reforms. The proportion of sales to the state at list prices began to decline immediately after the 1979 price rise, while the proportion of sales at both the premium and the negotiated prices ballooned. Consider, for example, the trend in grain procurement. In 1978 most grain sales to the state went at list price, and less than one-third took the premium price. But by 1983 nearly three-quarters of grain sales were fetching the premium and negotiated prices, while the lower list price applied to only one-quarter of the sales (table 5).

State leaders quickly scented trouble. True, the bumper harvests of the early reform period would have created *some* shift of procurement into the higher prices. After all, reform policy was calculated to provide just such an incentive to peasants. But the magnitude of the price shift greatly exceeded the leaders' expectations, and they

Table 5. Grain Sales to the State by Prices

	List Price (%)	Premium Price (%)	Negotiated Price (%)
1978	68.5	31.5	0
1981	45.2	38.2	16.6
1983	27.6	72.4	

Sources: Qiao Rongzhang, "Jiage butie de jige wenti" (Some problems with price subsidies), *Jingji yanjiu ziliao* 1982: 11, p. 9; Guojia wujia ju nong chanpin jiage si (State price Bureau, Agricultural Product Price Section), "1981 nian quanguo zhuyao nong chanpin chengben shouyi chubu fenxi" (Preliminary analysis of nationwide costs and profits for major agricultural products in 1981). *Jingji yanjiu ziliao* 1983: 3, p. 26; and Terry Sicular, "Plan and Market in China's Agricultural Commerce," *Journal of Political Economy* 96: 2 (1988), p. 290.

soon realized that peasant duplicity was behind it. The proof of the peasants' connivance in manufacturing this exaggerated price shift was readily at hand: each year from 1978 to 1982 the state reduced the size of the basic quota for grain, but peasants nonetheless kept failing to fulfill it, with a larger shortfall every year; in spite of such shortfalls, however, the total procurement of grain (in all price categories) went up each year.[40] In other words, while peasants couldn't find enough grain to meet their low-price basic quota, they inexplicably found plenty of grain to sell in the more remunerative extra-quota and negotiated procurements. Nationwide, on a massive scale, peasants were cheating.

The losses to peasants getting extra cash from this price shift glared in the state's accounting ledgers. The breakdown of the state's procurement bill for all crops by different price categories shows a relentless shift of state expenditure toward the more costly categories of procurement (table 6). One can readily surmise, as state leaders

40. The nationwide total size of the basic grain quota was reduced from 37.75 million metric tons (trade weight) in 1978 to 35 million tons in 1979, 34.33 million tons in 1980, 30.38 million tons in 1981, and 30.32 million tons in 1982. At the same time, basic quota fulfillment dropped to 94.6 percent in 1979, 82.4 percent in 1980, and 80 percent in 1981. Terry Sicular, "Plan and Market in China's Agricultural Commerce," *Journal of Political Economy* 96: 2 (1988), p. 290.

Table 6. State Procurement Expenditures by Price Category, 1978–1984 (in Billions of Yuan)

	List Price	Premium Price	Negotiated Price	Total
1978	47.24	4.42	1.02	52.68
	(89.7%)	(8.4%)	(1.9%)	
1979	51.17	11.94	3.50	66.61
	(76.8%)	(17.9%)	(5.3%)	
1980	54.22	15.10	8.00	77.32
	(70.1%)	(19.5%)	(10.5%)	
1981	55.56	20.00	11.00	86.56
	(64.2%)	(23.1%)	(12.7%)	
1982	62.22	22.50	12.50	97.22
	(64.0%)	(23.1%)	(12.9%)	
1983	60.70	35.50	17.00	113.20
	(53.5%)	(31.4%)	(15.0%)	
1984	48.78	48.39	20.70	117.87
	(41.4%)	(41.1%)	(17.6%)	

Sources: *Statistical Yearbook of China [1984]* (Hong Kong: Economic Information and Agency, 1984), p. 365; *Statistical Yearbook of China [1985]* (Hong Kong: Economic Information and Agency, 1985), p. 479.

Note: This series, which the State Statistical Bureau stopped releasing after 1984, includes the value of the agricultural tax collected in kind along with the procurement quotas, as well as procurements by state commercial, industrial, and foreign trade departments. The series originally included direct purchases from peasants by urban residents, but I have deducted that sum from the totals in order to get a better approximation of the state's procurement bill.

did with alarm, what these figures meant: every year peasants were obtaining a higher average price for their crops.

The State Fights Back: The Backlash of 1985

With all the peasant schemes for subverting procurement and raising the price level of farm goods, state officials faced an immense problem. A staggering number of peasants were thinking up ways to defraud the state. How was the state to deal with such massive manipulation of the price system? State leaders believed there were simply too many peasants with larcenous hearts and ingenious minds to track down. Worse still, many of the offenders were themselves cadres in the rural bureaucracy, playing their habitual double role: guardian of state policy one moment, and village leader cheating the state the next. Despairing of catching all manipulators of the reformed procurement system, central officials instead moved to deny everyone the means for raising prices.

Energy for a backlash against peasants began to gather in the central government as early as 1983.[41] Central officials easily recognized that most schemes for artificially raising procurement prices involved shifting output into the higher price categories. The state therefore moved to eliminate the premium and negotiated prices. Experiments in freezing premium-price procurements began with oilseeds in 1983. By that year peasants were already selling 60 percent or more of their oil crops in the premium price category. To hold the line against further price increases, the state froze the proportion of basic-quota to extra-quota sales at 40:60.[42] No matter how much oil a farmer sold to the state, 40 percent would go at the list price, and only 60 percent would fetch the premium price.[43] In effect this change eliminated both the list and premium prices, establishing in their place a single price higher than list but lower than the premium price at which peasants had been selling most of their oil crops. In 1984 the state tried a similar formula to restrict cotton prices.

41. Proponents of a move against farmers argued for lowering procurement prices, raising the price on relief grain sold in rural disaster areas, or eliminating the meager 10 percent of the state subsidy bill that made producer goods cheaper for agriculture. For an early example of promotion of the backlash against the countryside, see Ji and Jia, "Gaiga jiage butie de shexiang," pp. 17–18.

42. The State Council announced at the beginning of 1983 that this policy would begin with rapeseed. Guojia wujia ju nong chanpin jiage si (State Price Bureau, Agricultural Product Price Section), "1981 nian quanguo zhuyao nong chanpin chengben shouyi chubu fenxi" (Preliminary analysis of nationwide costs and profits for major agricultural products in 1981), *Jingji yanjiu ziliao* 1983: 3, pp. 22–31.

43. The same formula applied to sesame, peanut, and rapeseed oils. For cottonseed the effort to arrest price rises was even harsher: the new price equaled 60 percent of the list price plus only 40 percent of the premium price. Guo Jinwu, ed., *Jingji da cidian: shangye jingji juan* (Dictionary of economics: commercial economy volume) (Shanghai: Shanghai cishu chubanshe, 1986), p. 479.

The success of this experiment in combating peasant price manipulation led to the major procurement reform of 1985. Heralded as
the abolition of the procurement system, this reform was badly misinterpreted as the state relinquishing its tight control over farm marketing. In its announcement of the new policies, Central Document
Number 1 for 1985 certainly seemed liberal.[44] It declared an end to
mandatory quotas and to most of the multi-tiered price system that
had gone with them. The unified procurement (*tonggou*) of grain, cotton, and oil under compulsory quotas was ended. Negotiated grain
procurement (*yigou*) was also eliminated and so was assigned procurement (*paigou*) of nearly all second-category goods. No longer would
the state send down production assignments to peasants, and the market was open to nearly everything. Instead the state would practice
"contract purchasing" (*hetong dinggou*), in which state grain departments and cotton companies would negotiate purchasing contracts
with peasants before each planting season.

Beneath these breathtaking changes, however, lay a very conservative intent. More than anything else, the 1985 reform was an attempt to put a stop to the higher payments being made to peasants.
At the heart of the reform was not freer marketing, but controlled
prices. As a study by the Ministry of Agriculture, Animal Husbandry, and Fishery put it, the purpose of the reform was to "eliminate
the policy of premium prices and wide open procurements, and adopt
a policy of suppressing prices."[45] Following the formula to suppress
prices that had worked in the earlier experiment with oil crops, the
state fixed proportionate prices that eliminated the price incentives
peasants had responded to since 1979. The new price regime also cut
out the possibility of further peasant schemes for switching crops to
higher price categories. For grain, the state decreed a single price
equal to 30 percent of the list price plus 70 percent of the premium

44. "Zhonggong zhongyang, guowuyuan guanyu jinyibu huoyue nongcun
jingji de shi xiang zhengce" (Ten policies of the Chinese Communist Central Committee and the State Council for further enlivening the rural economy), Central
Document No. 1 for 1985, *Renmin ribao*, Mar. 25, 1985, p. 1.

45. Gao Hongbin et al., "Chang xian zengzhang, yihuo fazhan chizhi"
(Normal growth or sluggish development), *Jingji yanjiu* 1987: 9, p. 49. The *Jingjixue zhoubao* openly admitted the same point, in its June 7, 1987, issue, p. 6.

price. Negotiated prices were eliminated, and any sales peasants made to the state after they completed their contracted grain sales at the proportionate 30:70 price would drop back down to the old list price. Oil would continue at the single 40:60 proportionate price established in 1983. Cotton price rises would also be held in check with a single proportionate price set at 60:40 in the south (equaling 60 percent of the list price plus 40 percent of the premium price) and 30:70 in the north.[46]

With this reform the state defeated peasants in the price war. Peasants had made great strides in outwitting the state during the six years of rural reform through 1984. They had successfully raised the average procurement price. They had also defied the state plan by sowing crops that would squeeze more money out of procurement agents. In both these successes peasants unnerved reform leaders and provoked a backlash from them.

The backlash reform brought prices back under state control. Only the state, not the peasants, could now influence prices. By 1986 payments to farmers were well below the premium prices they had been getting before the first proportionate prices were established in 1983: 10 percent lower for grain, 13 percent lower for oil crops, and, for cotton, 12 percent lower in the north and 13 percent lower in the south.[47] In at least half the regions of China peasants' receipts on their whole mix of crops fell.[48]

Grain growers, many on farms with little crop diversification, were particularly badly hurt. Although the glut from the record 1984 grain harvest brought prices in many free markets down to the list price, the disappointing harvests of the rest of the 1980s drove free-market prices back up again. In 1986 alone, free-market prices for grain leapt by 29 percent.[49] Thus the historic gap between low pro-

46. These proportionate prices were all announced in "Zhonggong zhong-yang, guowuyuan guanyu jinyibu huoyue nongcun jingji," p. 1. The government continued to adjust these proportionate prices through the end of the 1980s. For details, see Terry Sicular, "Agricultural Planning and Pricing in the Post-Mao Period," *China Quarterly* 116 (December 1988), pp. 674–75.

47. Sicular, "Agricultural Planning," p. 693.

48. Joseph Fewsmith, "Agricultural Crisis in China," *Problems of Communism* 27 (November-December 1988), p. 84.

49. Liu Sunhao, "Lun woguo liangshi wenti de chulu" (The solution to China's grain problem), *Nongye jingji wenti* 1987: 8, p. 3.

curement prices and higher market prices reopened immediately with the 1985 reform. Once again, grain farmers were losing money every time they had to sell to the state instead of on the free market.

The point for state leaders was not simply that they paid peasants a lower average price. The point was that the state was in control. Once the state fixed the base prices under the new system, peasants could not raise them using the old ruses that had been responsible for most of their higher farm receipts. After 1985 the state could exercise discretion in procurement prices, and did raise them substantially— at least on paper. The inflation that raged from 1985 on offset the price rises in the second half of the decade, negating them completely except in 1987 and 1988 (table 3). The important fact is that whatever rises did occur were strictly in the state's control.

Chapter Six

Obsessions of State: Finance and Control

Why didn't peasants do better in the marketing fight? They did greatly expand their marketing choices in the 1980s, but at the end of the decade the state continued to extract goods under compulsory quotas. And the state decisively beat back peasant efforts to raise procurement prices. In this frustrated struggle for higher prices and marketing autonomy, peasants used the same methods that had succeeded in the move toward family farming. In both cases they connived in conspiracies, colluded with local cadres, defied orders, and manipulated policy to their own ends. In both family farming and marketing they achieved early, quick successes. Yet in the end the outcomes were different. Family farming triumphed, while the peasant initiative in marketing made little progress after the backlash reform of 1985. Why did peasant power not prevail in both cases?

This puzzle is even more intriguing in light of state actions. By 1985 reform had brought such an astounding reversal in Chinese agriculture that some foreign development economists believed China was faking its production figures (table 7). The record grain output in the 1984 harvest was 100 million tons larger than in 1978, the last year before reform—a colossal increase of one-third. In the same six-year period the production levels of oil crops more than doubled, and cotton nearly tripled. And even more important to the state, peasants were marketing more of these crops than ever in Chinese history. (For the enormous increase in grain marketing, see table 2, on page 122.) Every word and deed of Deng Xiaoping's reform coalition indicated

Table 7. Output of Major Crops, 1971–1989
(in Millions of Metric Tons)

	Grain[a]	Cotton	Oil Crops
1971–77[b]	269.2	2.22	4.20
1978	304.8	2.17	5.22
1979	332.1	2.21	6.44
1980	320.6	2.71	7.69
1981	325.0	2.97	10.21
1982	354.5	3.60	11.82
1983	387.3	4.64	10.55
1984	407.3	6.26	11.91
1985	379.1	4.15	15.78
1986	391.5	3.54	14.74
1987	403.0	4.25	15.28
1988	394.1	4.15	13.20
1989	407.6	3.79	12.95

Source: Zhongguo tongji nianjian [1990] (Statistical Yearbook of China) (Beijing: Zhongguo tongji chubanshe, 1990), pp. 363–64.

[a]Unprocessed weight.

[b]Annual average.

that this was precisely the result it had been striving for: to move an abundance of farm goods into the general economy and feed the voracious modernization drive. One of the crucial stimulants for this flood of goods was the changed marketing system. The state's procurement reforms, magnified by the peasantry's manipulation, had produced a new incentive structure. Farmers responded to the new incentives eagerly, making marketing reform a success beyond the reformers' wildest dreams.

Yet state leaders were not satisfied. The conservative reformers, who dominated the coalition in the second half of the 1980s, revolted against the liberal direction policy was taking at mid-decade.[1] For the conservatives, the brilliant success of rural reform was darkened by peasant gains in the marketing fight. They abhorred the way peasants

1. A resurgence of conservative power within the reform coalition began in 1985. Drawing their power mainly from the old-guard group in the original coalition, the conservatives succeeded in ousting their chief liberal rivals: Hu Yaobang, in 1987, and Zhao Ziyang, in 1989.

illicitly elevated farm-good prices and evaded the procurement system to make their own planting and marketing decisions. And so in 1985, led by Chen Yun, the ascendant conservatives reversed the policy trend that had brought their reform program so much success. The backlash reform of 1985 curtailed the price incentives that had enlivened the system from 1979 to 1984. In 1985 the conservatives also tried to arrest the trend toward peasant autonomy in planting and marketing. After dramatically announcing that compulsory procurement would henceforth be "abolished" (*quxiao*), the state effectively perpetuated mandatory quotas for China's three most important crops—grain, cotton, and edible oil.[2]

Here, then, is the puzzle. Peasants using the same methods to manipulate policy won in the case of family farming but were stalled (after great gains) in the case of marketing. And in containing this peasant effort to loosen the marketing system, the state reversed policies that had brought it spectacular success in its basic domestic program. Why did peasant power falter? And what drove the state to this Pyrrhic victory?

The reasons for the backlash of 1985 derived from the anxieties lurking in the heart of the state's relationship to the peasantry. The conservative reformers who forced the backlash were driven less by reasons of state than obsessions of state: obsession with finance and control.[3] In finance, conservatives believed that rising farm-good prices jeopardized both industry and the central state budget. This turned them against the peasantry, for the administrative structure of the economy locked the state into a financial alliance with industry against agriculture. And in the question of control, the conservative reformers were obsessed with central suzerainty over peasant labor and decision-making.

---

2. On compulsory quotas in the 1985 reform, see Joseph Fewsmith, "Agricultural Crisis in China," *Problems of Communism* 27 (November-December 1988), pp. 85–86; and Terry Sicular, "Agricultural Planning and Pricing in the Post-Mao Period," *China Quarterly* 116 (December 1988), p. 700.

3. A third obsession, birth control, did not touch on the farm marketing question but did cause state power to intrude deeply in the lives of rural people, especially women. See Tyrene White, "Postrevolutionary Mobilization in China: The One-Child Policy Reconsidered," *World Politics* 43 (October 1990), pp. 53–76.

Farm Marketing and Central Finance

The state's first retaliation against peasants in the fight over farm marketing came when the conservatives eliminated the higher price categories from the procurement system. This ended the peasantry's sustained, successful effort at raising the average price paid by the state for farm goods. At the same time, of course, this change killed the incentives that had fueled the reform period's dramatic recovery in the volume of farm procurement.

The attack on rising incentives for farmers had roots in the state's financial interests, which were tangled in a three-way relationship between agriculture, industry, and the state itself. Industry and agriculture had very unequal degrees of influence upon the state's fiscal welfare—state finance depended much more on industry than on agriculture. This financial alliance between the state and industry is a key to the state's puzzling intransigence against liberalizing farm-good prices. The state always subordinated farm pricing policy to two financial goals: protecting the financial interests of industry and the state, and extracting capital from the countryside.

Protecting Industry and the State

The state's habitual tool for safeguarding the financial health of industry was price subsidies. Price subsidies were special benefits the state financed in order to shield specific sectors of the economy from rising prices. The mechanism was simple: the state would buy goods in one sector and sell them in another sector at a lower price. The state financed this money-losing transaction with an expenditure of revenue, often absorbing the transport, storage, and handling costs of the goods as well. The beneficiary of the subsidy was the final buyer of the goods. With this mechanism, the state mediated the deepest division in Chinese society: between agriculture and the countryside on the one hand and industry and the cities on the other. The state's handling of price subsidies laid bare its own strong preference for protecting urban and industrial interests.

The state began using subsidies to shield the urban sector from rising food prices in 1961. At that time the state increased procurement prices for grain and edible oil without raising their urban selling prices. The central budget absorbed the loss represented by the difference, which amounted to 2 billion yuan that first year.[4] Thus the state began subsidizing urban consumption and initiated what would become a nightmare of irrational pricing. Over the years price subsidies expanded to cover dozens of items, including a few manufactured inputs for farming.[5] But the great bulk of these price subsidies was devoted to keeping food and raw material prices in the cities artificially low. Subsidies on grain, cotton, and edible oil—which the state sold mainly to urban consumers and state-owned light industries—accounted for 70 percent of the subsidy bill.[6]

With the reform period's leap in agricultural procurement prices, subsidies to urban buyers of farm goods soared. By the early 1980s urban price subsidies on food alone were devouring nearly one-fifth of state expenditure.[7] All subsidies taken together were costing the state budget some 32 billion yuan per year early in the decade, and this annual expenditure would pass the 50 billion yuan mark before 1990.[8] (Total state revenue was approximately 100 billion yuan each year in the early 1980s, and around 200 billion yuan at the end of the decade.) State leaders were appalled at this hemorrhage in the central budget. At mid-decade they tried to stanch the losses by retaliating against peasant manipulations of the harvest price. Hence the backlash reform of 1985. This solution—holding the line against rising peasant income instead of ending subsidies to the richer urban populace—was symptomatic of the state's relations with urban and rural China.

Price subsidies served the state's special political needs in urban centers.[9] State leaders dreaded unrest in the crowded cities and had

4. Peng Ziqin, "Youguan wending shichang wujia de jige wenti" (Several problems in stabilizing market prices), *Jingji yanjiu cankao ziliao* 1982: 122 (Aug. 11), p. 21.

5. For a detailed list, see Qiao Rongzhang, "Jiage butie de jige wenti" (Some problems with price subsidies), *Jingji yanjiu ziliao* 1982: 11, p. 8.

6. Wen Yejing, "Dui jin ji nian caizheng shouru zhan guomin shouru bizhong xiajiang wenti de fenxi" (Analysis of the problem of revenue declining as a proportion of national income in recent years), *Jihua jingji yanjiu* 1983: 21 (July 25), p. 13.

7. Terry Sicular, "Grain Pricing: A Key Link in Chinese Economic Policy," *Modern China* 14 (October 1988), p. 479.

8. Qiao, p. 8; *Far Eastern Economic Review*, July 13, 1989, p. 71.

9. On the effect of price subsidies on urban-rural income differentials, see

tried to insulate workers from swings in living costs since 1949. For urban Chinese, one of the most alarming memories of the Republic's disintegration in the late 1940s was hyperinflation. (In Shanghai from 1946 to 1949 consumer-goods inflation ran in the millions of percent.) In contrast, the new Communist government won an early measure of confidence by quickly establishing price stability.[10] Decades later, after the urban warfare of the Cultural Revolution, Deng's reform leadership was even more committed than its predecessors to keeping the cities quiet through political repression and low living costs. The leaders' anxieties were well founded, for urban Chinese in the reform years remained sensitive to minute variations in consumer prices, especially for food. Every rise in food prices caused political controversy. When the cities first felt the effect of the procurement price increases in 1979, such underground journals as *Beijing Spring* began to monitor prices.[11] In Tianjin, workers were reported to have a "bitter reaction" to the price hikes on nonrationed foodstuffs.[12] Because of the influence of rural reform on consumer prices, said one liberal scholar, "urban residents have formed certain bad impressions of the reforms."[13] In 1987 another source warned: "For many years now the price of grain in China has been relatively stable, and this has helped create a state of harmony and unity. If grain prices fluctuate widely within a short period of time, the result will be more than people can bear and the state of harmony and unity will be shattered."[14] The government accordingly paid 27.6 billion yuan in 1988 just to subsidize urban grain sales (mainly rice, bread, and flour).[15] Thus through-

Mark Selden, *The Political Economy of Chinese Socialism* (Armonk, N.Y.: M. E. Sharpe, 1988), pp. 159–62, 174.

10. On the early Communist success in arresting inflation, see Peter Schran, "China's Price Stability: Its Meaning and Distributive Consequences," *Journal of Comparative Economics* 1 (December 1977), pp. 367–88.

11. "Price Investigation," *Beijing zhi chun* 1979: 4, translated in *Chinese Law and Government* 14 (Fall 1981), pp. 64–65.

12. Peng, "Youguan wending shichang wujia," p. 22.

13. Chen Yizi et al., "Dui nongcun renmin gongshe tizhi gaige de jidian kanfa" (A few opinions on reform of the rural people's commune system), *Nongye jingji congkan* 1982: 4, p. 16.

14. *Jingjixue zhoubao*, Mar. 1, 1987, p. 1, translated in JPRS-CAR-087–012 (June 30, 1987), p. 85.

15. *Far Eastern Economic Review*, July 13, 1989, p. 71.

out the 1980s the state clung to the price subsidies, selling procured farm goods to city dwellers at a loss.[16]

The reformers also perpetuated the expensive price subsidies, paradoxically, for financial reasons, believing that money spent for price subsidies on farm goods eventually found its way back to the state. The subsidies sheltered the urban and industrial economy from rising agricultural prices, which enabled industry to deliver heavier fiscal flows into state coffers.

The precondition for this circular flow of funds was that subsidized farm goods had to raise industrial income. Price subsidies on farm goods inflated industry's profits by making food cheaper for urban residents. The availability of cheap food permitted industry to pay a lower wage bill, thus raising profits. The state then took a hefty share of these enhanced industrial earnings through taxes and direct profit remissions into the central budget. Furthermore, the price subsidies provided light industry with a cheap supply of the economic crops needed for raw materials, such as cotton, tobacco, and hemp. Lower production costs for light industry encouraged growth; the state could then either export the expanded light industrial product or sell it domestically, mainly back to the countryside in the form of high-priced consumer goods. In the end the state benefited from bigger taxes or profit remissions from industry, and higher foreign exchange earnings.[17]

16. One dissenting voice inside the coalition was that of Xue Muqiao. Xue, an influential economist, was disgusted with the urbanites' blindness to the fact that their living standard had improved even if prices had gone up. He was equally disgusted by the government's pandering to urban grumbling. In a 1986 speech he said, "What situation is better—the early 1960s, when prices were stable and many non-staple foods had to be rationed? Or these past two years, when prices were de-controlled and rose a bit, thereby doubling and redoubling the supply of non-staple food? In the past several years, people have eaten much better and worn much prettier clothes than they did during the 1960s and 1970s, and the furniture of the average worker and clerical family is much better than before, too. Reforms truly have markedly improved the people's standard of living. So why are we afraid to publicize these facts?" Xue Muqiao, "Do a Good Job in Price Propaganda Work," *Jiage lilun yu shijian* 1987: 2, translated in JPRS-CAR-87–047 (Sept. 14, 1987), p. 67.

17. For one version of this argument that the state recouped its losses on transactions with farm goods through higher income from industry, see Zheng Yiwen, "Guanyu gaige woguo nong chanpin shougou zhidu de ruogan wenti"

Driven by these economic calculations and by fear of angering the massive cities, the reformers kept paying the ever-mounting price subsidies. It was not until 1992, long after the reform coalition had disintegrated, that the State Council finally decided to end the subsidy on grain (although apparently leaving the other subsidies in place). With the city population terrorized after the military attacks on civilians in 1989, state officials felt safe in raising the urban selling price for grain. Announcing the price increase, Finance Minister Wang Bingqian made it clear that the purpose was to stop the drain on the central budget.[18]

Before the 1989 massacre, however, the reform coalition's solution to budgetary losses on subsidies for city dwellers was to contain payments to farmers. This lopsided treatment of the tension between procurement prices and urban subsidies made sense for the reformers. They were simply pursuing interests dictated by the state's position in the politics of finance. For beneath the surface, state leaders had unequivocal fiscal priorities: the state, then industry, and agriculture last. This ranking was determined by the structure created to run China's economy after 1949, in which the state's financial interests were tied directly to industry but only indirectly to agriculture.

The state's unequal financial links to industry and to agriculture derived from the distinctive forms of ownership prevailing in the two sectors. By the 1980s China had three kinds of ownership: private, which applied to personal property and small businesses, including most aspects of family farming;[19] collective, covering much of the rural economy plus some urban enterprises; and ownership by the whole people, which covered state industry. Private and collective ownership in the relatively simple rural economy meant that the people who tilled the land and operated rural enterprises were answerable for their own profits and losses. Large-scale industry, however, was an entity of greater technological sophistication and sociological com-

---

(Several problems regarding reform of our country's farm goods procurement system), *Jingji yanjiu cankao ziliao* 1983: 136 (Sept. 3), p. 7.

18. *New York Times*, Mar. 22, 1992, p. 4.

19. Technically the land that a family contracted belonged to the collective. But the usufruct rights that most families had over their land, combined with the right to transfer it to others for payment, came close to de facto ownership.

plexity and therefore required the more advanced form of ownership by the whole people—that is, by the state.

This division of the economy into a private or collective agricultural sector and a state-owned industrial sector may seem like an arcane theoretical nicety, pleasing to Party ideologues but of no interest to anyone else. But the assignment of different ownership categories to industry and agriculture had far-reaching practical consequences, the most important of which was the state's financial bond with industry.

State ownership in the industrial sector tied state revenue directly to industrial performance. State industry delivered revenue to the central budget through a mix of channels that changed over time. In the 1970s, for example, the state took a high volume of profit remissions from industry. At the beginning of the 1980s, Deng Xiaoping's government introduced a major reform intended to make income taxes the main channel for revenue from state-owned enterprises into the central budget.[20] Because fluctuations in enterprise income made this system unreliable, the reformers switched in 1987 to a "negotiated tax" or "fiscal contract" system. (Rather than taxing uncertain profits, this system required state enterprises to turn over fixed sums according to a multiyear schedule, regardless of actual profit in any given year.)[21] Whatever the mix of channels for delivering these revenues, the source was the same: the central budget remained dependent on industrial performance. Every year throughout the 1970s and 1980s the state obtained at least 80 percent of its revenue from some combination of industrial profit remissions, industrial and commercial tax, and income taxes on state-owned enterprise.[22] In contrast, the agricultural tax accounted for only 4 percent of state revenue in the 1970s and fell to about 2 percent per year by 1990.

20. This reform brought a 55 percent income tax on major enterprises and an eight-grade progressive tax on smaller ones. *Beijing Review,* May 23, 1983, p. 4. See also Elizabeth J. Perry and Christine Wong, "Introduction: The Political Economy of Reform in Post-Mao China: Causes, Content, and Consequences," in Elizabeth J. Perry and Christine Wong, eds., *The Political Economy of Reform in Post-Mao China* (Cambridge: Harvard University Press, 1985), p. 12.

21. *Far Eastern Economic Review,* Apr. 5, 1990, p. 38.

22. *Statistical Yearbook of China [1984]* (Hong Kong: Economic Information and Agency, 1984), pp. 417–18; *China Statistical Yearbook [1989],* The China Statistics Series (New York: Praeger, 1989), pp. 565–68.

In reforming procurement prices, Deng's coalition had to avoid jeopardizing state revenues from industry. Virtually every aspect of agricultural price policy was therefore subordinated to the financial interests of industry. To protect industry, state leaders believed they had to keep farm-good procurement prices low. Peasants knew that depressed agricultural prices underwrote a better life for city people. Barred from residing in the cities and denied the urbanites' privileges in education, health care, pensions, and welfare, peasants resented their own second-class status. But they had equally strong feelings against the second financial function of the pricing system: squeezing capital out of agriculture.

Extracting Capital from the Countryside

Because the procurement system undervalued the farm products it demanded from peasants, every procurement transaction contained an implicit tax on the countryside. After selling their goods at artificially low prices, peasants had to purchase industrial products (both consumer and producer goods) at artificially high prices. As China's most prestigious economics journal pointed out, "peasants take a loss whether they are buying or selling."[23] The net effect of this unequal exchange was a transfer of resources from agriculture to industry. Funds for modernization thus accumulated in the industrial sector, or in state hands via industrial taxes and profit remissions. The fundamental purpose of the procurement price structure was "to make peasants supply the state with accumulation."[24]

Prominent economists like Xue Muqiao readily admitted that the state relied on skewed prices to tax the peasantry. In an agrarian country like China, Xue said, "It seems unavoidable that the peasants have to contribute more to national construction before industry can provide the state with large sums of accumulation."[25] The real policy issue was the question of pace and method: how quickly and by what

23. Jiang Xingwei, "Tantan gong nong ye chanpin jiage jiandaocha wenti" (Discussion of the problem of the price scissors between industrial and agricultural products), *Jingji yanjiu* 1980: 4, p. 73.

24. Ibid., p. 76.

25. Xue Muqiao, *China's Socialist Economy* (Beijing: Foreign Languages Press, 1981), pp. 276–77.

means should the government extract capital from the countryside? Critics of price policy conceded the necessity of squeezing the peasantry, but objected that "the amount of funds accumulated from agriculture through price channels is excessive," and this "is one of the main reasons why peasant income and accumulation are so low."[26] In answer to such criticism, the reformers claimed they had a new, benign way of absorbing capital from agriculture. This new method would still accumulate funds through price channels, but it would work by enriching peasants with consumer goods instead of impoverishing them.

The chief advocate of this refined strategy was Chen Yun. Chen believed that before reform the material incentives for farmers were too low to be effective. Following his advice, Deng had boosted procurement prices. But that was not enough, according to Chen, who pointed out that material incentives are worthless if they are paid in money when there is nothing to buy: "The peasants are selling their agricultural products at high prices and accumulating money. If we cannot think of a way to make an exchange to recover it, then peasants will just end up with more and more paper money in their hands. Then there will be the danger that the peasants may become unwilling to continue selling their farm products to the state."[27]

Chen proposed a simple remedy. The state would offer peasants an array of consumer goods at inflated prices. With the enticement of manufactured goods, peasants would be willing to sell their output to the state. As procurement agents paid out more for larger crops, the state could recover the extra expenditure by expanding the volume of high-priced consumer goods sold to peasants.[28] The more consumer goods peasants bought, the faster the state could accumulate capital from the countryside. Hence the pleasant irony that Chen Yun enjoyed pointing out: "So long as the vast number of peasants have a

26. These quotations are from Fang Jing, "Sanshi nian lai woguo cheng xiang chabie de yanbian" (The evolution of the town-country gap in our country over the last thirty years), *Jingji yanjiu ziliao* 1982: 5, p. 21; and from Zheng, "Guanyu gaige," p. 3. To support their point, these critics wielded a variety of economic measures (often derived from arcane calculations using the labor theory of value).

27. Chen Yun, quoted in Peng, "Youguan wending shichang wujia," p. 22.

28. Fang, "Sanshi nian," p. 21, and Zheng, "Guanyu gaige," pp. 8–9.

higher consuming power, the state need not worry about having enough money to use."[29]

This strategy represented a refinement of the price mechanism used to extract capital from the countryside in the 1960s and 1970s. In those years the Chinese economy offered peasants virtually nothing in the way of consumer goods. In order to recover its outlay on farm procurement, the state offered producer goods at high prices, with a predictably deleterious effect on farm output. The expensive price tags on farm machines and chemical fertilizers had only retarded China's economic growth by putting modern farm technology out of many peasants' reach. Reversing this practice, Chen intended to overprice consumer goods while holding down prices on producer goods. "While consuming power is increased," he said, "a large amount of money can be withdrawn from circulation in order to accumulate more capital for industrial and urban development purposes. We can practice the policy of having low prices in one sector and high prices in another sector. To sell [farm inputs] at low prices is to patronize production, and to sell [consumer goods] at high prices is to get back more money for the sake of accumulation."[30]

This strategy—innovative as it appeared—was actually an idea recast from Mao Zedong's theoretical writings of the 1950s.[31] But Mao never put the idea into practice, for after 1958 his policies placed almost no new supplies of consumer products in peasant hands. In contrast, Deng Xiaoping's coalition delivered the goods. An explosion in rural demand occurred as soon as the first enlarged procurement payments reached peasants in 1979. By many accounts a revolution in peasant aspirations occurred practically overnight: "In the past, the peasants' primary demand was 'enough food to be full and enough clothes to be warm.' Now they demand to 'eat well, be well dressed, and have good housing.' "[32]

29. Chen Yun, "Chen Yun's Speech at the CCP Central Committee Work Conference," translated in *Issues and Studies* 16 (April 1980), p. 95.

30. Ibid., p. 97. I have made very slight corrections here in a garbled translation.

31. Mao pointed out that light industry could supply goods to improve rural life, and peasants purchasing these goods would be turning capital over to the state/industrial sector for development. See Mao Zedong, "On the Co-operative Transformation of Agriculture," *Selected Works of Mao Tsetung*, vol. 5 (Beijing: Foreign Languages Press, 1977), p. 197.

32. Peng, "Youguan wending shichang wujia," p. 22.

This revolution caught industry completely unprepared. For years peasants' cash income had been so pitiful that factories had come to ignore the rural market.[33] As late as 1981 factories in Wuhan, the huge industrial center of Hubei, produced mainly higher-quality goods that could compete successfully in the established markets—that is, in the cities. They were largely ignorant of the enormous demand right in rural Hubei for items that city people scorned, such as rubber shoes and mechanical alarm clocks.[34] The durable goods that peasants craved—sewing machines, radios, watches, and bicycles—were already quite common among Hubei's urbanites, according to the Wuhan Central Department Store. Hubei peasants also wanted to buy more building materials (especially glass for windows), leather shoes, powdered milk to replace ersatz infant formula made of rice-flour and sugar, manufactured cigarettes with filters, bottled beer, and toys for their children. All of these things were in too short supply to meet rural demand.[35] One study concluded that "even if the entire present product of light industry were put into the rural market, it would still not meet demand."[36]

33. Nicholas Lardy reported the cash component of collectively distributed income as only thirteen yuan per person annually in 1974–78; Nicholas R. Lardy, *Agriculture in China's Modern Economic Development* (Cambridge: Cambridge University Press, 1983), p. 161. Another source said that cash was less than half of net per capita peasant income in 1978, but jumped to two-thirds in 1981; "Nongmin shouru lianxu san nian da fudu zengzhang" (Peasant income increases by a big margin three years in a row), *Nongye jingji congkan* 1982: 6, p. 55.

34. *Hubei ribao*, Sept. 10, 1981, p. 3.

35. The information on demand for goods in rural Hubei is from *Hubei ribao*, Dec. 1, 1980, p. 2, and Apr. 26, 1981, p. 1. For a comparison with peasant demand in a richer rural area (in Jilin Province), see Wei Jinkui et al., "Guanyu Yingkou xian Yong'an gongshe qunzhong xuqiu qingkuang de diaocha" (Investigation of supply and demand among the masses at Yong'an Commune, Yingkou County), *Jingji yanjiu ziliao* 1982: 3, pp. 62–64. The survey by the Wuhan Central Department Store is reported in *Hubei ribao*, Mar. 26, 1981, p. 1. On the scarcity of goods in rural areas, see all the articles above, plus Ma Renping, "Nongcun shixing shengchan zeren zhi hou chuxian de xin wenti" (New problems that have appeared since the implementation of the production responsibility system in the countryside), *Jingji guanli* 1981: 8, pp. 6–7. Of course for some goods (such as synthetic and woolen clothing) demand jumped in both city and country in the reform period. See the study of income elasticity of demand for a variety of products in rural and urban Hubei by Yang Xiaokai et al., "Hubei sheng weiguan jingji muoxing ji yingyong" (Microeconomic models for Hubei province and their application), *Jingji yanjiu cankao ziliao* 1982: 175 (Nov. 13), pp. 22–42.

36. Yang Chengxun, "Lun nongcun shichang dui woguo xiandaihua jianshe

Chen Yun saw that the state's enlightened self-interest lay in meeting this demand. The coalition therefore expanded consumer production geared to peasants from the outset of reform. Rural morale enjoyed a boisterous upsurge as a result of rising living standards, and the state procured a hugely enlarged farm product below free-market prices. Yet peasants remained skeptical. Paying what they recognized as inflated prices for industrial goods, they felt cheated out of their higher farm receipts. From the early 1980s onward, peasants objected that the state used the skewed urban-rural price mechanism to take back the benefits of the procurement price rises. One of the earliest of these reports, from Wujiang County, Jiangsu, said that by 1983 farmers were already losing three-quarters of their gains from higher procurement prices to inflated prices for manufactured goods.[37] And contrary to Chen Yun's intentions, peasants were convinced that the state was securing their funds by over-pricing producer goods, not just consumer items. Farmers in Jianyang County, Fujian, compared their procurement receipts against higher prices on chemical fertilizers, insecticides, farm machines, and tools, and concluded, "The state gave us some material benefit and then walked off with it again."[38]

As a strategy for extracting capital, then, the reform coalition's push to offer more industrial goods for sale in the countryside was successful. But as a means for alleviating peasant discontent with the procurement system or for disguising the extraction of rural capital, it was not. Peasants continued to resent the low prices at which they were forced to sell their goods to the state. As far as they were concerned, state procurement was an onerous, poorly disguised tax.

---

de cujin zuoyong" (The function of the rural market in advancing the construction of modernization in China), *Jingji yanjiu* 1982: 3, p. 21.

37. Wujiang xianwei nong gong bu lianhe diaocha zu (Combined Investigating Group of the Agriculture and Industry Department of Wujiang County Party Committee), "Nong fu chanpin tijia hou nongmin dedao le duoshao haochu?" (How much benefit have peasants gotten out of the price increases on agricultural and sideline products?) *Nongye jingji congkan* 1983: 6, p. 42.

38. Chen Yixiang and Xie Guohua, "Guojia gei de shihui you bei nazou le" (The benefits given by the state were taken away again), *Nongye jingji congkan* 1983: 6, p. 49.

"The Imperial Grain Tax"

If one ignores state procurement of farm goods, then rural taxation in China appeared to be minimal under Deng. The main exaction was the agricultural tax, a fixed levy payable in kind or in cash. The predominant form of payment was grain, though cash became somewhat more common in the late 1980s. The Chinese press made much of the fact that the agricultural tax declined over a long period, from over 10 percent of agricultural output in the 1950s to only 4 percent in the 1980s.

But the agricultural tax was a red herring. Much heavier was the disguised tax in the form of the state procurement quota assigned to each field. This indirect tax, not the agricultural tax, was the principal levy on peasants. As Xue Muqiao said, through indirect taxes "the state has obtained several times more from the peasants."[39] To farmers growing crops undervalued by the procurement system, the quota assignment represented a public claim on the land just like the agricultural tax—only much larger. For this reason peasants nicknamed state procurement "the imperial grain tax."[40]

Even after the official price rises of 1979–81, the procurement burden was often too heavy, especially in grain farming, which engaged a greater proportion of the peasantry than any other kind of production. With procurement prices set well below free-market prices, the state had to rely on coercion to get grain planted. In spite of the huge expansion in grain output during the reform period, grain farmers enjoyed much smaller gains than peasants raising economic crops, not to mention those pursuing lucrative sideline enterprises.[41] Investigators in Zhejiang Province found that peasants had "little enthusiasm" for grain because "the costs in grain cultivation are high, risks are large, income is low, and profit is small."[42]

39. Xue, *China's Socialist Economy*, p. 277.

40. Chen Yan and Jiang Taiwei, "Nongye jihua tizhi bixu shiying nongye 'shuangbao' hou de xin xingshi" (The agricultural planning system must be suited to the new situation in agriculture after the "two contracts"), *Jihua jingji yanjiu* 1983: 33 (Nov. 30), p. 24.

41. On the differential returns to grain and economic crops, see Guojia wujia ju nong chanpin jiage si (State Price Bureau, Agricultural Product Price Section), "1981 nian quanguo zhuyao nong chanpin chengben shouyi chubu fenxi" (Preliminary analysis of nationwide costs and profits for major agricultural products in 1981), *Jingji yanjiu ziliao* 1983: 3, pp. 22–31.

42. Zhu Nailiang et al., "Zhejiang Jiaxing diqu zhuanrang chengbao tudi de

In the south-central rice-growing belt of which Zhejiang is a part, oppressive grain quotas in the 1980s even drove peasants to the unthinkable extreme of abandoning land.[43] Across the region, among the most fertile and overpopulated in China, it was reported that "there is land nobody wants, land that is abandoned and left to go out of cultivation."[44] In a prosperous southern Hubei county, for example, grain cultivators "try to think of any way they can to get rid of their responsibility fields."[45] In Yuanjiang, a productive rice-growing county in Hunan, the only way officials could keep peasants from abandoning land was by cutting their procurement assignments in half. The quotas there had stood at a crushing 3,000 kilograms per hectare—well over half the harvest.[46] Such debilitating quotas were not necessarily the rule, however. In other localities, the grain assignments were light. If anything, the incidence of procurement quotas struck peasants as capricious. It was no coincidence, for example, that Chuxian and Guzhen in Anhui Province, touted as models during the reform years, both had extremely light burdens: the quota for Chuxian Prefecture averaged 540 kilograms per hectare, and that for Guzhen County was only 270 kilograms.[47] These localities could

qingkuang" (Transfer of contracted land in Jiaxing Prefecture, Zhejiang), *Nongye jingji congkan* 1983: 5, p. 32. Cf. Liang Xiufeng, "Lao shangpin liang chanqu nongmin gongxian da shouru shao de qingquang zhidi zhuyi" (Cases of peasants in old commodity grain production areas making a big contribution but getting little income deserve attention), *Nongye jingji congkan* 1982: 6, pp. 40–41.

43. On peasants attempting to abandon land in Zhejiang, see Xu Jinbiao et al., "Nongmin weishenme bu yuanyi zhongtian?" (Why aren't the peasants willing to till the land?) *Nongye jingji congkan* 1984: 1, pp. 57–58.

44. Zhu et al., "Zhejiang" p. 32.

45. This was in Honghu County. Zhou Yegao, "Yao zhongshi jiejue liangshi zhuanye hu, zhongdian hu fazhan zhong yudao de wenti" (Pay attention to solving the problems that specialized grain households and keypoint grain households run into in the course of development), *Nongye jingji congkan* 1983: 5, pp. 60–61. On land being abandoned elsewhere in Hubei, see *Renmin ribao*, Aug. 6, 1983, p. 2.

46. Xu Qingshan, "Caiqu zhengce cuoshi, baohu nongmin zhongtian jijixing" (Take policy measures to protect the peasants' enthusiasm for tilling the land), *Nongye jingji congkan* 1984: 1, p. 53.

47. As of 1981, when central propaganda was celebrating these two districts' farming successes. The propaganda never mentioned the low procurement duty as a prime factor in making success possible. Anhui shengwei nongcun gongzuo bu (Rural Work Department of Anhui Provincial Party Committee), "Anhui sheng nongcun wan hu jingji qingkuang de diaocha" (Economic survey of ten thousand

achieve model status partly because the state's low-priced procurements took a relatively small bite out of their income. As with any tax, the size of the procurement burden was an important determinant of farmers' net income.

How much capital was actually extracted from the countryside through procurement is a complex question on which neither Chinese nor Western economists agreed.[48] Peasants themselves habitually reckoned the disguised tax by subtracting their procurement receipts from what they could have gotten for their crops on the free market. By this method of calculation their losses were enormous. Even after the procurement price increases, free market prices exceeded state list prices by over 40 percent from 1980 through 1984. For grain and edible oil, market prices were 90 to 100 percent above list prices.[49] Using this method, Secretariat economists in 1983 calculated transfers to the state through grain procurement alone at 15 billion yuan per year (about five times the value of the agricultural tax), while the Ministry of Agriculture in 1988 estimated the transfer at 10 billion yuan annually.[50]

---

households in Anhui Province), *Jingji yanjiu cankao ziliao* 1982: 126 (Aug. 18), pp. 21–22.

48. For discussions about measuring the tax implicit in procurement, see Song Guoqing et al., *Guomin jingji de jiegou maodun yu jingji gaige. Di er bufen zhi yi: Cong chanpin tonggou dao dizu dishui* (Economic reform and contradictions in the structure of the national economy, a section of part 2: From unified purchase of products to land rent and land tax), vol. 2, printed by Zhongguo nong-cun fazhan wenti yanjiu zu (Research Group on Problems of Chinese Rural Development), April 1983, pp. 35–36; Thomas P. Bernstein, "Cadre and Peasant Behavior Under Conditions of Insecurity and Deprivation: The Grain Supply Crisis of the Spring of 1955," in A. Doak Barnett, ed., *Chinese Communist Politics in Action* (Seattle: University of Washington Press, 1969), p. 366; Lardy, *Agriculture*, pp. 119–20; Alexander Eckstein, *China's Economic Revolution* (Cambridge: Cambridge University Press, 1977), p. 119; and Dwight H. Perkins, "Constraints Influencing China's Agricultural Performance," in U.S. Congress, Joint Economic Committee, *China: A Reassessment of the Economy* (Washington, D.C.: Government Printing Office, 1975), pp. 363–64.

49. Andrew Watson, "Reform of Agricultural Marketing in China Since 1978," *China Quarterly* 113 (March 1988), p. 12 n.

50. Song Guoqing et al., *Guomin jingji* (2 vols.), vol. 2, pp. 35–36; Grain Problem Unit, Economic Policy Research Center, Ministry of Agriculture, Animal Husbandry, and Fishery, "The Grain Shortage and Readjustment of Economic Policies," *Nongye jingji wenti* 1988: 5, translated in JPRS-CAR–88–040 (July 26,

State leaders treated the disguised-tax phenomenon as a political problem of the utmost gravity. This was evident in their resistance to the idea of a straight land tax. Younger, university-educated reformers deplored the inefficiency of the procurement system as a vehicle for taxation. They proposed scrapping the whole unwieldy system of procurement plus tax-in-kind and replacing it with a straight land tax payable in cash.[51] But central leaders rejected a simple land tax as politically risky. The danger they saw was this: to get the same amount of revenue through a land tax as the state already obtained indirectly through procurement would mean revealing just how huge the transfer of capital out of the countryside really was. If peasants found out the real magnitude of their tax burden, state leaders feared, their fury would bring political catastrophe.

This caution at the top betrayed a certain obliviousness to what was happening at the bottom of rural society. It was no secret to peasants that procurement concealed a tax. From the beginning of family farming, peasants had treated procurement as a tax pure and simple. To see the peasants' point of view, remember that each year procurement quotas were divided among the provinces, which redivided them among their prefectures, counties, and so on down to the villages. By the time individual households got their procurement assignments, the quotas had been divided so many times that some were irrationally small. A peasant family might be assigned a fairly large quota for grain or cotton, plus quotas for some dozen other products in quantities too small to be grown economically.[52] As an example, here are the

1988), pp. 30–31. The problem with these calculations is that they beg the question of how much free market prices were inflated because of the very existence of the procurement system. After all, if state procurement were shut down completely, then the flood of goods entering the free market would drag prices down. For this reason the implicit tax was probably somewhat less than the state estimates.

51. For one of the best examples of the argument for replacing procurement with a land tax, see Song Guoqing et al., *Guomin jingji de jiegou maodun yu jingji gaige* (Economic reform and contradictions in the structure of the national economy), printed by Zhongguo nongcun fazhan wenti yanjiu zu (Research Group on Problems of Chinese Rural Development), February 1983. This is a separate printing from the two-volume work by Song Guoqing et al. cited above.

52. Officials accepted these tiny quota assignments in order to share the implicit tax burden evenly. Because the gap between procurement price and market price differed widely among farm goods, the magnitude of the implicit tax also

procurement quotas assigned to families in a village in Suining County, Sichuan, for 1982:[53]

rice	66.5 kilograms	peanuts	2.7 kilograms
wheat	52.5	chicken eggs	2.0
cotton	46.0	barley	0.9
cotton seed	43.5	soybeans	0.7
rapeseed	11.0	mung beans	0.4
corn	9.0	sesame seeds	0.1
sorghum	8.0	pigs	2 head

The economist who compiled these figures commented, "This is not a joke. It is the result of every administrative level having to take the State Planning Commission's plan, and divide it up and share it out."[54]

Peasants called these absurd lists of tiny procurement quotas "opening a department store."[55] Because of them peasants uncovered the tax hidden within the procurement system. Only fools would use their time so inefficiently as to grow a quota of 0.9 kilograms of barley or 0.7 kilograms of soybeans. So instead, peasants bought the required quantities of goods, paying free-market prices. Then, to meet their quotas, they sold the same goods to the state procurement stations at the low list price. Thus procurement became a cash transaction. Peasants paid out one yuan for some product in the market, then got back less than one yuan for it from state agents. In this transaction the truth could not have been more transparent: procurement was only a disguised way of giving up cash for the sake of the state. It was a tax.

Although the practice was usually illegal, peasants had been buying goods on the market for resale to state procurement agencies at

varied across different products. No one wanted a procurement assignment heavy in goods with a larger implicit tax, so the quotas tended to be parceled out evenly by each administrative level.

53. Song Guoqing et al., *Guomin jingji* (2 vols.), vol. 2, p. 46. For other examples of irrationally small quotas, see Sichuan sheng Changshou xian gong shang xingzheng guanli ju (Administrative and Management Office for Industry and Commerce, Changshou County, Sichuan), "Changshou xian de nong shang san ji jingji hetong zhi" (Changshou County's three-level contract system for rural commerce), *Jingji yanjiu ziliao* 1982: 10, p. 28; also see Chen and Jiang, "Nongye jihua," p. 22.

54. Song Guoqing et al., *Guomin jingji* (2 vols.), vol. 2, p. 46.

55. Sichuan sheng Changshou xian gong shang xingzheng guanli ju, p. 28.

least since the early 1970s. By the 1980s large rural units habitually divided their quotas into the portion they would meet directly by growing the product themselves and the portion they would fulfill by buying goods on the market.[56] Not only individual peasants, but communes and even counties were mired in such draining cash transactions. Peasants had no illusions about the losses they suffered under this system. One source reported their feelings this way:

> As far as the peasants are concerned, grain procurement is simply "the imperial grain tax." From the local cadres down to the village children and old men, this idea is crystal clear.... Who is ready to accept the notion that procurement is just an equal exchange? Only the people in the cities believe that. The state provides over twenty billion yuan every year in price subsidies on agricultural and sideline products [for city people]. The city and the country will never agree on this. The city people look upon the official prices for farm goods as an exchange. The peasants see it as the imperial grain tax.[57]

As a tax, as a conduit for capital accumulation, and as part of the structure supporting the alliance between industry and the state, the procurement system was critical to the state's financial interests. State leaders believed that peasants manipulating the procurement price system threatened those interests. No matter how counterproductive the effects of suppression, therefore, the state was not prepared to allow peasants to win the price war.

Farm Marketing and State Control

But peasants had another way of resisting procurement: evasion and disobedience. By planting the wrong crops or by delivering fewer crops, farmers fell short of their quotas and cut their losses in the procurement transaction. Like the price war, this effort to evade state command aroused one of the leadership's most intense obsessions: the desire to control peasants. Farm marketing policy gave the state powerful indirect control over what peasants did on their farms. By restricting peasants' marketing

---

56. Song Guoqing et al., *Guomin jingji* (2 vols.), vol. 2, pp. 49–50.
57. Ibid., vol. 2, p. 51.

choices, the procurement system controlled their cropping decisions and labor. Peasants resisting procurement were fighting this control. All reform rhetoric aside, the idea of ordinary peasants making independent decisions about marketing and cropping—and thus keeping control over their own labor—was not acceptable to the coalition leaders. The peasants' struggle for liberalization of farm marketing was at heart a fight against state control.

Peasant Control of Crop Selection

The most direct way to resist state control was outright defiance. In the early reform period some village cadres began to whittle away at procurement volume to minimize the implicit tax. A 1982 report from North China said, "Clashes between cadres and the state over procurement assignments have increased. Cadres are now unwilling to accept procurement assignments that they would have completed before, or else they are trying to reduce them. The demand with regard to procurement assignments now is the smaller the better."[58] Individual farmers went even further. In Hubei it was reported that peasants "haggle when they get their procurement assignments, trying to cut down the basic quota. And when selling grain to the state they hold back the good grain and sell the bad, or even adulterate it with some foreign substance." [59] Such direct forms of resistance had only a marginal effect on overall procurement, however. For the countryside as a whole, and for any individual farmer, the more effective means for reducing the procurement burden was to switch crops.

The crop that farmers wanted most to avoid planting was grain.[60]

58. These clashes were in Henan and Shandong. Xu Daohe and Gong Qiao, "Shandong, Henan yi xie diqu nongye jihua qingkuang de diaocha" (An investigation of agricultural planning in a few districts of Shandong and Henan), *Jingji yanjiu cankao ziliao* 1982: 134 (Aug. 31), p. 36.

59. Hubei sheng nongwei (Hubei Provincial Agricultural Committee), "Da li jiaqiang he gaishan nongcun sixiang zhengzhi gongzuo" (Greatly strengthen and improve rural ideological and political work), *Shehui kexue dongtai [Hubei]* 1983: 2 (Jan. 10), p. 21.

60. Price parities between grain and other crops did vary, and at certain locations and certain times grain was more attractive than some economic crops. By 1990, for example, cotton no longer held the appeal over grain for some farmers that it had in the first half of the 1980s. But as a general rule, throughout the 1980s grain was the crop to escape.

Undervaluation of grain by the procurement system loaded it with a heavy implicit tax. Before the reforms, this underpricing was so severe that grain cultivation was a losing proposition. The *Economics Weekly* estimated that in 1978 farmers lost one to two yuan for every *mu* (one-fifteenth hectare) of rice they planted, five yuan on each *mu* of corn, and over eight yuan on each *mu* of wheat. The initial Third Plenum reforms brought a brief period through 1982 when grain was profitable, but after 1982 grain production costs went up so quickly that farmers lost heart within one or two seasons.[61] Following the record harvest of 1984, planting grain for the state became as unattractive as ever. In major grain-producing areas the gap between procurement prices and market prices ranged from 50 to 100 percent from 1985 on.[62] At the same time, with the excessive issues of currency after 1984, returns to grain fell precipitously against the steep rise in the general price level.[63] A commentator for the state admitted in 1987 that "stagnation in grain is a fact . . . the price motivation for the peasants is weak. Besides, as the means of production are in short supply and expensive, the peasants grow grain mainly to fulfill their patriotic duty"—that is, to fulfill a forced quota.[64] The state tried to reverse the situation in 1988 with an 18 percent increase in grain procurement prices.[65] But this increase, large as it was, amounted to running hard just to stay in the same place. It fell short of the year's 18.5 percent rise in the retail price index and barely kept pace with the 1988 jump in prices for agricultural producer goods (16.2 percent).[66] Farmers finished out the decade with repugnance for growing China's most important crop.

Farmers fleeing from grain planted economic crops instead. Throughout the decade of reform, light industry craved the raw ma-

61. *Jingjixue zhoubao*, Mar. 1, 1987, p. 3.

62. Gao Hongbin et al., "Chang xian zengzhang, yihuo fazhan chizhi" (Normal growth or sluggish development), *Jingji yanjiu* 1987: 9, p. 51.

63. Chen Jian, "Lijie he bawo muqian Zhongguo nongcun xingshi de yaoshi shi shenme" (What is the key to understanding the current situation in rural China"), *Nongye jingji wenti* 1987: 8, p. 23.

64. *Xinhua ribao*, June 14, 1987, translated in JPRS-CAR-87–027 (July 30, 1987), p. 73.

65. *Far Eastern Economic Review*, July 13, 1989, p. 71.

66. *China Statistical Yearbook [1989]*, pp. 591, 596.

terials found in economic crops. This surging demand caused farmers to switch crops in great waves. Cotton was the first wave—rising in the wake of the Third Plenum price increases, cresting in 1984, and breaking with the crash of price incentives in the second half of the decade. A wave of tobacco planting swelled in mid-decade, followed by a wave of ramie when its price skyrocketed by several hundred percent, causing the government to complain in 1987 that peasants had been crazed by a "ramie-planting fever."[67]

The rise of cotton typified these waves. The Third Plenum tried to reverse the historic underpricing of cotton, with spectacular results. Within five years China doubled its cotton output, becoming the world's biggest producer by 1983. The record 1984 harvest exceeded domestic demand and China became a major exporter. But the cotton surge brought new trouble: the state could no longer get peasants to grow the grain commanded by the state plan. In Shandong Province, for example, team, commune, and even county cadres colluded to expand cotton area at the expense of grain, reducing the grain sown area in some prefectures by over 40 percent.[68] Shandong farmers who faithfully fulfilled their grain quotas instead of switching to cotton suffered serious losses, while their disobedient neighbors profited plentifully.[69] Fearful of cotton taking over grain fields nationwide, the state decided to reverse itself and cut incentives for cotton. Farmers responded—by the end of the decade cotton output had fallen to barely two-thirds of the 1984 peak (see table 7). In 1990 textile mills had trouble obtaining sufficient supplies of cotton, for it could no longer compete with the price incentives on other cash crops.[70]

Yet the state never succeeded in regaining the land for grain. Grain was so underpriced that per-hectare returns reached only a fraction

67. *Jingjixue zhoubao,* Apr. 12, 1987.

68. Xu and Gong, "Shandong, Henan," p. 33. For a detailed analysis of the Shandong cotton problem, see the study by the Shandong Academy of Social Sciences in Deng Guibin, "Wending paijia, gaige jiajia, tiaozheng jiangli cuoshi" (Stabilize the official price, reform the premium price, and adjust the reward measures), *Jingji yanjiu cankao ziliao* 1983: 136 (Sept. 3), pp. 55–67.

69. Liang, "Lao shangpin liang," pp. 40–41.

70. *Far Eastern Economic Review,* Feb. 22, 1990, p. 66; Wu Nanbing, "Several Problems in Cotton Procurement Policies that Merit Attention," *Jiage yuekan* 1987: 5, translated in JPRS-CAR–87–033 (Aug. 13, 1987), pp. 109–13.

Table 8. Area Sown to Grain and to Economic Crops
(in Millions of Hectares)

Area	1978	1988	Change 1978–88	Percentage Change
Grain	120.6	110.1	−10.5	−8.7
Economic crops	14.4	21.5	+7.1	+49.3
Total[a]	150.1	144.9	−5.2	−3.5

Source: *China Statistical Yearbook [1989]*, The China Statistics Series (New York: Praeger, 1990), pp. 158–59.

[a]The residuals are accounted for by vegetables and other crops.

of what they would have been if the same land were planted to jute, hemp, tobacco, ramie, sugarcane, or other economic crops.[71] Economic crops as a group encroached further every year onto the land once planted to grain, even as China's total sown area underwent a dangerous drop (table 8).

The economic liberals led by Zhao Ziyang felt some trepidation about this trend, but they had reason to feel heartened as well. Peasants had clearly shown that they were very sensitive to price incentives and market signals. This ratified the fundamental policy theory guiding the liberals: that prices could be a more subtle, efficient, and productive way to guide agriculture than heavy-handed central planning. The liberals had demonstrated that with a certain mix of farmgate prices, input costs, and procurement quotas, they could elicit a predictable and even quick response from peasants making cropping decisions. To the liberals, the decline of grain did not prove their experiment a failure; it only showed that the price signals for grain were inadequate. Rather than bludgeoning peasants into planting grain, they advocated raising prices and requiring city people to buy their grain on the free market. Then, at last, China would be sending market signals to farmers telling them how massive the demand for grain really was.[72]

71. For an early analysis of returns of grain versus economic crops, see Guo-jia wujia ju nong chanpin jiage si, pp. 22–31.

72. One outlet for the liberals' view was the *Economics Weekly*. See *Jingjixue zhoubao*, Apr. 12, 1987, p. 6; June 30, 1987, p. 3.

Where the liberals saw hope and progress, however, the conservative reformers saw only a deplorable spectacle. The decline in grain was a calamity in their minds, and further surrendering state control to the independent marketing decisions of peasants lay somewhere between irresponsibility and madness. The conservatives saw bad omens everywhere. In the second half of the 1980s China continued to lose some 200,000 to 300,000 hectares of farmland every year to housing, urban expansion, and industrial use. The average farm size for a peasant family of four was less than an acre. With this pressure on arable area and peasant resistance to planting grain, the nation did not match the peak grain year of 1984 (407 million tons) until 1989. Meanwhile, population grew at a natural rate of 10 to 15 million per year, requiring (according to Vice-Premier Tian Jiyun) about 10 million tons more grain each year.[73] Furthermore, Chinese were consuming grain in a much more direct, unprocessed form than people in developed countries. Any enrichment of the diet (meaning conversion of grain into meat, eggs, liquor, or dairy products) would require still more grain. According to one farm journal, a 25 percent increase in per-capita grain output would be necessary for the average Chinese "if he wishes to drink beer and Maotai or eat more meat."[74] Industry also clamored for more grain, because it was required for the production of solvents, sizing, alcohol, starch, and pharmaceuticals. Yet year after year recalcitrant peasants fell short of their basic grain quotas. Angry and alarmed, the conservative wing of the reform coalition propelled itself into action.

Reassertion of Control by the State

Chen Yun led the conservative reaction. Infuriated with peasant defiance, Chen was ready to reverse his own advice against coercing the peasantry to get the farm product. He opened his attack with a rare public criticism of current policy in a speech at the National Party Conference in September 1985. Before all the top leaders gathered in

73. Tian Jiyun, "China's Current Agricultural Situation and Policy," *Beijing Review*, Jan. 8–14, 1990, p. 19.

74. Fu Min, "Correctly Treat the Readjustment of the Structure of Agricultural Production," *Nongcun gongzuo tongxun* 1985: 1, translated in JPRS-CAG–85–015 (May 21, 1985), p. 31.

the Great Hall of the People in Beijing, Chen complained that "some peasants are no longer interested in growing grain," because "peasants engaged in industry and business earn more than those who grow crops. They are not even interested in raising pigs and vegetables." Unless peasants were brought under control, he warned, "grain shortages will lead to social disorder." The only way for the state to assert itself was through central planning: "Planning is the essence of macroeconomic control." Chen condemned markets as a destructive substitute for planning, and claimed that they caused the economy to become "chaotic." He charged that "market regulation involves no planning, blindly allowing supply and demand to determine production."[75]

Chen was striking back at the liberal wing of the reform coalition. Nine months before Chen's speech, the liberals had won major concessions on farm marketing policy in the procurement reform of 1985 promulgated in January. This backlash reform had largely been a conservative victory, for it had squelched peasant schemes for raising prices. But the reform was also something of a compromise, in which the liberals had gained, too—against Chen's wishes. The reform was meant to liberalize the procurement system by releasing all second-category goods to the market and proclaiming the end of compulsory procurements of grain, cotton, and oil. The compromise formula called for grain marketing to run under a "dual track system" (*shuang gui zhi*) combining state procurement with the free market. Now, later in 1985, Chen was fighting for a conservative interpretation of this compromise, one that would keep the state dominant in agriculture, with free marketing in a minor adjunct role at most.

Asserting this conservative control meant opposing the apparent intent of the 1985 reform. Under the new rules, instead of submitting to compulsory quotas, farmers were supposed to sign freely negotiated contracts with state grain departments for the amount of grain they actually wished to sell. These contracts finally brought to agriculture the norms established by one of the landmark laws of the re-

75. The excerpts are all from "Speech Delivered at the National Conference of the Communist Party of China," Xinhua, translated in Foreign Broadcast Information Service, *Daily Report: China*, FBIS-CHI–85–184, Sept. 23, 1985, p. K14.

form period, the Economic Contract Law, adopted in 1981. The law stated: "In concluding an economic contract, the principles of equality and mutual benefit, consensus through consultation, and compensation at equal value must be followed. Neither party may force its will upon the other, and no unit or individual may illegally interfere."[76] Applied to farm procurement in 1985, the law meant that peasants could no longer be forced to accept contracts with quotas for sales they did not want to make. In the ensuing years, Chen and conservative officials at all levels prevented this reform from taking real effect. Mandatory quotas may have been "abolished," but they flourished under other names. In the late 1980s localities all over the country told of using "administrative methods"—the standard euphemism for coercion—to get peasants to deliver grain and other goods to the state.[77] The principle of letting peasants enter freely into contracts was routinely violated, in spite of regular lip service in its honor. For example, in a 1990 interview a county-level Hebei official told me, "Peasants here have free choice to plant whatever they want." Yet when I asked what would happen if a peasant family refused to sign the procurement contract, he replied simply, "They must sign." And when asked if peasants got the chance to negotiate what went into their contracts, the official rolled his eyes, saying, "If we consulted every peasant about his contract we couldn't finish talking to all of them in a whole year."[78] As another report from northern China put it, "Contracts are drawn up as administrative orders that do not represent the principles of willingness and equal rights and obligations for both parties. They are merely a form."[79]

The mutuality and equality celebrated in the new contracts shat-

76. Fifth Article of the Economic Contract Law (adopted at the fourth session of the Fifth National People's Congress, December 13, 1981) from Wang Zhong, Li Quanyi, and Zhou Zhiyuan, eds., *Jingji hetong fa shouce* (Handbook of Economic Contract Law) (Changchun: Jilin daxue chubanshe, 1984), p. 4.

77. For examples of coercion, see Fewsmith, "Agricultural Crisis in China," especially pp. 85–86.

78. Interview with Agricultural Bureau official of Xinji *zhen* (formerly Shulu County), Hebei, June 1990.

79. Hu Qiufa and Yuan Zhijun, "Some Suggestions Regarding the Emphasis on Grain Production," *Nongye jishu jingji* 1985: 12, translated in JPRS-CAG–86–010 (Mar. 27, 1986), p. 17.

tered against an ingrained official mentality of control and domination. A 1987 report said, "Because of the lasting effects of many years under the old procurement system (*tonggou*), the signing of a grain procurement contract still carries a heavy flavor of coercion, with peasants cast in a passive, subordinate position. This inequality in legal status leads directly to unequal contract obligations. The contracts frequently lack any means for controlling the state commercial departments."[80] Grain procurement departments remained notorious for squeezing peasants, who sometimes derided their staffs as "grain extortion officials" (*cui liang guan*). Arbitrary additions to quota assignments continued to be a common abuse, with extra procurement demands passed down through the bureaucracy level by level.[81] Another 1987 report said that when peasants refused to sell, "then the administrative departments and grain procurement departments at every level pull out the same old administrative methods, rigidly dictating grain cropping areas, using coercion to procure grain, imposing many methods of punishment, and even calling out the militia and the police to ransack [peasant homes] for grain."[82]

The state bureaucracy resorted to coercion to procure grain throughout the late 1980s. Shaanxi officials warned farmers that their children would be expelled from school if they did not make their 1988 grain quotas.[83] The *People's Daily* reported in 1987 that the whole northeast was gripped in a "grain war" between farmers and the state.

> The tense atmosphere of the "grain war" simultaneously filled Liaoning, Jilin, and Heilongjiang provinces. Some localities in Jilin adopted coercive measures to purchase grain, such as imposing fines and repossessing the land. Some villages in Liaoning hired ensembles to blow wind instruments in the peasants' courtyards on the eve of the spring festival, disturbing those who refused to deliver grain.

80. Shu Hua, "Liangshi dinggou hetong falü yiju de zhiyi yu duice" (Questions and solutions regarding the legal foundation of grain purchasing contracts), *Nongye jingji wenti* 1987: 11, p. 44.

81. For one example, see Shanxi Provincial Service, Apr. 26, 1987, translated in JPRS-CAR-87–010 (June 23, 1987), p. 110.

82. Lu Wen, "Nongcun jingji fazhan zhong de xin dongtai" (Recent trends in rural economic development), *Nongye jingji wenti* 1987: 12, p. 3.

83. *Wall Street Journal*, Jan. 19, 1988, p. 1.

They even took away the peasants' television sets and washing machines. To purchase grain, the cadres of some villages in Heilongjiang quarreled and exchanged blows with the peasants.[84]

To sweeten this coercion, the government adopted a program of incentives in 1986 called the "three-link" policy (*san guagou*). Peasant sales of grain, cotton, and certain other crops to the state were "linked" to three rewards: coupons to buy cheap diesel, coupons to buy cheap chemical fertilizer, and cash advances in the spring planting season. These were huge incentives. Diesel and fertilizer shortages plagued all farmers, as did a cash squeeze every spring. But the government could not make good on the promises. Procurement agents, for example, could only pay the springtime cash advances by getting credit from the Agricultural Bank, which was in the clutches of the credit crisis that pervaded rural China in the late 1980s. Procurement agents could not even get funds to pay for farmers' actual deliveries at harvest time, let alone for the cash advances.[85] Of sixteen provinces surveyed in the summer procurement season in 1988, for instance, only half had the funds needed to pay peasants for their deliveries. Throughout the late 1980s chagrined peasants received promissory "white slips" (*bai tiaozi*) instead of cash for their crops.[86]

If the government's failure to follow through on the cash advances disappointed peasants, reneging on the other two "links" —cheap diesel and fertilizer—enraged them. Yields declined dramatically when peasants were denied chemical fertilizer, and without diesel for the water pumps to irrigate the fields at the right moment, crops like rice could be lost entirely. Peasants were infuriated because officials took the cheap diesel and fertilizer promised to peasants and sold it at full market prices or used it as bribes. The Xinhua News Service covered many incidents of this official embezzlement to try to shame authorities into carrying out the three-link policy properly.[87] Meanwhile, angry peasants took things into their own hands.

84. *Renmin ribao*, July 7, 1987, p. 2, translated in JPRS-CAR-87-034 (Aug. 14, 1987), p. 92.

85. Heilongjiang Province Branch Bank, "Devote Major Efforts to Successfully Supplying Funds for Purchasing Agricultural Sideline Products," *Nongcun jinrong* 1985: 18, translated in JPRS-CAG-86-010 (Mar. 27, 1986), pp. 26–27.

86. *Far Eastern Economic Review*, July 13, 1989, p. 71.

87. On diesel, for example, see the Xinhua story in *Renmin ribao*, Apr. 30,

In Sangzhi County, Hunan, for example, more than 2,000 peasants gathered over three days in June 1987 to buy their promised chemical fertilizer at the county warehouse. A county government official informed them, "There is no fertilizer in the warehouse." In fact, all the fertilizer had already been allotted in sales to county and township (*xiang*) cadres with connections, including officials from the public security bureau, the county court, and the county government. Outraged, the mob of peasants stormed the warehouse.[88] This was not an isolated event. Some 170,000 Hunan peasants, unable to buy their subsidized fertilizer, raided fertilizer plants and retail outlets. In all there were over 200 incidents of plundering fertilizer in Hunan in the summer of 1987. Twelve people were killed, scores injured.[89]

Yet even though the state reneged on the promised incentives, it still got the grain. Ultimately, peasants had no one else to sell to. Although the reform coalition legalized free markets for grain in 1979, there was no national network of private traders to haul peasants' grain away. The bulk of private grain marketing remained local, leaving millions of peasants in the heavy grain-growing districts with inadequate outlets for private sales. "After all," as one local Hubei official said, "you can't sell grain in the village if everyone else is a grain farmer too."[90] After the record grain year of 1984, when peasants had trouble selling their huge output, grain slumped in the second half of the 1980s. The low price incentives and controls over marketing cut peasant enthusiasm for grain production. Output did not equal the 1984 harvest again until 1989 (table 7). When output finally crept up again, the conservative reformers claimed that their coercive methods had worked. But it was not the rampant bullying of peasants that brought the grain in, any more than it was the three-link policy or the appeal to peasants' patriotic duty. Rather, the con-

1987, p. 1. On chemical fertilizer and diesel, see Beijing Xinhua English Service, July 3, 1987, translated in JPRS-CAR-87-038 (Aug. 25, 1987), pp. 98–99; also *Renmin ribao*, June 17, 1987, p. 1.

88. *Renmin ribao*, July 28, 1987, p. 2.

89. *Far Eastern Economic Review*, May 25, 1989, p. 69. For more on the "three link" corruption in Hunan, see Hunan Provincial Service, June 1, 1987, translated in JPRS-CAR-87-015 (July 6, 1987), pp. 77–78.

90. Interview at Huashan Commune, Wuhan Municipality, Hubei, September 1983.

servatives' procurement policies succeeded on one basic principle: denying peasants any marketing alternative.

The Underlying Source of Control

Before the reforms, the local coercive apparatus was the key to extracting crops. Without coercion, peasants would just eat their grain season after season in circumstances of poverty. But the peasantry's prereform method of resistance—consuming the grain themselves—only worked in conditions of bare subsistence. Once farmers moved beyond subsistence, as they did in huge numbers during the 1980s, they could obtain the consumer goods they wanted for a better life only by taking their crops to market. This need among peasants for marketing outlets gave the state a method of control more subtle than overt coercion.

The control that the state imposed through the procurement system worked by denying peasants alternative buyers for their crops. The power inherent in the state's position as monopsonist buyer was neither mysterious nor secret. The state openly paraded this power and encouraged its purchasing agents to impress upon peasants just how dependent on the procurement stations they were. Employees of the supply and marketing cooperatives, for example, were instructed: "You must make the peasants realize, through the course of their practical lives, that in buying and selling they cannot do without you; in processing their output they cannot do without you; and in storage and transport they cannot do without you."[91]

The waste caused by this form of control peaked with the record harvest of 1984. What happened in 1984 was unprecedented, even bizarre: a crisis of abundance. The lines of peasants laden with farm produce outside the procurement stations that year exceeded anything anyone had ever seen. In many places the lines were several days long. Some people misinterpreted the crowds as evidence of peasant enthusiasm for selling to the state. In fact, most farmers had no choice. They were desperate to sell their hard-won harvest before they lost

91. Wang Zhuoru, "Gongxiaoshe zenyang jinxing tizhi gaige?" (How should the supply and marketing cooperative system be reformed?) *Shangye gongzuo* 1983: 10, p. 9.

it. Whatever grain peasants could not sell to the state was likely to rot, said the *Anhui Daily*, for shabby peasant homes made poor storage facilities, "with so many rats and birds in the house."[92] But without enough free markets to handle the overflow from the big harvest, procurement stations were swamped. They stopped buying. In one among many thousands of cases, the Chenliang grain station in Funing County, Jiangsu, refused peasants' excess grain. The procure-agents there, said the *Xinhua Daily*, "used the excuse that the grain was not dry, and time and again demanded that the peasants sun-dry their grain at the grain station for up to ten days. This caused the peasants to suffer indescribably from the heat during the daytime and mosquito bites at night. At approximately 4:00 P.M. on the seventh of July, a large thunderstorm struck and a lot of the grain was washed away."[93]

The image of grain disappearing in a downpour captures the crisis of 1984. The irony of that successful year—a huge harvest that many peasants could not sell—forced state leaders to realize their dilemma. The modernization program demanded large harvests from peasants, but the system for controlling peasants turned abundance into waste—grain that the state could not buy just washing away in the rain. If the state could not buy the new surpluses, then continued suppression of markets to force peasants to deliver their quotas could only have one result: depression in farm production. This dilemma gave great impetus to the liberals' efforts to open up the rural market. Market growth accelerated in mid-decade. By 1988 there were over sixty thousand rural markets, double the number in 1980.[94] Nothing else posed as great a challenge to the state's rural authority.[95]

Conservatives fought hard against the free-market trend in the late 1980s. Throughout the chain of command, provincial and local officials met the challenge with blockades and repression. Some acted

---

92. *Anhui ribao*, Nov. 16, 1984, p. 1.
93. *Xinhua ribao*, July 20, 1984, p. 1, translated in JPRS-CAG–85–012 (Apr. 15, 1985), p. 105.
94. Wu Xiang, "Shenhua gaige, qianghua nongcun jingji xin tizhi" (Deepen the reforms and strengthen the new rural economic system), *Nongye jingji wenti* 1988: 1, p. 11.
95. Andrew Watson, "Reform of Agricultural Marketing," pp. 1–28.

out of loyalty to the conservative leadership wing in Beijing. Others were just protecting their bureaucratic bailiwicks. All were imbued with the compulsion for control. Procurement officials from the provincial level down fought tenaciously to hold on to their positions of monopsony. Still faced with purchasing quotas to fill, they could not abide competition. "If the grass so much as sways in the breeze," said one report, "they instantly sense trouble procuring grain, and clamp down their monopoly power."[96] Procurement officials barred competitors from the market, set up tax offices to harass rivals, and erected administrative blockades.[97] Bureaucrats threw up barriers to the movement of farm goods at every level of administration. In 1988 and 1989 it was said that Hebei called out the militia to patrol the provincial border and prevent its cotton from being traded for coal from Shanxi. Elsewhere counties and prefectures set prohibitive prices for grain that might leave their jurisdiction. Some provinces tried to keep grain from crossing their borders at all. For example, the *People's Daily* reported in 1987 that the northeast was awash in an "ocean" of corn. The three northeastern provinces each adopted a policy of "control" (*guanzhu*), erecting blockades to keep the corn from escaping the procurement system. They barred corn from export to other provinces and prohibited transport of grain by rail or highway without explicit provincial permission.[98]

This late-1980s conservative reaction against the market had a chilling effect on peasant attempts to escape state control. An agricultural economics journal sent out an alarm:

> As forced grain procurements have grown more severe, other fields of circulation have retrogressed too. Many things that had already been freed to the market have been re-subjected to compulsory procurement and to regional blockades. Free buying and selling of tea,

---

96. *Renmin ribao*, July 8, 1987, p. 2.

97. This was the behavior commonly exhibited by "main-channel managers" (*zhu qudao jingyingzhe*), occupying positions in state commerce departments, grain departments, and supply and marketing cooperatives. See Zhang Lechang and Wen Yuanlun, "Nong chanpin liutong tizhi gaige zhong de liyi moca" (Conflicts of interest in reforming the circulation of farm commodities), *Nongye jingji wenti* 1988: 3, p. 27.

98. *Renmin ribao*, July 7, 1987, p. 2.

for example, was already in practice, but as sales became brisk recently, it was brought back under state control. Regional blockades against wool have been thrown up, with great wool wars breaking out. Silk marketing was liberalized at one time and now is controlled again as tight as could be. Some places have returned to compulsory procurement of pigs, and many have set up blockades. Throughout the marketing process there are people who are not only failing to help peasants succeed in the circulation of commodities, but are intensifying the attack against them and strangling markets. . . . The clamor to restore and fortify compulsory procurement is very loud.[99]

This somber passage was written at the end of 1987, the year that the liberal head of the Party, Hu Yaobang, was thrown out of power. Within two years Zhao Ziyang was deposed as well. Their downfall did not mean the end of the marketing struggle, of course. The leadership rivalry between liberals and conservative planners would continue into the 1990s. If anything, the effect of reform in the 1980s appeared to portend only further market development, and, consequently, further difficulty in controlling peasants. But the conservatives in power at the time of the Beijing massacre in 1989 showed no sign of giving up the fight. They succeeded in at least stalling efforts to loosen state control in the second half of the decade, denying peasants victory in the long battle over farm marketing.

The Limits of Peasant Power

The analysis of family farming earlier in this book concluded with two requisites for peasants to wield influence on a strong state. One was a state for which the top priority was balanced economic growth. The second was something to make peasant action cohesive in the absence of autonomous political organization. In the fight over farm marketing, these two conditions certainly prevailed. The state was unswervingly dedicated to the economic growth demanded by its modernization program, and peasant action exhibited cohesion in widely uniform responses to price

99. Lu, "Nongcun jingji," p. 4.

signals. (Indeed, the same peasant schemes to manipulate the price system existed almost everywhere in China.) Yet even though these two conditions prevailed in the struggles over both family farming and agricultural marketing, the outcomes were starkly different. In the case of family farming, peasants demonstrated startling effectiveness in moving the state to change the basic form of rural social life. In the marketing fight, the state put an end to peasants' influence over prices and stalled their drive for autonomy in selling and cropping decisions. Obviously, the first two requisites for peasant power suggested above were inadequate. A third stipulation must be added, and that is that peasants cannot threaten what state leaders perceive as the security of the state itself.

This stipulation may appear at first to limit peasant power to too narrow a sphere to be meaningful. Leaders of states are often paranoid. They are likely to perceive even mundane issues of domestic policy as potential threats to state security. Circumscribed by the perceptions of such suspicious adversaries, peasant power must be severely restricted. This is indeed the case: peasant power is narrow. It lacks any coercive force. Yet even within these limits, peasant power is nonetheless real and effective. Noncoercive peasant power might include the ability to influence state policy choices. More important, it could include the power to make the state consider and finally elect policy choices the state had not originally conceived of, choices that were of the peasants' own creation. Peasants demonstrated both these types of power in the establishment of family farming.

Peasants succeeded in promoting family farming because they were able to cast their preferences in a form that state leaders could eventually perceive as serving, rather than threatening, fundamental state interests. This does not mean there was no conflict. On the contrary, peasants who took up family farming had to fight hard against state officials at all levels. In resisting suppression of experiments in family farming, peasants bought time in which to prove the productive merit of their innovations. In this way peasants succeeded in making their challenge to state authority appear to serve the state goal of increased farm output. Thus peasants exercised their limited power. Conflict with the state was unavoidable, but peasants managed both consciously and inadvertently to steer the conflict in a way that did not threaten the leaders' sense of security.

Peasants failed in the marketing struggle because they could not keep that conflict from threatening the leadership's sense of state security. Peasants wanted higher farm-gate prices, plus the freedom to make their own cropping decisions based on open market choices. These goals provoked two of the deepest obsessions of the conservative reformers. The peasantry's successful campaign for higher prices incited the leadership's first obsession, the fear of fiscal rout. In the perpetual budget crisis of the reform decade, the conservatives believed peasant activism in the price war could bring about the financial ruin of the state. Burgeoning agricultural prices meant a triple threat—to state industry, to fiscal flows into state coffers, and even to political quiescence in the crowded cities. To the conservatives, these matters all touched the security of the state. The conservative reformers therefore retaliated against the peasants' price victories with the backlash reform of 1985.

The peasants' striving for marketing autonomy inflamed the state's other obsession, the mania for control. Conservatives wanted control over farm output, over peasant labor, and over peasant cropping decisions. With peasants ensconced in private farms, conservatives felt the only control left was the state plan and the procurement system. Fearful leaders like Chen Yun saw the peasants' attempt at autonomy in production and marketing as a threat to this last secure authority over the countryside. Peasant autonomy violated basic precepts of the conservatives' vision of order. Following cropping commands, fulfilling the procurement duty, and having faith in the state plan were all fundamental acts of obedience to the state. If the state could not elicit even this level of compliance, then its authority was under challenge. Conservatives at all levels of the state apparatus tried to fight this challenge and keep state control over the movement of essential goods.

Peasant initiatives in marketing thus ran into stiffened resistance in the conservative will to defend the state. Reasonably or not, conservatives deemed state security to be at risk from the peasantry, and they were resolved to protect it. To breach this determined opposition among state leaders was beyond the limit of peasant power. The conservatives' rivals in the liberal wing of reform may have preferred not to fight the peasants over procurement at all. For the liberals feared a deadening effect if the state pressed its control of market outlets too aggressively. After the disappointing farm performance in the second half of the 1980s, the conservatives could not really reply that the output figures vindicated their policy. (As shown in table 7, output for major crops in 1989 was only about what it had been five years before.) But the conservatives could claim that they had held off the perceived peasant threat to state security—and in doing so had demonstrated the limits of peasant power.

Chapter Seven

The Logic of
Privatization

Although their power was limited, Chinese peasants succeeded in creating the major innovations of the reform era. The state, for its part, was also committed to change. But when reform came, it was not the tame follower of anyone's vision. It was not fully subject to the new-found initiative of the peasantry or to the dictates of the central state. Reform took on a life of its own. Capitalist countries have occasionally seen reform run out of control. But the tendency is more pronounced in state-socialist systems, where rigid bureaucracies tie up potential change for years on end. The first innocent reform that a state-socialist system approves is likely to set loose a stampede of other changes that were waiting to happen. In China, the splendid demonstration of this tendency for reform to gallop out of control was privatization in the countryside.[1]

Privatization occurs when publicly owned resources and enterprises are turned over to private control. The move from public to private control took place on a vast scale during China's rural reforms. A large proportion of the land, machinery, factories, credit, animals, trucks, and human labor—in other words, a large part of practically everything necessary for production in the rural economy—became

---

1. Parts of chapters 7 and 8 of this book appeared in a much shortened form in Daniel Kelliher, "Privatisation and Politics in Rural China," in Gordon White, ed., *The Chinese State in the Era of Economic Reform: The Road to Crisis* (London: Macmillan, 1991), pp. 318–41.

privately controlled. In carrying out this privatization, China was part of a pattern gripping the whole world in the last quarter of the twentieth century. After wide expansion of state economic power around the world dating from the late nineteenth century, governments were surrendering economic power to private citizens and the market. Governments as diverse as those of the United Kingdom, Chile, Sri Lanka, and all the nations of the Warsaw Pact were eager to retreat from direct administration of their economies. Like China, they had concluded that state power in the economy had expanded to the point where it harmed production.

Deng Xiaoping's reform coalition first reached this conclusion with regard to agriculture, believing that state control over the rural economy had grown so pervasive and intrusive that it was stifling development. Coalition leaders decided that the ministries, planning commissions, county officials, procurement agents, and local cadres of the far-flung state apparatus had made Chinese agriculture stagnate. Farmers left to their own devices, they believed, could do better. As they began to grant economic powers to private rural citizens, the reformers improvised a program that relied on the classic prescriptions of privatization. They cut the powers of unwieldy administrative organs (the communes). They put primary resources (the land) into private hands (family farms). They leased or sold public enterprises (commune and brigade operations) to private investors. They turned management over to the immediate producers (peasant entrepreneurs and farmers), and expanded the market's scope for allocating goods, labor, capital, and income.

In adopting such policies, China's government unwittingly began to follow a "logic of privatization." The logic of privatization in a state-dominated economy can be expressed as a straightforward proposition: when one aspect of economic life is turned over to private hands, gains in productivity and efficiency are often impeded unless other aspects of economic life are also privatized. Consequently, when reformers in a country like China are bent on maximizing production, privatization begets more privatization, as one reform makes a subsequent reform seem so logical as to appear inevitable. The result is a chain reaction of policy changes. More than other types of reform, therefore, privatization tends to snowball, careening beyond whatever limited goals the leaders initially envisioned. In this chapter I will demonstrate this phenomenon at work in China, in the transformation of four aspects of the rural economy: land tenure, credit, labor, and entrepreneurship. The logic of privatization drove China's government to policy positions in each of these areas that astounded everyone, the reformers most of all.

The Rebirth of Private Land Tenure

Privatization's original foothold in rural China—and its base for all later conquests—was the family farm. From this tiny area of private control, a system evolved that mimicked the features of private land tenure. The legal basis of this new system was the land contract, which gave a peasant household control over a piece of collective land in return for meeting a quota of sales to the state. Starting from this contractual basis (known as the "responsibility system"), the extent of the farmers' claim on the land grew rapidly during the reform period. At first the rules governing land contracts restricted peasants' prerogatives: "Commune members only have the right to cultivate their contracted land; they have no ownership rights over it, they are not permitted to rent it out, buy it or sell it, transfer it, abandon it, or hire other people to cultivate it."[2] Yet peasants learned almost instantly to commit all these forbidden acts with their contracted land. They leased it, rented it, and sold it. They built homes on it, hired labor to work on it, and used it as security for loans. In other words, peasants treated their land as private property, in spite of repeated and ultimately ritualized reminders from the state that it was still owned by the collective. Within a few years peasants with no more legal title to their farms than a temporary usufruct contract possessed virtually permanent claims on the land. They even gained the right to bequeath the family farm to their children. By the mid-1980s, central leaders—either explicitly or tacitly— condoned this quick evolution toward a nearly private system of land

2. "Renzhen jiejue bao gan dao hu hou chuxian de xin wenti" (Conscientiously solve new problems that arise after contracting work to households), *Nongcun gongzuo tongxun* 1981: 11, p. 2.

tenure. How could a state-socialist government, even a government of Communist reformers, come to approve of such a system?

From Protecting Land to Protecting Property

This evolution in the direction of private land tenure occurred unplanned, step by step. The first step came at the end of the initial year of legal family farming, in the state's response to the disturbingly small investment peasants were making in their new farms. The first land contracts, which had been legally adopted in a few parts of China as early as 1980, were awarded for one-year terms, with the expectation that the land would then be reapportioned. As the first contract year drew to a close, however, officials feared that if peasants anticipated a reshuffling of their plots they might neglect the fall planting of crops like winter wheat and green manure.[3] Most places therefore renewed each household's contract for the same land it held already, this time for a three-year term.

Once peasants had three-year contracts in hand, they did begin to invest, but it was the wrong kind of investment. They built houses. "Encroaching on the land to build houses has become a universal phenomenon," said one report, ". . . [as] peasants mistake their rights over contracted land for ownership rights, and build houses on their responsibility fields."[4] Officials decried this destruction of arable land to no avail: one survey after another found that residential construction was the first priority for peasants with rising income.[5] Since more than half of China's peasants still (as of 1981) lived in homes of mud-brick and thatch, this desire for new houses was natural.[6] But the "house-

3. Hubei sheng nongwei diaocha zu (Investigative Group of the Hubei Provincial Agricultural Committee), "Ruhe shixing shuidao lianchan jichou zeren zhi" (How to practice a responsibility system with output linked to reward in wet rice cultivation), *Nongcun gongzuo tongxun* 1981: 1, p. 11.

4. *Hubei ribao*, Oct. 25, 1981, p. 1.

5. For example, see Sun Xiangjian and Pei Changhong, "Lun dangqian woguo nongye de neibu jilei" (On internal accumulation in our nation's agriculture today), *Jingji yanjiu cankao ziliao* 1983: 27 (Feb. 19), p. 8; and Hubei sheng nonghui, shehui kexue yuan diaocha zu (Investigative Group of the Hubei Provincial Peasant Association and the Hubei Provincial Academy of Social Sciences), "Dui xian jieduan nongmin duiwu de guji" (An appraisal of the peasant ranks in the present stage), *Nongye jingji congkan* 1983: 2, p. 35.

6. Fang Jing, "Sanshi nian lai woguo cheng xiang chabie de yanbian" (The

building fever," as disapproving officials called it, signified something more. It represented peasants' hopes and fears for their newly acquired land. As an expression of hope, building a private home on a field contracted from the collective was an aggressive act of possession, an assertion of individual control over the land. On the other hand, pouring earnings into a house also expressed peasants' fears that they might lose the land. They guessed that if policy changed and the collective repossessed the land, they would at least be allowed to keep their new house, because dwellings had been private even under the commune system. Thus instead of investing in the land, peasants chose the more prudent course of investing in an asset they thought they could retain.

That this wave of housing investment added nothing to agricultural productivity worried officials far more than the symbolic issue of encroachment on collective land. One of the principal motives for permitting family farms had been to give peasants a private stake in building up a piece of land (with fertilizers, improved irrigation, and so on). If they did not make these improvements on the land, the whole strategy was ruined. Worse still, the accustomed channel for putting resources into the land was in a shambles because of decollectivization. Investment in the land had always depended on collective funds; it was endangered now that the collectives were in decline. Collective accumulation funds had previously paid for soil nutrients, field capital construction, local waterworks, and all the other investments that maintain the productivity of farmland. But with the advent of family farming, contributions to these collective funds plunged as peasants diverted resources from collective investment to housing construction. In 1980, the first year in which startled officials noticed this problem, peasants' housing expenditures soared to 17.5 billion yuan, while their contributions to the collectives shrank to 10.5 billion yuan. As family farming spread in 1981, this diversion of investment funds became even more alarming, with housing costs reaching 21 billion yuan while collective contributions dwindled to 8.9 billion yuan.[7] Collective investment was sinking, and peasants—unsure of

evolution of the town-country gap in our country over the last thirty years), *Jingji yanjiu ziliao* 1982: 5, p. 18.

7. The estimates on housing construction are from Sun and Pei , "Lun dang-

their tenure on the land—were failing to fill the gap with individual investment.

The danger that the land might lose productivity forced central leaders to decide whether to offer peasants much longer land contracts. When the first three-year contracts were coming to a close in 1983, a debate broke out over giving peasants semi-permanent control over their land. The leaders reasoned that peasants would only invest in land when they knew they would reap the rewards, that is, when they expected the land would still be theirs in ten or fifteen years. Places that eschewed three-year contracts and reapportioned the land annually from 1980 to 1983 were said to have suffered declines in output.[8] The press claimed that most peasants backed longer contracts, and attributed speeches like this one to peasant spokesmen: "If the contracts don't change for one year, we'll apply chemical fertilizer. If they don't change for two years, we'll plant green manure. If they're good for three years we'll spread pig and cow manure. Under four-year contracts we'll haul pond sludge to the fields. If it's five years we'll repair the waterworks. And if the contracts don't change for ten years, then we could transform sand dunes into good fields."[9]

People concerned with fairness and equity argued against granting farmers such long-term possession of the land. Birth, death, marriage, or occupational change among family members would inevitably change people-to-land ratios. While these changes could

qian woguo nongye," p. 8. The collective contribution figures are from Nongye bu renmin gongshe ju (Ministry of Agriculture, People's Communes Office), "1980 nian nongcun renmin gongshe de shouru he fenpei" (1980 income and distribution in rural people's communes), *Nongye jingji congkan* 1982: 3, p. 58; and Nong mu yu ye bu shedui qiye guanli ju (Collective Enterprise Management Office, Ministry of Agriculture, Animal Husbandry, and Fishery), "Quanguo nongcun renmin gongshe jiben hesuan danwei 1981 nian shouyi fenpei qingkuang" (The national situation in 1981 for distribution of income in basic accounting units of rural people's communes), *Nongye jingji congkan* 1982: 6, p. 52.

8. This argument, with examples of such a decline in a Henan commune, appears in Lan Baoqing, "Tantan lian chan chengbao zhong dikuai de wending wenti" (The problem of stabilizing land in production contracting), *Nongye jingji congkan* 1983: 4, p. 55.

9. "Tudi chengbao qixian guo duan bu li shengchan," (When the time limit on land contracts is too short, it is bad for production), *Nongye jingji congkan* 1983: 6, p. 53.

work to ease the pressure on the land for some families, others would be plunged into land shortage and hardship. Only by periodically re-apportioning land among households could such inequities be limited. But other people argued that the only way to guarantee higher productivity was to settle families permanently on plots of land. In the political climate of the reform period, any issue that pitted fairness against productivity had a foregone conclusion. So it was with this debate on land tenure.[10] Central Document Number 1 for 1984 closed the question with the announcement that peasants would get land contracts of fifteen years or longer.[11] Some peasants hailed this as the "Second Land Reform."[12]

Thus the first step in privatization—short-term private control over land parcels—led to the second step—virtually permanent tenure. Establishment of long-term tenure was not an accident. It was a necessity once the state committed itself to family farms held for any duration. For in order to protect the productivity of individually held land, the state was compelled to protect the land as property. In this way the "responsibility system" of the early reform years evolved into a new system of land tenure based on semi-permanent family farms. This set the stage for the next, more startling act of privatization.

The Revival of Land Rent

Once China's vast agricultural population was settled semi-permanently on individual farms, the reappearance of land rent was inevitable. With virtually permanent landholdings, peasants needed some mechanism for transferring land between households. Without such a mechanism, the new land tenure system would have been rigid and inefficient, incapable of responding to new commercial developments or population changes. In the mid-1980s, central leaders tacitly chose to let localities figure out their own solutions to this problem. In areas where the collective administration remained strong, the local officials worked out methods for transferring land between families.

10. A succinct summary of the debate is presented in "Tudi chengbao qixian guo duan bu li shengchan," pp. 53–56.

11. *Hubei ribao*, Mar. 3, 1983, p. 1.

12. "Tudi chengbao qixian guo duan bu li shengchan," p. 55.

By 1990, for example, the government of Jiucheng *zhen* in Hebei had established a regular mechanism for reapportioning land between families. This mechanism adjusted procurement assignments up or down according to household population change and also transferred small pieces of land between families to maintain equity.[13] Elsewhere, however, where the collectives did not weather the jolts of the reform period so well, peasants developed their own method for adjusting land needs between families: they privately arranged transfers of land, lubricating the transaction with some form of payment.

In this way a market in land rental sprang up. The amounts of land involved were small. A national survey in 1983 showed private transfers involving from 1 to 10 percent of cultivated land in different counties.[14] Thus tenancy showed no signs of dominating land tenure, as it did in southern China before the Revolution. But even as a form of marginal adjustment, land rent showed the power of privatization to gradually suffuse the economy.

Because land rent was one of the great forms of exploitation attacked in the Revolution, many Chinese publications discussing the alienation of land tried to avoid the word meaning "rent" (*zu*) in preference for the more neutral term "transfer" (*zhuanrang*; or sometimes *zhuanbao*, "transfer of contract"). In some cases "transfer" was indeed more accurate—for example, when a household pursuing a specialized business returned its contracted land to the collective for reassignment to someone else. However, the term "transfer" only disguised what was happening when one household privately yielded its land to another for payment. Some Chinese sources delicately omitted any reference to such remuneration, even though some 85 percent of all land transfers involved payments of rent.[15] Other Chinese sources were not so squeamish about these matters, and spoke openly about rent paid in money (*zujin*) or in grain (*zugu*).

13. These transfers were carried out within a system in which peasants held land contracts of fifteen years. Interviews with local officials, Jiucheng *zhen*, Xinji *shi* (formerly Shulu County), Hebei, July 1990.

14. "Nongye jingji ziliao huiji (ba): ruogan diqu tudi zhuanbao qingkuang tongji" (Compilation of materials on agricultural economics [eight]: statistics on the circumstances of land transfers in several districts), *Nongye jingji congkan* 1984: 1, pp. 63–65.

15. Ibid., p. 63.

Specific rental agreements varied. The tenant's first obligation to the landlord (that is, the person who contracted the land from the collective) was to fulfill the state procurement duty attached to the land. In many instances—especially if the land was sown to grain—the tenant made little profit producing the procurement quota and delivering it to the state. In such cases the labor involved in freeing the original contract holder from the procurement duty represented a service by the tenant, and in some instances this was the tenant's only obligation to the original holder of the land. In other cases, the tenant also made an additional payment of rent. Rent was paid in money or grain, although grain was by far the more common form of payment. The grain payment could be a fixed amount or a percentage of the harvest. Sometimes it was paid in the form of a sale of grain to the landlord at a discounted price, in which case the rent equaled the amount of the discount below the market price. The magnitude of the rent varied widely, but it could be as steep as 20 to 40 percent of the harvest.[16] In 1983 in Lishui Prefecture of Zhejiang, for example, new landlords rented out wet-rice land in exchange for discount-price grain sales worth 58 yuan for every *mu* (one-fifteenth hectare) of rented land, when the net income per *mu* was only 145 yuan. In the same prefecture, rice land rented out for lump-sum grain payments was going for 150 kilograms per *mu* when total yields were approximately 750 kilograms per mu.[17]

Even with these expensive terms, it is easy to understand why farmers wanted to rent more land. China had only about one-tenth of a hectare of cultivated land for every member of the rural population in the 1980s.[18] In the central and southern rice growing regions the allotment of contracted land per peasant was generally even smaller, about one *mu* or less. Each *mu* of rice land took only about forty labor-days per year to farm, so land-tilling families faced severe

16. These rents were not as severe as those prevailing before the Revolution, which could be as high as 50 to 70 percent of output.

17. Zhou Qiren et al., "Tudi zhuanbao de diaocha he chubu fenxi" (An investigation and preliminary analysis of the transfer of contracted land), *Nongye jingji congkan* 1983: 5, pp. 26–27.

18. "Zhongguo guoqing cankao ziliao" (Reference materials on national conditions of China), *Shehui kexue dongtai [Hubei]* 1981: 24 (Aug. 20), p. 29.

problems of underemployment.[19] Families with little land also faced low income. One study asked why people had higher income in Chuxian and Suxian prefectures of Anhui than in Anqing and Huizhou prefectures. The strongest explanatory factor turned out to be amount of land held: "Whoever had more land got a faster rise in income."[20] The high-income prefectures had an average of 0.15 hectare of cultivated land per person; the low-income prefectures had only 0.04 hectare.[21] Farmers with such tiny landholdings saw few ways out of poverty. Not every family had the skill, market access, capital, or wits to start a nonfarm business, so renting more land was often the only way for a land-tilling family to raise its income.

The motives for renting out one's land were more complicated, and they were connected to the rise of private entrepreneurship.

Land Rent and Entrepreneurship

Looking at the puny, dispersed strips of land that most people received as so-called farms, state leaders recognized that China's newly divided arable was too scant to support a nation of smallholders. The underemployment that had been somewhat disguised under collectivized agriculture came into the open with the rise of individual farming. To relieve the land pressure, and to diversify the rural economy, the state began early in the 1980s to give every encouragement to private entrepreneurs who departed from traditional, self-sufficient farming. These new entrepreneurs were peasants who took advantage of the commercial thrust of reform to set up specialized businesses

19. If the allotment of land per household was *too* small, however, a land rental market was unlikely to develop, because tilling the land took so little time that it was no obstacle to running an additional, nonfarm business. This was the case in areas near Canton with very high prerevolutionary tenancy rates that might otherwise have been expected to be early leaders in the development of land rent in the reform period. See Zhong Luoran, "Guangdong sheng Nanhai xian Dali gongshe zhuanrang chengbao tudi de qingkuang" (Transfers of contracted land in Dali Commune, Nanhai County, Guangdong Province), *Nongye jingji congkan* 1983: 5, p. 38.

20. Anhui shengwei nongcun gongzuo bu (Rural Work Department of Anhui Provincial Party Committee), "Anhui sheng nongcun wan hu jingji qingkuang de diaocha" (Economic survey of 10,000 households in Anhui Province), *Jingji yanjiu cankao ziliao* 1982: 126 (Aug. 18), p. 21.

21. Ibid., p. 21.

instead of tilling the land for a living. Most of the earliest entrepreneurs were "specialized households" (zhuanye hu), who commonly chose not to work their contracted farmland and devoted their energy to family-sized businesses instead.[22] (By 1990 it was also common to hear geti hu ["individual household enterprise"], originally an urban term, applied to these same rural family businesses.)[23]

The revival of land rent in China was tied not only to the privatization of farming but also to the rise of these small private entrepreneurs who left farming. The Chinese press cited a variety of minor reasons for people renting land to their fellow villagers, including that some land was too dispersed or inconveniently located and that some families were too short of labor, too old, or too sick to cultivate it.[24] But by all accounts the most common reason peasants rented out land was that they had some alternative calling—either factory work or an independent enterprise from which they could make more money. In spite of reports in the late 1980s of peasants actually selling land to run a business, peasants who went into private business generally considered it more prudent to maintain rights to contracted land by renting it out. The new entrepreneurs preferred this arrangement, for they regarded land as insurance against both policy change and business failure.[25] The rental market served individual entrepreneurs particularly well. They could rent out their contracted fields—unloading the headache of the procurement duty on the land and getting a rental payment to boot—and then devote their full time to a pursuit more lucrative than farming.[26]

22. A minority of specialized households did remain directly engaged in agriculture, but unlike ordinary farmers, they specialized in a single crop grown for the market, not for their own consumption.

23. Interviews in Xinji shi (formerly Shulu County), Hebei, June and July 1990.

24. "Nongye jingji ziliao huiji (ba)," p. 63; also Zhong, "Guangdong," pp. 38–39.

25. Wall Street Journal, Jan. 19, 1988, p. 16.

26. In some cases this meant that land changed hands faster where there were more opportunities for setting up specialties besides cultivation. For example, in Lishui Prefecture of Zhejiang, where duck-raising was a big independent enterprise, more than 10 percent of the land had already been transferred between households by 1983. See Zhou et al., "Tudi zhuanbao," p. 26. However, because other factors—such as the people-to-land ratio and the size of the procurement

This added benefit for rural entrepreneurs gave the reform leaders yet another reason to acquiesce in the revival of land rent, for they were committed to private entrepreneurship and wanted to give specialized households every encouragement to plunge full-time into new businesses. The situation did, however, raise a troublesome question for the reformers: Why should specialized households be paid rent for their contracted fields? To defend new policies against ideological attack, the reformers had always claimed that the basic collectivist structure of rural life had not changed. Thus they insisted that peasants had no ownership rights over their farms: only the collective could own land. This fiction was hard to maintain if specialized households could turn their contracted fields over to other families and pocket the rent as if they owned the land. Yet the reformers chose to ignore this quandary, and condoned the practice of private rent payments for transferred fields.

People who worried about a widening gap between rich and poor objected. They conceded that when a family took in land relinquished by a specialized household, a rent payment might justifiably go to the collective (that is, the legal owner)—but surely not to the specialized household. Such private rental payments broke traditional Communist strictures against profiting from the plight of land-poor families. Rent violated even the looser principles of the reform period, such as more pay for more work. "The person who transfers the land is after rent, paid in money or in rice," said one critic. "This means profiting by other people's labor, and it amounts to exploitation through land rent. It goes against the system of public ownership of land and the principle of distribution according to work."[27]

The reform leadership rejected this line of reasoning, and for all practical purposes abandoned the pretense that land was not privately held. Publicly it was claimed that specialized households who rented out their land were "the vigorous, energetic masters of today's rural co-

burden—affected tenancy rates, there was no dependable correlation between the tenancy rate and the number of alternative opportunities for commercial ventures in a given district.

27. Zhu Nailiang et al., "Zhejiang Jiaxing diqu zhuanrang chengbao tudi de qingkuang" (Transfer of contracted land in Jiaxing Prefecture, Zhejiang), *Nongye jingji congkan* 1983: 5, p. 32.

operative economy. . . . Even if the people who use the [rented] land were to pay the collective, the collective should still turn the payment over to the household that originally contracted for the land. This is only reasonable: for in reality, payment for the transfer of contracted land has the positive effect of encouraging the growth of specialized, socialized production."[28] This stance on rent was consistent with the leadership's view of specialized households as the progenitors of a modern rural economy. In the leaders' eyes, rent was a legitimate reward to people advancing state policy. And as a practical matter, rent paid to the new entrepreneurs had the added benefit of concentrating investment funds among the people most aggressively developing the economy.

Opponents worried that renting out land might be the first step toward a full-blown private land market. "If things continue in this way," they said, "everybody will be out to get land."[29] At the outset of the reforms, in the late 1970s, a market in land was entirely unthinkable. Yet in a few short years land became what a private tenure system makes it—namely, a commodity: a transferable asset, something that can be rented or even sold. It is doubtful that the reform leaders initially envisioned anything approaching private land tenure. But there is a certain imperative in privatization. Peasants were given land in hope that they would work it harder and nurture it with investments of savings and labor. To promote productive investment (as opposed to house-building) the leaders lengthened the contract period from one year to three years and on to fifteen years and more, ever deepening the peasants' private stake in their land. Peasants naturally came to treat the land as their own, and transfers between families became private transactions. When private entrepreneurs arose and wanted to unburden themselves of their land, those in need of land were ready to pay to put crops on it. When the state finally felt moved to defend these payments of rent to the entrepreneurs, it was simply acknowledging the extent to which land tenure had become entangled

28. Zhou et al., "Tudi zhuanbao," p. 30.
29. "Shidang tiaozheng chengbao tian shi wanshan shengchan zeren zhi de xuyao" (Appropriate adjustments in contracted fields are necessary for perfecting the production responsibility system), *Jihua jingji yanjiu* 1983: 33 (Nov. 30), p. 39.

in private control. Though the reform leaders may never have intended to permit private land tenure, the logic of privatization carried them ahead. Along the way, obtaining the fruits of one step of privatization meant acquiescing in the next step.

Credit

With individual farming and independent entrepreneurship on the rise, the development of a private credit market was the natural next step. A whole new territory opened for individual credit after the new land tenure system left farmers to fend for themselves. This was not the intention of the early reforms, which foresaw collectives sharing with individuals the costs of farming. The original idea behind the responsibility system was to "unite what is best united, divide what is best divided, and strike an appropriate balance between the two."[30] In other words, the land and other inputs might be parceled out, but certain costs, investments, and tasks would still be managed collectively. In practice, however, this intended partnership of family farm and collective support died at birth. The collectives were on their way out. The new land tenure system shifted farming costs to individual peasant households who would now need credit to farm.

Before reform, peasants made annual contributions to collective funds for welfare, education, cadres' stipends, and other expenses. The largest of these funds was the public accumulation fund, which covered fixed investment and current operating costs in agriculture. With the first hint of individual farming, peasant contributions to all these collective funds hit a steep decline, dropping from a national total of 11.7 billion yuan in 1979, to 10.5 billion in 1980, to only 8.9 billion in 1981—well before the official abandonment of the communes in 1983 and 1984.[31] Public accumulation funds, along with welfare funds, bore the brunt of this decline.[32] The most extreme case

30. Sun Benyao et al., "Ba jiti de youyuexing he geren de jijixing jieheqilai" (Combine the superiority of the collective with the enthusiasm of the individual), *Nongcun gongzuo tongxun* 1981: 9, p. 15.

31. Nongye bu renmin gongshe ju, p. 58; and Nong mu yu ye bu shedui qiye guanli ju, p. 52.

32. Anhui shengwei nongcun gongzuo bu, pp. 24, 27.

was Anhui, where contributions to public accumulation funds simply collapsed, falling by over 90 percent from the mid-1970s to 1981.[33] Although few other provinces matched Anhui's crash, most collectives around the country reported declining accumulation funds, and many stopped collecting at all.[34] The press published reports from all across China of collectives falling apart, becoming "empty shells" or "dead things." In 1982 a report from Shandong said, "The burden of buying many of the means of production is left to the peasant households. Then the funds contributed to the collective are even smaller. Some units have only enough for the allowances for cadres, local teachers, barefoot doctors, and welfare relief. They have no money left to consolidate or develop the collective economy. Even collective property is divided up or ruined, so the collective becomes a 'mere skeleton.'"[35] Such collectives were too enfeebled to buy fertilizer, pumps, tools, machinery, or draft animals, or to organize collective labor to repair dikes and dredge irrigation canals. When one Hubei unit tried in vain to gather farmers for collective land improvement, a local man said, "They've already divided up the fields. Nobody would come in for flood-control work. The cadres beat the gong until it split."[36]

This decline of the collectives left peasants to meet farming costs by themselves. Brawls broke out between families competing to use the collective draft animals on the newly divided fields, and peasants quickly realized they would have to control their own inputs to get by.[37] Many inputs, especially expensive ones like tractors, irrigation

33. Ibid., p. 24; and Sun and Pei, "Lun dangqian woguo nongye," p. 7. Both these sources based their Anhui findings on a survey of some 2,500 cadres in sixty-nine Anhui counties at the beginning of 1982. The survey reported that contributions to public accumulation funds fell from about 7 percent of gross income in 1976 to less than 0.5 percent in 1981.

34. Sun and Pei, "Lun dangqian woguo nongye," p. 7.

35. Xu Daohe and Gong Qiao, "Shandong, Henan yi xie diqu nongye jihua qingkuang de diaocha" (An investigation of agricultural planning in a few districts of Shandong and Henan), Jingji yanjiu cankao ziliao 1982: 134 (Aug. 31), p. 34.

36. Hubei ribao, Nov. 3, 1980, p. 2.

37. For an account of such a conflict in Shanxi, see Zhonggong Ji xian xianwei bangongshi (Chinese Communist Party, Ji County Party Committee Office), "Liugou dadui you baochan dao hu zhuan dao zhuanye chengbo zeren zhi" (Liugou Brigade switches from bao chan dao hu to a specialized contract responsibility system), Nongcun gongzuo tongxun 1980: 11, p. 13.

equipment, and draft animals, were beyond the means of single families.[38] Even smaller implements had to be purchased anew, since individual farming requires considerable duplication in tools. Some households tried to ease their costs by sharing, each buying "a leg" (a one-quarter share) of a draft animal, for example. But most peasants were wary of the risk in such joint purchases, noting the Chinese proverb that if two people share the cost of feeding a horse, the horse gets thinner.

The result, of course, was that farmers had to rely on credit. Unfortunately, China's banking system had never provided agriculture with sufficient funds, even in the collective period. With millions of farmers now knocking at its doors, the official credit system was hopelessly inadequate. The rural credit network had two arms. One was the Agricultural Bank (revived again in 1979), which devoted most of its lending to rural commerce and industry. Over half of its loans funded state procurement agents buying the harvest, and the bulk of the rest went to township industries and businesses (*xiangzhen qiye*). Only a tiny portion of its loans (perhaps 5 percent) went to farmers.[39] The second arm of the rural credit network was the credit cooperatives, the main official source of loans for farming collectives and individuals. Theoretically the credit cooperatives were independent organizations managed by peasant shareholders. "But in fact," critics charged, "the Agricultural Bank has always treated the credit cooperatives as their own primary-level organs. The credit cooperatives have no authority over personnel, finances, or business, and basically, they have no autonomy."[40]

Keeping the credit cooperatives under the thumb of the Agricultural Bank undermined both the cooperatives themselves and the Chinese farmers dependent upon them. Credit cooperatives obtained

38. Nong mu yu ye bu nongjihua guanli ju (Agricultural Mechanization Management Office of the Ministry of Agriculture, Animal Husbandry, and Fishery), "Nongmin siren goumai shiyong tuolaji de qingkuang" (Private purchase and use of tractors by peasants), *Nongye jingji congkan* 1983: 1, pp. 64–65, 51.

39. On-Kit Tam, "Rural Finance in China," *China Quarterly*, 113 (March 1988), p. 67.

40. Wang Ming and Li Shusheng, "Several Issues Concerning Rural Financial Structural Reforms," *Nongye jingji wenti* 1987: 3, translated in JPRS-CAR–87–032 (Aug. 12, 1987), p. 82.

nearly all their funds from peasants' interest-bearing time deposits. But the cooperatives lost control over much of these rural savings, for they were required to place 30 percent of their funds as reserves at the Agricultural Bank.[41] This reserve requirement meant that a large portion of savings collected from farmers was lost as a fund of farm credit. This money was redirected away from farming in two ways. First, the Agricultural Bank itself was required to place reserves in the central People's Bank or the Bank of China, which had the effect of removing farmers' savings from the rural economy entirely. Second, because the Agricultural Bank's loan portfolio was devoted almost exclusively to rural industry and commerce, even the funds it did lend out in the countryside did not reach farmers in need of credit.

After placing their reserves of 30 percent at the Agricultural Bank, the credit cooperatives also had to keep 5 to 8 percent of their funds on hand as ready money for their depositors to withdraw.[42] Theoretically, once they met these reserve and ready-cash requirements, the credit cooperatives were then free to use the rest of their funds as loans to peasants. But since the cooperatives were caught in the mesh of the state banking system, their real loaning capacity was subject to further restrictions commanded by the state.

Official credit for farmers and peasant entrepreneurs began to be strangled in 1985, when the state—alarmed at excessive investment throughout the economy—imposed more controls on rural loans as part of its effort to tighten the money supply. As a result, according to a Ministry of Agriculture research unit, "banks and rural credit cooperatives only accepted deposits but did not issue loans. In some areas, credit organizations were on the verge of paralysis, and circulation of currency nearly came to a standstill. The whole rural economy sustained heavy damage."[43] By 1987 the entire banking sys-

41. The Agricultural Bank paid lower interest rates than the cooperatives had to pay their own peasant depositors, but until 1987 the Bank also promised to bail the cooperatives out if they were losing money.

42. Interviews with officials of the Agricultural Bank, the People's Bank, and the Bank of China, Hebei Province, July 1990.

43. Gao Hongbin et al., "Chang xian zengzhang, yihuo fazhan chizhi" (Normal growth or sluggish development), *Jingji yanjiu* 1987: 9, p. 50.

tem of China was badly overextended, and banking officials blamed the credit cooperatives (which made many unsecured loans to peasants) for the drain. As part of a general austerity, the banking system in 1989 set ceilings on credit cooperatives' lending. These ceilings were enforced even if a cooperative had its required reserve deposited at the Agricultural Bank and had sufficient deposits left over to support more loans to peasants. Barred from exceeding its ceiling, the credit cooperative had to turn the money over to the Agricultural Bank instead, further restricting the credit available to farmers.[44]

In their subordinate relation to the Agricultural Bank, the credit cooperatives could never be what they were supposed to be: genuine cooperatives controlled by peasants for peasant interests. The 1980s saw a move to save the cooperatives from the domination of the Agricultural Bank and let them be responsive to farmers' needs. But critics said the reforms toward this end amounted to "token gestures," such as "distributing a few cents' worth of dividends, inviting everybody out to dinner, or going through some symbolic voting procedure or other formalism."[45]

Private credit became the only way out for peasants all over China. Given the inadequacy of the official credit system to meet the needs of millions of newly independent farmers and rural entrepreneurs, a private loan market became, as the Chinese press likes to say, "an objective necessity." Although some official organs still inveighed against moneylenders as a matter of long habit, the government tacitly decided to tolerate private credit from the early 1980s on. The vast number, small size, and informal arrangement of private loans were beyond the state's policing capacity. Usurious interest rates quickly became normal. While bank and credit cooperatives issued loans to individual farmers at 0.3 to 0.7 percent monthly interest, private lenders charged 2 to 4 percent, and even 5 percent a month was not unknown.[46]

---

44. Interviews with officials of the Agricultural Bank, the People's Bank, and the Bank of China, Hebei Province, July 1990.

45. Wang and Li, "Rural Financial Structural Reforms," p. 85.

46. Some sources reported the norm as 3 or 4 percent, others as 2 or 3 percent. *Nongmin ribao*, Jan. 20, 1988, p. 2; Chen Lian, "'Shuangbao' hou nongcun jinrong gongzuo de bianhua" (Changes and problems in rural finance work since "*shuangbao*"), *Nongye jingji congkan* 1982: 1, p. 39; Zhao Qiuxi, "Several Issues

On an annual basis these were staggering rates. For example, the common monthly rate of 3 percent meant a burden of over 40 percent annual interest—a rate as high as those prevailing in pre-revolutionary China.[47] The Shaanxi provincial branch of the Bank of China tried unsuccessfully to regulate these private loans with guidelines restricting monthly interest to 1.5 to 2 percent per month (somewhat higher than limits the Communist Party had mandated in liberated areas during the Revolution).[48] Later the government conceded that the only result of such efforts to restrict interest was that "free loan activities have become more hidden." Recognizing that farmers needed this credit, the government turned a blind eye on extortionate interest. One official in 1985 urged his colleagues to do so, saying, "Even when interest rates are on the high side, we must not regard them as usurious loans. It is unsuitable to use the name of the government to stipulate the standards for interest rates of free loans, or to regard those interest rates which surpass the standards as usurious."[49]

In spite of the heavy interest rates, the new private credit market provided a service that farmers and entrepreneurs found indispensable. Whereas personal loans in the collective era had taken the form of grain to see families through hard times, loans now were in cash and their primary use was in "production and circulation." A multi-province survey delivered at the 1984 National Conference on Rural Work reported that private loans already accounted for half of peasants' operating expenditures.[50] Other surveys from the same year indicated an even bigger role for private credit, with banks and credit cooperatives accounting for only one-quarter of peasant borrowing.[51]

---

on the Rural Funds and Credit and Loans Policies," *Nongcun jinrong* 1985: 5, translated in JPRS-CAG-85–019 (June 11, 1985), p. 42.

47. Arthur H. Smith reported monthly interest at 2.5 to 4 percent during his years in Shandong Province at the end of the Qing Dynasty. Arthur H. Smith, *Village Life in China* (1899; reprint, Boston: Little, Brown and Co., 1970), p. 112. See also Lloyd E. Eastman, *Family, Fields, and Ancestors: Constancy and Change in China's Social and Economic History, 1550–1949* (New York: Oxford University Press, 1988), p. 75.

48. Chen Lian, "'Shuangbao' hou,'" p. 40. Cf. Mark Selden, *The Yenan Way in Revolutionary China* (Cambridge: Harvard University Press, 1971), p. 230 n.

49. Zhao, "Rural Funds and Credit," pp. 42, 43.

50. Ibid., p. 42.

51. Gao Hongbin et al., "Chang xian zengzhang," p. 50.

In small cities private credit became more formalized, with actual banks springing up. The leader in full-scale private banking was Wenzhou, the small Zhejiang city that achieved national fame as the prodigy of privatization. A city of half a million serving a surrounding rural population of six million, Wenzhou had private banks operating openly (though illegally) as early as 1986. These private banks, whose formula was copied by dozens of upstart banks elsewhere in Zhejiang, made profits by specializing in loans to the small entrepreneurs scorned by the official banking system.[52] Private credit had become a normal part of the more privatized economy.

For a time the government applauded this development. The leaders were pleased at the way private lenders gathered idle funds in the countryside and put them to productive use. Besides, the leadership knew that the official credit apparatus which it controlled had failed to channel funds into vital farm production, and the money had to come from somewhere. It was only toward the end of the 1980s that some in the government became disenchanted with private credit. By then moneylenders had developed more sophisticated methods for generating larger loans while lodging the risk with people other than themselves. Collecting deposits from individual peasants for interest, they reloaned the money at higher rates. When the loans (nearly always unsecured) went bad, the depositors lost their savings. By 1990 many repetitions of this personal catastrophe for peasants soured banking officials on private credit, and the government became less willing to countenance unofficial lending. But, as before, there was nothing to take its place, and it lived on.[53]

Chinese analysis of private credit in the 1980s frequently remarked upon how naturally the phenomenon had crept into the rural economy.[54] In fact there was nothing mysterious about this radical change. Private farming engendered private borrowing, as a matter of necessity. Privatization was rolling heavily over the reformers' original intentions, propelled by its own weight. Moneylenders' victimization of peasants was only one of the revived prerevolutionary

52. *New York Times,* Aug. 5, 1988, sec. A, p. 4.
53. Interviews with banking officials, Hebei, July 1990.
54. For examples, see *Nongmin ribao,* Jan. 20, 1988, p. 2; Wang and Li, "Rural Financial Structural Reforms," pp. 82, 83; and Zhao, "Rural Funds and Credit."

abuses in which the Communist Party of the 1980s found virtue. Hired labor was another.

Hired Labor and the
Precariousness of Family Farms

Just as the move toward private land tenure and private credit proceeded step by step, China's passage to private hiring of labor grew naturally out of other features of privatization. With hired labor, the logic of privatization was straightforward. Once farms and other rural businesses began to operate on their own, they needed a private labor market. Without a ready pool of labor, private enterprises could not maintain their flexibility, independence, and productivity. The rapid growth that many of China's rural entrepreneurs achieved in the early 1980s came partly because they were willing to break the long-standing strictures against privately hiring labor. Once it became clear that further growth spurred by entrepreneurship would require an unfettered labor market, the government struck down the restrictions. The need for such a move was simple and clear. What is less obvious is that the expansion of hired labor was tightly connected to the inviability of China's new family farms.

The main source of rural hired labor was farm households. Households that could not make ends meet on their contracted land were forced to hire out some or all of the family members as laborers. For some, particularly grain farmers, sowing the fields was not profitable enough for a living. Others had too little land—either the village did not have enough land to go around in the first place, or the family outgrew its original share. Some peasants had been assigned deficient land, which was poorly irrigated, infertile, or subject to waterlogging. Even peasants deemed to have "sufficient" land rarely had enough. If China could have carried out the most perfect and fair land distribution conceivable, people would still have had to hire themselves out as laborers. There just was not enough farmland. Rural China had a huge surplus of labor that the land could not absorb. The most commonly cited Chinese estimate of rural surplus labor during the 1980s was 100 million people.[55]

55. For example, see *Jingjixue zhoubao*, Apr. 5, 1987, p. 3.

Peasants who had to turn to wage labor sought it from old collective enterprises still in operation or from the independent entrepreneurs, that is, the specialized households and larger private ventures. Hiring by land-tilling peasants was less common. Individual landholdings were too small and profit margins too slim for farmers to hire much labor. When they did, it was for seasonal or short-term work, such as irrigation improvements or "double rush" (*shuang qiang*), when one rice crop had to be harvested and another transplanted within a few days. As a general rule, crop-growing families were afraid to hire labor because the weather made it too risky. In a bad year the fixed cost of a hired laborer could put a farm into the red.

Hired laborers' prospects depended mainly on what local resources were available to support businesses. Coastal provinces with plentiful resources and access to rich markets developed extraordinarily successful industrial enterprises in the 1980s. In Jiangsu, Zhejiang, Fujian, and Guangdong, these enterprises offered wages that gave rural workers much more prosperity than they enjoyed as farmers. But in areas without such resources, hired laborers faced harder times. Because crop cultivation employed few laborers, peasants forced onto the labor market from heavily agricultural districts had to migrate to find work. Itinerant laborers were usually young males (aged twenty or younger), although middle-aged people too sometimes had to take to the road. They were likely to end up in areas with good transport and a variety of resources that could support different enterprises.

One such destination was Yangxin, a Hubei county on the southern bank of the Yangtze River. Yangxin County had a relatively sparse population in an area rich in resources for aquatic production, various industries, and small coal operations. These enterprises were predominantly private, and they hired labor from counties north of the river. The counties supplying the laborers (Xishui, Huangqu, Qichun, and Guangji) were almost exclusively agricultural, but suffered from a desperate shortage of cultivated land—less than 0.01 hectare per person, leaving many peasants little choice but to leave home for a temporary job in Yangxin.[56]

---

56. Chen Wenke et al., "Muqian Hubei sheng wu diqu qi xian nongcun siren gugong jingying diaocha" (A survey of rural operations that privately hire labor in

Laborers throughout China in such situations were usually un-skilled people with little education.[57] Working outside their own villages, they lacked the connections and clout (the *guanxi*) necessary to improve their lot. Peasants who made their way to the large cities were especially easy targets for unscrupulous employers. Shanghai's Bureau of Industry and Commerce reported in 1987 that large private employers "hire out-of-town peasants unfamiliar with market conditions at patently depressed wages in order to jack up their own profits. These peasants do not do any less work than their local counterparts, yet earn one-third to one-quarter less."[58] Working conditions nearly everywhere were poor and dangerous. In both urban and rural settings, the private businesses that most commonly hired peasants were light industry, handicrafts, transportation, and housing construction. With the exception of a few skilled master workers (*shifu*), peasant employees did manual labor for subsistence wages.[59] Private entrepreneurs hiring laborers for one or two yuan a day could make very large profits. For example, four brothers pioneering private production in Guangdong contracted for collective factory equipment to produce bicycle rims. They hired 180 workers at 60 yuan per month, paid themselves monthly wages of 360 yuan apiece and split year-end profits of 9,000 yuan each. In another instance, a man in a Zhejiang township set up a workshop to assemble electrical switches. He hired nine peasants at 1.5 yuan per day and worked them long hours to produce a high volume, accumulating the enormous sum of 150,000 yuan in profit.[60] Employers considered notorious by Chinese for their profiteering were the labor contractors, or labor gang bosses (*baogongtou*). Labor gang bosses might control forty to one hundred laborers, hiring them out and taking a third or more of their wages off the top.[61]

---

five districts and seven counties of contemporary Hubei), *Shehui kexue dongtai [Hubei]* 1983: 28 (Oct. 1), pp. 3–4.

57. Ibid., p. 4.

58. Hu Guohua et al., "Profit-Driven Individual Entrepreneurs Evade Taxes and Take Advantage of Other Loopholes in Public Policy," *Liaowang* 1987: 51, translated in JPRS-CAR-88–006 (Feb. 19, 1988), p. 26.

59. In the early 1980s such wages were one to two yuan per day. Lu Wen, "Guanyu nongcun siren gugong wenti de tantao" (Inquiry into the question of private hiring of labor in the countryside), *Nongye jingji congkan* 1983: 3, p. 25.

60. Ibid. For other examples see Chen Wenke et al., "Muqian Hubei."

61. For a fictionalized description of life under labor bosses, see Dai Hou-

The income gap between laborers and employers inspired endless debate in Chinese intellectual circles over whether hiring labor amounted to exploitation.[62] Regardless of what intellectuals might have thought, the reform leaders came to regard hired labor as a permanent institution. The cohesion and efficiency of the more privatized economy demanded it. And more important, the reformers' benign attitude toward hired labor masked a latent hostility against the centerpiece of the reforms: the family farm.

The private labor supply was both a consequence of the family farm's efficiency and a token of its failure to meet China's development needs. On the positive side, individual farms generated surplus labor because they used labor too efficiently to absorb a family's entire work supply. On the other hand, this apparent efficiency was also an artifact of small farm size. Many of China's family farms were too small to support the whole family—too small, in other words, to be viable. If people were forced off the farm into wage labor, the reform leadership did not object. In the first place, the reformers were eager to get the vast rural populace out of farming and into diversified lines of production. Hired labor was a necessary part of that hope. In the second place, even though the reform leaders put the peasantry back onto private landholdings, they had no love for traditional family farms. Agriculture in China still bore the earmarks of peasant farming, in which the family has only a small amount of land for the main crop and pursues half a dozen sidelines to make ends meet. In contrast to modern farming, this kind of family farm is unspecialized and self-sufficient. The farm is "small but complete," as the Chinese put it.[63] And as far as the reform leaders were concerned, this small but complete farm was a stubborn barrier to China's future development. In 1987, 70 percent of Chinese family farms were smaller than two-thirds

ying, *Ren a, ren!* (Ah, humanity!) (Guangzhou: Guangdong renmin chubanshe, 1980), pp. 33, 44–48. For details on a specific labor gang, see Lu Wen, "Guanyu nongcun siren gugong," p. 25.

62. A summary of this debate appears in Xu Yongqing, "Dangqian nongcun gugong wenti de jizhong butong guandian" (Several different points of view on the current question of hiring labor in the countryside), *Nongye jingji congkan* 1983: 1, pp. 19–23, 14.

63. Gui Jianping, "Woguo nongcun fengong wenti qian xi" (A simple analysis of the problem of the division of labor in our nation's agriculture), *Jingji yanjiu cankao ziliao* 1983: 175 (Nov. 14), p. 37.

of a hectare (about 1.5 acres). Worse still, the average family farm was not a consolidated field as Americans might envision, but scattered strips and bits of land—nine or ten different parcels on the average making up a "farm."[64] The family farm was pitifully small, dispersed, and unsuited for large-scale modern farming.

The reformers were blunt about the fate of traditional peasant agriculture. "This small peasant economy is an economy without a future," said one reform economist.[65] Peasant farms might have been private, but the reform coalition did not value privatization for its own sake; rather, privatization was a strategy for development that they stumbled into, perhaps half-knowingly. The leaders studied foreign agriculture and knew that modern private farms looked nothing like the so-called natural peasant household, producing for its own needs and engaging only minimally in the broader economy. What the reformers desired was not self-sufficient cells of stagnation, but economic units engaged in rich and complex transactions with the whole economy.

To create that more complex interaction, the reformers considered two ways of replacing the family farm. One way was to recollectivize agriculture. No one was contemplating a return to the communes, but the reformers did envision some sort of cooperatives: units large enough for mechanized farming and efficient enough to operate as businesses. In one such model, Doudian Village (Fangshan County, Beijing), which was promoted at the Thirteenth Party Congress in 1987, villagers collectively worked with modern machinery on land consolidated into farms of roughly twenty-five hectares.[66] The second way the reformers hoped to phase out the family farm was to further encourage small entrepreneurship of the type represented by the specialized households. Entrepreneurship moved peasants out of farming and into pursuits that reformers believed would enrich the network of internal connections in the economy. What attracted the reformers to specialized households was their very lack

64. Lu Wen, "Nongcun jingji fazhan zhong de xin dongtai" (Recent trends in rural economic development), *Nongye jingji wenti* 1987: 12, p. 5.

65. Yu Guoyao, "Woguo nongye de jiating jingying he jiating jingji" (Family management and the family economy in our nation's agriculture), *Jingji yanjiu cankao ziliao* 1983: 100 (June 30), p. 11.

66. *Wall Street Journal*, January 19, 1988, p. 16.

of self-sufficiency. Unlike traditional farmers, these small entrepreneurs had to be engaged in the wider economy: they relied on the market both to buy their output and to supply their consumption goods. The leaders considered specialized households a model that was not only widely attainable given China's poverty, but the perfect vehicle for "speeding up the disintegration of the rural natural economy."[67]

Privatization re-created many of the features of the natural economy that had been eradicated or suppressed by the collectivist interlude. In re-creating what the Communist Party had once destroyed, the reformers were acting without nostalgia. They regarded small family farms as a dead end for China. They had no illusions about the charms of life as a hired laborer. (Indeed, class analysis by the Party before Liberation reckoned rural laborers to have the most miserable lives of all Chinese.) But in the newly privatized countryside, both the family farm and hired labor found a new context and, in the eyes of the reformers, a changed meaning. Small farmers in the late twentieth century, desperately short of land, were bound to have a precarious existence. For the economy as a whole their way of life held no promise of future development. If the insecurity of smallholding and the growth of private enterprise combined to draw peasants off farms onto a private labor market, then the reform coalition was not going to stand in the way. On the contrary, reformers enthusiastically promoted private hiring of labor as half the solution for consolidating farmland and freeing China from the ghost of the traditional peasant economy.[68] And if half the solution was labor for hire, the other half was entrepreneurs to do the hiring.

Celebration of Entrepreneurship

One of the most startling reverses brought by Deng Xiaoping's government was the unrestrained enthusiasm of the state toward rural entrepreneurs. During the quarter-century of collectivized farming in China, no one had been vilified or

67. Xu Chongzheng and Chen Daokui, "Chuxian diqu zhuanye hu fazhan de diaocha" (Investigation into the growth of specialized households in Chuxian Prefecture), *Lilun zhanxian* 1983: 181 (May 15), p. 4.
68. Lu, "Nongcun jingji fazhan," pp. 5–6.

abhorred quite like those who tried to make more money for themselves. Now the government practically made heroes of them. From 1979 on, the government arranged a huge onslaught of publicity promoting entrepreneurship, introducing new phrases into the language. The first new term, *zhuanye hu* ("specialized household"), saturated rural news reporting. These entrepreneurial households became ubiquitous media heroes, celebrated in the newspapers and romanticized in the movies. *Wan yuan hu,* or 10,000-yuan households, were another new category, made of families whose annual income reached the fabulous level of ten thousand yuan—roughly ten times the income of most peasant households. Another neologism was *jingji lianheti,* which translated awkwardly as "economic association," but had a meaning closer to "joint-stock company." This term referred to businesses on a larger scale that pooled capital from several or many households and paid out dividends and profits according to investment shares.[69] All these businesses engaged in every conceivable type of production and service. Some were built from the ground up. Others contracted for the use of collective resources, such as ponds, mills, orchards, or factories. If their businesses grew large enough, these entrepreneurs were the people who privately hired labor in the countryside.

In its enthusiasm for entrepreneurship, the government claimed that specialized households had grown so explosively that by 1984 they represented a fantastic 14 percent of the peasant population.[70] Pressure was so heavy for local officials to demonstrate their districts' advances in entrepreneurship that some set up fake specialized households. In one delightful example, Yuhuan County, in Zhejiang Province, boasted a specialized household "raising five hundred ducks and getting an income of more than ten thousand yuan." In fact the supposed business genius behind this success was a fraud, posing to make

69. For more on the early "economic associations," see Wang Guichen, "Dui xin de jingji lianhe de jidian renshi" (Several points to be understood about new economic associations), *Nongye jingji wenti* 1982: 4, pp. 17–19; and Huang Yuehui, "Zenyang kan nongmin xin de jingji lianhe?" (How should we look at the peasants' new economic associations?) *Xinhua wenzhai* 1982: 1, pp. 69–70.

70. For example, see *Zhongguo baike nianjian* (Chinese encyclopedic yearbook) (Beijing: Zhongguo da baike quanshu chubanshe, 1984), p. 362.

the local cadres look good. With the cadres' help, he had rented hundreds of ducks from other peasants at 0.3 yuan a day, losing a sizable sum of money but amassing all the ducks in one place to look like a grand business. "Thus," reported the *Peasant Daily*, "when the inspectors came, they could see lots of ducks."[71] In 1985, after a closer look at the situation nationwide, the government released revised figures showing that only 2.3 percent of peasant families had bona fide businesses qualifying as specialized households.[72]

In village society, this entrepreneurial minority was controversial from the outset. The entrepreneurs' earliest troubles grew out of their very success. After the government embraced the slogan, "Let some peasants get rich first," the new entrepreneurs did just that. As a vice-secretary of the Hubei Party Committee pointed out, "The majority of the peasant households who have gotten rich first are specialized households"[73]—that is, entrepreneurs, not ordinary farmers. The trouble was that the entrepreneurs' sudden wealth inspired resentment among neighbors and local officials alike.

Local cadres were the first to vent their antagonism. When the new businesses first appeared amid the policy confusion of the early reform period, cadres could not tell what was allowed and what was not. Perceiving the new businesses as a vague threat to local authority, cadres felt compelled to interfere.[74] They began to bully entrepreneurs by "extending a hand" (*shen shou*), or demanding a share.[75] Cadres also made unspecified threats through symbolic actions. One example concerns a Hubei peasant who contracted with his collective for the use of a local pond. He hired four laborers from outside the

71. *Nongmin ribao*, Jan. 5, 1985, translated in JPRS-CAG-85-010 (Mar. 11, 1985), p. 25.

72. Xinhua Domestic Service, Nov. 4, 1985, translated in JPRS-CAG-85-033 (Dec. 12, 1985), p. 10.

73. From a speech by Provincial Vice-Secretary Shen Yinluo, reported in *Hubei ribao*, Jan. 16, 1984, p. 1.

74. Hubei sheng nongwei (Hubei Provincial Agricultural Committee), "Da li jiaqiang he gaishan nongcun sixiang zhengzhi gongzuo" (Greatly strengthen and improve rural ideological and political work), *Shehui kexue dongtai [Hubei]* 1983: 2 (Jan. 10), p. 20.

75. Yan Nong, "Hubei sheng nongcun 'liang hu yi lian' de fazhan qing-kuang" (The development of "two households and one alliance" in rural Hubei), *Shehui kexue dongtai [Hubei]* 1983: 16 (June 1), p. 8.

village at thirty yuan per month and made a tidy profit growing fish, clams, and pearls. Soon the local cadres began to show up at his house every evening at dinner time. They never said anything and never threatened to take away the pond. They only ate, but for free—a way of demonstrating power in China. The cadres' unspoken message was, "We can shut down your operation any time we like, so don't cross us."[76] Cadre harassment of entrepreneurs did not always take the form of extortion and threats, however. The cadres' antagonism was sometimes just the expression of community norms of equality, shared by a majority of villagers. For instance, a Zhejiang entrepreneur whose family made it as a 10,000-yuan household testified that the local cadres beset him not for their own personal gain, but to enforce the village egalitarianism: "In 1982, I built a three-story house in our village. But the village leaders said: All the houses in our village are two-story houses except yours. Why did you build the 'additional' third floor? With your house higher than the others, you are taking away the good fortune of all the other villagers. Thus the third floor of my house was peremptorily pulled down by some villagers who lacked common sense, and the house was 'brought down to the same level' as others in this way."[77]

Harassment led by cadres diminished after state support for entrepreneurship became unequivocal. Central Document Number 1 for 1983 came down in January of that year with a sweeping endorsement of commercial activities. The document gave entrepreneurs approval for private hiring of labor, private purchase of large-scale producer goods (for example, processing equipment, tractors, trucks), and pooling of capital in private investment.[78] Rural entrepreneurs had engaged in all of these practices before 1983, of course, but the legality of their activities was always doubtful, and they had to bribe local cadres to ward off bullying. After the promulgation of

76. Interview with economists, September 1983, Wuhan.

77. *Nongmin ribao*, Jan. 5, 1985, translated in JPRS-CAG-85-010 (Mar. 11, 1985), p. 24. I have made minor corrections in a garbled translation here.

78. The document was entitled "Dangqian nongcun jingji zhengce de ruogan wenti (1983 nian 1 hao wenjian)" (Several problems in current rural economic policy [Central Document No. 1 for 1983]), and extensive excerpts from it were published in *Renmin ribao*, Apr. 10, 1983, pp. 1–2. In particular, see section 4 and section 6.

Central Document Number 1, they could proceed with the blessing of the state. Cadres who opposed entrepreneurship did not know what to do. In Hubei, cadres froze up when faced with decisions about specialized households: "They don't nod their heads yes, they don't shake their heads no; and if anything goes wrong they make themselves scarce."[79]

Such irresolution among cadres opposed to reform gave way to defections into the ranks of the entrepreneurs once cadres realized how profitable entrepreneurship could be for them.[80] A widely publicized Shanxi survey found that by the end of 1983 former commune cadres comprised a huge proportion (43 percent) of specialized households.[81] At the time, many Chinese discounted this survey (which Vice-Premier Wan Li had highlighted in a speech), saying it was only an attempt to mollify cadres hurt by the reforms, and to encourage them to "get rich first" as well. But before the end of the decade it was clear that the evolution of entrepreneurship had in fact served cadres very well.

The more savvy cadres did not waste their energy on family-sized businesses; they moved to take control of the old collective enterprises. A 1982 national survey of large rural businesses (averaging assets of about three hundred thousand yuan and employing a mean of about forty workers) showed that most (59 percent) started by leasing the productive assets of collective enterprises. In these newly privatized enterprises, the organizers, owners, and managers who got the leases were commonly the former cadres who had been involved in the enterprise when it was run collectively. As the decade wore on, the predominance of these formerly collective enterprises in private business declined steadily and swiftly. But in the critical opening period of competition, ex-cadres enjoyed an unbeatable advantage in their special relationship to the old collective enterprises.[82]

79. Yan, "Hubei sheng nongcun," p. 11.

80. On the ways in which commercialization changed cadres' lives, see Jean C. Oi, "Commercializing China's Rural Cadres," *Problems of Communism* 35 (September-October 1986), pp. 1–14.

81 The survey was from Ying County, Shanxi. See *Renmin ribao*, Jan. 18, 1984; and *South China Morning Post*, Jan. 30, 1984, p. 6.

82. Liu Xiaojing, "Issues Pertaining to the Healthy Development of Private Enterprises: An Empirical Study of 130 Private Enterprises in 18 Provinces," *Nong-*

Later, the predominant form of large business shifted from leases on collective assets to enterprises begun with purely private assets. Seventy percent of large rural businesses running in 1987 had gained their starts using only private capital and assets, with no connection to former collective enterprises. By that time, however, cadres had already gotten a head start from their business experiences in the early 1980s, and they now represented a greatly disproportionate number of the owners and managers in the dominant, privately capitalized companies. Furthermore, former cadres as owners still had special competitive advantages—for example, in getting credit. Banks and credit cooperatives in the second half of the 1980s restricted their private-sphere lending to larger businesses; in the tight credit market this lending followed the path of personal alliances, enhancing the power of cadres-turned-entrepreneurs.[83]

Whatever their failings in managing the old collective economy, cadres did well for themselves under reform. After all, they had the connections. They knew best where to find local resources; they had the most personal contacts and management skills; they knew how to use telephones and they had the best access to market information. Their skills as brokers and middlemen, gained during years of experience under the commune system, made China's rural cadres natural aspirants to success under privatization.[84]

While cadre antagonism against private business therefore diminished with time, entrepreneurs still had to remain on guard against resentment from ordinary peasants. "Households doing conspicuously well," said one Hubei report, ". . . are afraid that once they are rich they will attract too much attention and invite trouble."[85] Trouble sometimes came anonymously, as theft, sabotage, or poisoning of animals.[86] One young woman in Anhui who built a successful poultry

---

ye jingji wenti 1988: 4, translated in JPRS-CAR-88-033 (June 23, 1988), pp. 33–37.

83. Ibid., pp. 33–37.

84. For a different analysis of the cadres' critical role in promoting or thwarting entrepreneurship, see Victor Nee, "Peasant Entrepreneurship and the Politics of Regulation in China," in Victor Nee and David Stark, eds., *Remaking the Economic Institutions of Socialism: China and Eastern Europe* (Stanford: Stanford University Press, 1989), pp. 168–207.

85. Yan, "Hubei sheng nongcun," p. 11.

86. Ibid., p. 13.

business (marketing a quarter of a million chickens annually) suffered losses from neighbors plundering her inventory. She testified: "Fishing is a popular sport, but people may not have heard about fishing for chickens. Quite a few of my chickens have actually been stolen by this type of 'fishing.' The fishermen baited their hooks with rice and then put the rods in the chicken coop. The chickens were captured when they ate the rice. I have suffered a loss of more than four thousand yuan over the past year because of this."[87] In other cases peasants physically threatened entrepreneurs. A Shaanxi peasant whose household became a 10,000-yuan household in 1982 by raising ducks (truly his own ducks) was warned by his neighbors, "You'd better stop before you go too far. Watch out or you might become an example." The peasant took heed, reluctantly, deciding that after he saved another ten thousand yuan in 1983 he "would stop getting rich."[88] Successful entrepreneurs were also victims of extortion perpetrated by fellow villagers. Reports from Anhui said peasants commonly asked members of specialized households for "loans" they had no intention of repaying—a form of extortion that "makes the hearts of the specialized household throb with terror."[89] All these expressions of resentment toward entrepreneurs led the Hubei Party journal to advise the rich not to indulge in higher consumption but to reinvest their profits and avoid attention.[90] The Party journal was not being overly cautious, for peasants were known to commit violence against members of the community prospering from private business. In one Jiangsu county, the public security forces were even called out "to protect the haves from the have-nots."[91]

In this fight between the haves and the have-nots, reform lead-

87. *Nongmin ribao*, Jan. 5, 1985, translated in JPRS-CAG-85–010 (Mar. 11, 1985), p. 24.

88. Yu Guoyao, "Nongcun zhuanye hu fazhan de qushi he wenti" (Trends and problems in the development of rural specialized households), *Jingji yanjiu cankao ziliao* 1983: 176 (Nov. 15), p. 22.

89. Xu and Chen, "Chuxian diqu," p. 8.

90. "Guanjian zai you li yu shengchan de fazhan" (The key lies in whatever helps to develop production), *Dangyuan shenghuo [Hubei]* 1983: 2, p. 10.

91. The county in question was Suqian; *South China Morning Post*, Jan. 30, 1984, p. 6. For a study of this type of conflict in a single Jiangsu community, see David Zweig, "Prosperity and Conflict in Post-Mao Rural China," *China Quarterly*, 105 (March 1986), pp. 1–18.

ers placed the interests of richer entrepreneurs before those of ordinary villagers. Policy on leasing collective property was the earliest sign of this preference. The state encouraged collectives to lease
out their assets with no limit on the profits entrepreneurs could
reap. For example, a Hunan man submitted a bid to lease his production team's brick factory, promising the team an annual income
of 14,100 yuan from the business. His personal profit from the
venture came to 2,700 yuan per year, five to ten times what he
paid each of his workers.[92] In many such leasing arrangements,
entrepreneurs plowed profits back into the business until the private portion of investment dwarfed the original collective share of
assets; the enterprise then fell entirely under private control.[93] In
addition to condoning such profitable private arrangements, the
state encouraged entrepreneurship by instructing local officials to
favor private businesses with tax holidays and preferential lines of
credit.[94]

Special access to official credit for entrepreneurs especially irked
farmers. The interest rates on bank and credit cooperative loans were
far below rates prevailing in the private credit market. Central policy
authorized lending officials to steer these loans toward private companies and specialized households. This gave entrepreneurs a great
advantage over other peasants. In the past the official credit system
had made only small loans to individuals, to see them through illness
or help them purchase grain in hard times. Now, with individual loans
on the rise, entrepreneurs received most of the benefit. Figures from
the Agricultural Bank of Yangxin County (Hubei) showed that spe-

92. Lu, "Guanyu nongcun siren gugong," p. 25.

93. This phenomenon is discussed in Chen Wenke et al., "Muqian Hubei,"
p. 13.

94. On tax policy, see Yan, "Hubei sheng nongcun," p. 13; and Zhongguo
nongcun fazhan wenti yanjiu zu (Research Group on Problems of Chinese Rural
Development), *Yi nongcun wei tupo kou shixing fenqu liti kaifa de gaige zhanlüe*
(Use agriculture as the breakthrough point and open up a differentiated, multi-
dimensional reform strategy) (August 1982, Mimeographed), p. 5. Tax policy on
private enterprise was confused and arbitrary, especially during the early reform
period. Some entrepreneurs evaded taxes entirely; others were subject to multiple
taxation; and some, fearful that they might be accused of tax evasion when there
were no taxes on the books that might apply to them, made up their own taxes
and donated them to the local tax bureau. See Yu, "Nongcun zhuanye hu," p. 22.

cialized households routinely obtained credit several times the magnitude of loans to ordinary peasants.[95] Nationwide, by the mid–1980s
rural credit cooperatives were devoting nearly half their lending to
specialized households, which represented less than 3 percent of the
rural population. Although banks and credit cooperatives claimed to
make some effort to be more responsive to the needs of land-tilling
peasants,[96] they preferred the fast turnover and high repayment rate
associated with entrepreneurs.[97] The larger entrepreneurial ventures
could safely be granted loans in amounts of one hundred thousand
yuan or more.

It puzzled peasants that these preferential credit policies favored
the people least in need of help. Indeed, people who became entrepreneurs seemed to possess advantages that other peasants could not
match. From the beginning, certain groups were in a superior position to take advantage of the commercial thrust of the reforms. One
group was ordinary farming families that happened to be at the peak
of their labor strength at the outset of reform. With more family
members to make the most of family farming, they quickly amassed
savings ahead of their neighbors.[98] In the ensuing entrepreneurial
boom they had both the capital and the labor necessary to get nonfarm businesses off the ground. A second favored group was educated
youths with scientific or technical knowledge. Surveys throughout
the 1980s showed that entrepreneurs had educational levels well above

95. When bank lending to individuals in the county suddenly expanded with
the new policies in 1982, reaching 90,000 borrowers, the average loan to specialized
households was 350 yuan; the average loan to land-tilling households was eighty
yuan. Yangxin xian nongye yinhang (Yangxin County Agricultural Bank), "Chong-
fen fahui yinhang zhineng, jiji zhichi 'liang hu yi lian'" (Bring the functions of
banks fully into play and actively support the "two households and one alliance"),
Shehui kexue dongtai [Hubei] 1983: 16 (June 1), pp. 14–17.
96. *Hubei ribao*, Aug. 18, 1980, p. 1; Jan. 24, 1981, p. 2.
97. Yangxin xian nongye yinhang, pp. 14–15, 18.
98. Hubei income surveys showed that against the background of the general
rural boom in the early 1980s, earning power jumped disproportionately for families with higher proportions of able-bodied adults. Li Xueceng, "Guanyu woguo
cheng xiang jumin shenghuo xiaofei jiegou de ruogan fenxi he chubu yuce (shang)"
(Some analysis and initial calculations on the composition of personal consumption
among the urban and rural residents in our country [part 1]), *Jingji yanjiu cankao
ziliao* 1983: 182 (Nov. 26), p. 48.

the rural average.[99]. Another group, demobilized soldiers, enjoyed a similar advantage. According to a Shanxi survey, ex-servicemen who had acquired special skills in the army enjoyed disproportionate representation among specialized households. So did older craftsmen.[100]

Although many private businesses failed, as a rule entrepreneurs had higher incomes than ordinary farmers. A national survey taken at mid-decade found that specialized households had more than twice the earning power of other peasant households. (In many counties just to be designated a specialized household, a family had to make a gross income well above the county average.)[101] Ordinary farmers composed the great majority of peasants, but certain disadvantages were clustered among them, in contrast to entrepreneurs. Lower education and lower income both correlated with farming. Among poor peasant households (those earning less than two hundred yuan per capita in 1986, representing 15 percent of the rural population) nearly two-thirds were farm families. Among richer peasant households (earning more than one thousand yuan per capita, representing 10 percent of the rural population) barely one-third were in farming.[102]

If entrepreneurs had so many advantages over the land-tilling majority, why did the state skew its economic policies to favor them above ordinary peasants? Considering the state's traditional claim of solidarity with the "poor and lower-middle peasants," why was it trying so hard to help this richer, privileged group?

The answer is that successful businesses served state interests. Privatization made entrepreneurs the logical group on which the state could pin its hopes for rural development. The goal of state policy was no longer to distribute wealth evenly but to put resources to-

99. For examples, see *Zhejiang ribao*, July 21, 1983, p. 3; and Liu, "Healthy Development of Private Enterprises," p. 35.

100. On the Shanxi survey, see *South China Morning Post*, Jan. 30, 1984, p. 6.

101. On the national survey, see Xinhua Domestic Service, Nov. 4, 1985, translated in JPRS-CAG-85-033 (Dec. 12, 1985), p. 11. On designation of special households see Fu Yuxiang, "Shitan 'liang hu' de biaozhun wenti" (On the question of standards for the "two households"), *Nongqye jingji congkan* 1984: 1, p. 61; see also Chen Zhiqiang, "'Zhongdian hu' de tifa yi quxiao wei hao" (It would be best to abolish the term "keypoint household"), *Nongye jingji congkan* 1984: 1, p. 45.

102. *Nongmin ribao*, Jan. 11, 1988, p. 2.

gether in more powerful and productive combinations. This goal gave central reformers little reason to object to the rise of a privileged group within the peasantry. The reformers believed that resources, investment, and encouragement should be concentrated where they would have the greatest effect. The strategy, as summarized by the Central Committee, was: "Don't spread things all around the same way you sprinkle pepper!"[103] Instead, said a Secretariat research report, policy should benefit a minority, the "groups of able people with the 'entrepreneurial spirit' [who] will spring up all over the countryside." The report emphasized that "not every peasant household has the technical level, the eye for management, or the ability to organize production that are necessary to branch out and develop commodity production. Therefore we must use all the existing resources to the maximum, so that those who have money use their money, those who have strength use their strength, and those with ability use their ability."[104]

The idea driving state support for privatization was that a group with "money, strength, and ability"—given free rein—could use these assets better than public officials tangled in procedures and hierarchies could. And in fact the entrepreneurs acted just as their champions in the reform coalition might have hoped. They broke across administrative boundaries, combining factors of production that formerly fell under separate jurisdictions. Tapping resources that had never before been joined, entrepreneurs advanced the production possibility curve in salients where the collectives had been too rigid to venture. By seeking out investors and employees, entrepreneurs also absorbed the surplus savings and labor created by the higher income and work efficiency of family farms. This alleviated the leadership's fear that idle farm resources might be dissipated in nonproductive investment. As a Secretariat research unit had warned in 1982, "Without other outlets, rural surplus labor and capital are bound to be thrown

103. "Zhonggong Zhongyang guanyu jiakuai nongye fazhan ruogan wenti de jueding (cao'an)" (Resolution of the Central Committee of the Chinese Communist Party on certain problems in the acceleration of agricultural development [draft]), reprinted by *Zhonggong yanjiu* 13: 5 (May 1979), p. 160.

104. Zhongguo nongcun fazhan wenti yanjiu zu, p. 5. This discussion paper had a heavy influence on Central Document No. 1 for 1983.

into activities like the 'house-building fever' and short-term invest-ments in which 'a profit is a profit, no matter how you get it.' Idle people, gambling, and superstition will increase day by day. There-fore, as long as the state's financial power is insufficient, we must take the countryside's own surplus labor, idle capital, and rich natural re-sources and put them in motion to form enormous productive power."[105] The new private businesses proved ideal for this purpose. In Hubei, for example, at one commune in Yingcheng County, 340 new businesses attracted investments totaling 214,000 yuan from some 1,900 households whose funds had been idle. In Yangxin County (also in Hubei), new entrepreneurial ventures absorbed 70 percent of the surplus labor, employing nearly one out of four able-bodied peasants in the entire county.[106]

All in all, the entrepreneurs fulfilled so many policy aims that the reformers portrayed them as practically the unofficial agents of state policy. According to the copious praise in the Chinese press, entre-preneurs put the countryside's resources to work: discovering unap-preciated productive assets, buying surplus labor, and investing countless bits of idle capital, and doing all of this more creatively and efficiently than the old collectives.

Privatization made the entrepreneurs the state's natural partners in the countryside. Was this, however, a partnership the state should desire? Privatization appeared to unfold as an apolitical, logical pro-cess, but it was creating a new structure of conflict in the Chinese countryside—a new interaction of social forces that would all clamor for the state's attention and backing. In the rural society remade by reform, the state would have to choose whose side it was on.

---

105. Ibid., p. 4.

106. Both examples are from Yan, "Hubei sheng nongcun," p. 9. For exam-ples of private enterprises employing idle capital and labor in Anhui, see Xu and Chen, "Chuxian diqu," pp. 1–10.

Chapter Eight

Privatization and
State Socialism

Privatization and reform brought
the Chinese state face to face with
a more differentiated rural popu-
lace. Although peasants in Mao's China had held different job assignments, nearly all had had the same relation to the means of
production. Commune members collectively owned the means of
production, except for minor sidelines and small private plots. In
practice collective ownership rights may have been meaningless, but
they gave all peasants the same status: each peasant was simply a
member of the collective. The contrast after the reforms was striking.
In the semi-market economy that emerged in the 1980s, the variety of
roles peasants could play was much more diverse. Although Western
debate on the effect of the reforms often centered on income stratification, the new, finer cleavages among peasants amounted to more
than just gaps in wealth.[1] Peasants now had quite different relations
to the means of production. Some were the virtual owners of private
farmland, others rented land, and a growing number left the land altogether. Those who left farming might lease erstwhile collective enterprises, buy shares in enterprises, or own enterprises outright. And
some peasants, owning nothing productive, had to sell their labor to
a luckier person who did control some productive asset. These differentiated roles in the economy created new relationships between peas-

1. On this debate, see Martin King Whyte, "Social Trends in China: The
Triumph of Inequality?" in A. Doak Barnett and Ralph N. Clough, eds., *Modernizing China: Post-Mao Reform and Development* (Baltimore: Westview Press,
1986), pp. 103–23.

ants: as competitors, as business partners, as debtor and creditor, as shareholder and manager, as landlord and tenant, as boss and employee.

These more refined cleavages posed a dilemma for the state. Facing a more complex peasantry, the state had to make repeated choices about which peasant groups to support, which interests to encourage, and which trends to oppose. In light of the Communist Party's traditional opposition to all trappings of rural capitalism, some of the choices the state made in the 1980s were astonishing. What drove these choices? In part, it was certainly the economic logic of privatization: the state wanted its policy choices to support the modernization program, and therefore acquiesced in one step of privatization after another. But a deeper compulsion also drove the state—the need to retain power. In the changed political economy of rural China, what means could the state now use to enforce its will upon the peasantry?

Privatization as a Threat to State Power

Outside the obvious coercive apparatus of the military and the Public Security Bureau, state power in the Chinese countryside at the beginning of the reforms operated through three main bases: the collective structure, the Communist Party, and a constituency among peasants who were slightly privileged by virtue of their class labels. Privatization and reform shook all three of these bases of power, driving the state to seek new sources of political power in rural China.

Undermining the Collective Structure

When privatization startled the reform leaders by accelerating their economic program, they were nimble enough to take steps to support it. Preserving the commercial rebirth sparked by privatization meant defending it against the political muscle of local officials in the collective bureaucracy. Therefore, five years into reform, in 1983, the leaders addressed the obstacle to commercial growth posed by the commune administration. Eager to give the rural economy more independence from political cadres, the leadership quietly abandoned the Party's hoary principle of "politics in command." Suddenly economic development gained unprecedented autonomy from political administration.

To protect this autonomy, central leaders decided to separate the economic and political lines of local administration. This meant disbanding the communes, which had always fused political and economic functions. To take over the communes' political operations, *xiang* governments were resurrected. The *xiang* (conventionally given the misleading translation of "township") was an administrative unit that had been superseded by the communes in 1958. In its 1980s revival, the *xiang* government covered roughly the same jurisdiction as a commune, embracing a population averaging about twelve thousand people.[2] Like the commune before it, the *xiang* government was responsible for civil government, public security, judicature, taxation, and enforcement of state policy. A unit below the *xiang* called the village people's committee (*cun min weiyuanhui*) was also created to cover about the same jurisdiction as the old brigade. Together, the *xiang* government and village committee oversaw such social policy areas as health, education, and family planning.[3]

The significance of this change lay in the reduced economic authority of rural administration. Compared to the communes, the new *xiang* governments exercised only narrow economic powers. Daily farm operations were already beyond the purview of local government when the *xiang* came back into being in 1983, for family farming had become a fact of life. With the *xiang*, this trend went further, removing the huge network of collective enterprises—including

2. A commune swollen to unwieldy proportions was sometimes replaced by more than one *xiang* government. Jean Oi calculated that the average "township" (*xiang* or *zhen*) had 11,886 people (in 1986) while the average commune had 14,720 people (in 1974). Jean C. Oi, *State and Peasant in Contemporary China* (Berkeley: University of California Press, 1989), p. 5.

3. The Chinese term for separating political and economic administration was *zheng she fenkai* ("separate the government from the commune"). Vivienne Shue's article, "The Fate of the Commune," *Modern China* 10 (July 1984), pp. 259–83, contains a succinct analysis of the reasons for the abandonment of the communes, as well as a detailed summary of the new functions and organizational structure of the *xiang* governments.

everything from manufacturing to forestry, construction, commerce, animal husbandry, and mining—from direct government control. Under the administrative reforms of 1983 and 1984, all these enterprises became independent companies. As a popular journal pointed out, "the rural government can no longer interfere in the substantive operational activities of these organizations by administrative fiat, as it did in the past."[4] In other words, the administrative reforms severely curtailed local government's day-to-day control over collective enterprises, at a time when local officials had already lost much of their authority over ordinary farming.[5] Commune cadres showed scant enthusiasm for relinquishing this economic power. The central government reported that cadres actively resisted the separation of economic and government functions, even though their superiors in the counties, prefectures, and provinces widely supported it.[6] The Central Committee and the State Council dashed the commune cadres' last hopes with a joint communiqué instructing the whole country to set up *xiang* governments by the end of 1984.[7]

The Central Committee recognized that without the communes certain management tasks might be neglected. Anticipating this problem, the Party had earlier published lists of former commune functions that would have to be performed by the new administrative structure or by private entities. These tasks included wholesale purchase of production materials, large-scale afforestation, major invest-

4. Chen Yan, "Problems of Separating the State from the Commune," *Liaowang* 1984: 47 (Nov. 19, 1984), translated in JPRS-CAG-85-015 (May 21, 1985), p. 77.

5. On early experiments with de-communization, see Li Yuzhu and Shao Taiyan, "Shibantan gongshe tizhi gaige de diaocha" (Investigation of systemic reform in Shibantan Commune), *Nongye jinqji congkan* 1981: 6, pp. 41–44, on Sichuan; and Zhou Zhenfeng, "Jiangsu sheng jueding jiakuai nongcun tizhi gaige bufa" (Jiangsu Province decides to step up the pace of reform in the rural system), *Jingji cankao* Mar. 1, 1983, p. 1, on Jiangsu. Along with Sichuan and Jiangsu provinces, Anhui was a forerunner in de-communization..

6. According to a survey carried out by the National People's Congress. Richer communes also protested more vehemently, while poor communes were more likely to favor the change. Chen Guang and Zheng Li, "Nongcun tizhi gaige chubu tansuo" (Initial investigation into reform of the rural system), *Nongye jingji congkan* 1982: 3, p. 25.

7. A summary of the communique appeared in *Renmin ribao*, November 23, 1983, p. 1.

ments, distribution of market information, response to natural disasters, and so on.[8] Many of these functions nevertheless fell into abeyance after 1984 until private entrepreneurs took them up. Where there was money to be made from formerly collective tasks, the wait for entrepreneurs was brief; in contrast, nonremunerative functions like social welfare often disintegrated. Reorganizing the collective enterprises on an independent footing was hastened, even stampeded, by privatization. Shortly before disbanding the communes, central leaders had declared that "as the reforms of rural government and commune are completed, the people's communes, brigades, and production teams will become discrete, independent organs of economic management."[9] Whether these discrete organs were required to keep all their assets public and collective was a blurry issue, however. Some former communes and brigades did maintain their enterprises as public entities. But others used their new independence to sell or lease collective enterprises to private takers. Capital-rich households and peasant companies were waiting to snap them up.

The odds of survival for the reformers' economic program probably rose sharply with the demise of the commune. Politically, however, decollectivization undermined the state's most intrusive tool for domineering daily rural life. Inside the commune structure, the teams had once superintended the most minute details of farming, and the brigades had dominated virtually all rural enterprise. Now farming and entrepreneurship were more private and independent, leaving the rural bureaucracy a much smaller kingdom over which to rule. This did not mean that the state had abandoned its authority to a burgeoning rural capitalism. Local cadres continued to act as

8. Such lists appeared first in the Party document "Zhonggong zhongyang zhuanfa 'quanguo nongcun gongzuo huiyi jiyao'" ("Summary of the National Conference on Rural Work," circulated by the Central Committee of the Chinese Communist Party), Central Document No. 1 for 1982, reprinted in *Zhongguo nongye nianjian 1982* (1982 Chinese agriculture yearbook) (Beijing: Nongye chubanshe, 1982), pp. 5–6; also in *Renmin ribao*, Feb. 19, 1982, p. 1; and in Chen Yizi et al., "Dui nongcun renmin gongshe tizhi gaige de jidian kanfa" (A few opinions on reform of the rural people's commune syetem), *Nongye jingji congkan* 1982: 4, p. 14.

9. Yan Nong, "Hubei sheng nongcun 'liang hu yi lian' de fazhan qingkuang" (The development of the "two households and one alliance" in rural Hubei), *Shehui kexue dongtai [Hubei]* 1983: 16 (June 1), p. 13.

brokers, just as they had before reform.[10] Some of the largest, most productive rural industries were still administered by public institutions, both state-run and collective. Although the collectives were much weaker than before, some Western scholars argued that this only made villages more vulnerable to a raw form of state power unmediated by the collective bureaucracy.[11] Yet the lines of direct government control were now drawn much more narrowly, explicitly excluding the daily economic activities of most of the peasant population.

The state's direct administration of rural life was consequently weaker. Before the dismantling of the communes was even complete, some localities were reporting that local administration was reduced to a "command vacuum."[12] By the end of the 1980s (according to the *Liaoning Daily*) the collective structure in Liaoning Province was so enfeebled that village cadres could not even command peasants to make their required contributions to the local coffers. "There is no other way for the village cadre but to humbly call on the households one by one to ask for it, and to do so again and again. They will run their feet sore and wear their lips thin, frequently put off again and again, and never hearing even one good word. Some village cadres say, one year has 365 days, of which we use one-third to collect the [fees]; we have alienated the peasants of the entire village, but have befriended the dogs of every household in the place."[13]

Such treatment stood in sharp contrast to the power that the state previously exercised through the village officialdom. The collective structure had once made local cadres the embodiment of state authority in the smallest village, with a command so far-reaching that it could knock at the front gate of every peasant household. Now only the dogs would listen.

---

10. See Jean C. Oi, "Commercializing China's Rural Cadres," *Problems of Communism* 35 (September-October 1986), pp. 1–14.

11. See Vivienne Shue, *The Reach of the State* (Stanford: Stanford University Press, 1988).

12. Chen Yizi et al., "Dui nongcun," p. 16.

13. *Liaoning ribao*, Feb. 1, 1988, translated in JPRS-CAR-88-033 (June 23, 1988), p. 58.

Undermining the Appeal of the Party

Unlike the collectives, the Communist Party did not suffer a major reorganization under reform; its structure remained the same. But it too was undermined as a base of state power because privatization subverted Party ideology and offered an alternative ladder to status.

The Communist Party, from the state's point of view, was the irreplaceable organization for maintaining state power. To peasants, however, it represented one of the only avenues for upward mobility. Before reform, peasants had meager opportunities for individual economic gain. Higher personal status could be achieved more readily through political advancement. Admittance into the Party depended on a cluster of political attributes, including class background, activism, and ideological commitment. Ambitious peasants (including sincere idealists) worked hard at political study and community service—and equally hard at personal connections—to advance their status in the Party.

The trouble with privatization was that it made this sort of political dedication irrelevant to personal advancement. In the first place, privatization directly assaulted the Party's old ideological appeal. Privatization suggested that personal wealth was a worthy goal in life, on a par with the self-sacrifice that Party ideology had once esteemed. Because personal wealth was an individual matter, inequality came with it—a development the Party endorsed with the slogan, "Let some people get rich first." Egalitarianism (*pingjun zhuyi*) became a negative, backward value, and was even used as an epithet, reversing the Party's public commitment to equality. Before reform, peasants were supposed to "prosper equally" (*pingjun fu*) and "prosper simultaneously" (*tongshi fu*). A household accumulating wealth ahead of its neighbors would be condemned as an "upstart trying to get rich quick" (*bao fa hu*), and would be criticized for making itself into a "fortified village" (*tu weizi*). With reform, however, peasants prospering conspicuously were lauded as "advanced" (*xianjin*). The old idea of helping poorer neighbors to catch up ("getting rich together") was disdained as "staying poor together" (*tongshi qiong*).

Promoting this ideological reversal meant the Party had to admit its culpability for the leftist (and now officially erroneous) ideology of the past. Trying to blame the ideological muddle on their predecessors, the reformers said the leftists had "pushed a false, big, and empty politics" that "damaged the Party's image and destroyed the prestige and fine traditions of political work." Unfortunately, according to the Party, revulsion against leftist ideology led people to "reject ideological-political work altogether," thus "going from one extreme to the other."[14] And in fact this was true. Even local cadres were sick of ideological work, which one characterized as, "Shout the slogans at the top of your lungs, hold the program high, and raise a terrific din just for form's sake." Village leaders were now ready to dispense with politics completely. To the Party's chagrin, their apolitical approach was, "If you handle the economy right, then ideology will take care of itself," and, "As long as policy is correct, there is no need for ideological-political work."[15]

Ordinary peasants also lost interest in the Party and its political concerns. To discover the extent of peasant indifference to ideology, state organs in the early 1980s undertook surveys to "appraise the peasant ranks" (*guji nongmin duiwu*). A number of these surveys, from Zhejiang, Hubei, Hebei, and other provinces, were published. The findings were consistent and sobering for the Party: indifference to politics was widespread, and worse, it was most pronounced among younger peasants. One survey concluded that younger peasants "have no ideals."[16] Another found young peasants without the

14. Zhao Yong, "Huifu sixiang zhengzhi gongzuo de chuantong" (Restore the tradition of ideological and political work), *Nongcun gongzuo tongxun* 1981: 2, p. 26.

15. "Quan dang dongshou, kaichuang sixiang zhengzhi gongzuo xin jumian" (The whole Party should get to work and open up a new phase in ideological and political work), *Dangyuan shenghuo [Hubei]* 1983: 3, p. 28. Central Party documents tried to combat this outlook. Central Document Number 1 for 1983 said: "If every item of rural economic work is done well, it can spur the development of ideological-political work, but in the end it cannot take the place of ideological-political work. Only strengthening ideological-political work can guarantee that each rural reform will enjoy healthy growth." "Dangqian nongcun jingji zhengce de ruogan wenti" (Several problems in current rural economic policy), *Renmin ribao*, Apr. 10, 1983, p. 2.

16. Hebei shengwei yanjiu shi (Research Office of the Hebei Provincial Party Committee), "Dangqian nongmin duiwu zhuankuang de diaocha" (Investigation of the state of the peasant ranks), *Nongye jingji congkan* 1983: 2, p. 41. Cf. Hubei sheng nongwei (Hubei Provincial Agricultural Committee), "Da li jiaqiang he gaishan nongcun sixiang zhengzhi gongzuo" (Greatly strengthen and improve rural ideological-political work), *Shehui kexue dongtai [Hubei]* 1983: 2 (Jan. 10), p. 21.

slightest notion of things the Party cherished: "A portion of the young people are absolutely ignorant—or know next to nothing—about the Motherland, the Communist Party, socialism, or the Communist tomorrow. They aren't interested in the future, ideals, belief, morality, values, and so on. Their political zeal isn't high, and there are not enough progressive people among them seeking admission to the Party or the [Communist Youth] League. They are not willing to take part in any kind of political activities in the village, or activities for the public good".[17] Recruiting for the Party was difficult among such indifferent youths. One 1983 survey of over ten thousand eighteen- to thirty-five-year-olds found less than one percent seeking Party admission.[18] The Communist Youth League, the main conduit for Party recruitment of young adults, sank into miserable straits in the countryside. The head of ideology for the Youth League's official journal admitted in 1983 that "in most rural areas the League has ceased to function." [19]

The main source of the Party's rural troubles was not the ideological crisis, however. It was a practical matter: reform and privatization created circumstances in which peasants saw paltry benefits in joining the Party. Privatization gave peasants an alternative set of values and aspirations. As one report said, "A large proportion of young unmarried men in the villages care most about making some more money, building a house, and getting married. All the unmarried women care about is 'wearing some nice clothes and finding a good husband.'"[20] Most peasants believed the Party could do little to further their pursuit of these materialistic goals. Young people in a poor Hebei village said "they figure it doesn't make much difference whether they join the Party or not."[21] Individual economic success could be achieved without the Party. Thus reform faced the Party ever

17. Hebei Tangshan diwei xuanchuan bu (Propaganda Department of the Tangshan Prefecture Party Committee, Hebei), "Qingnian nongmin sixiang qingkuang de diaocha" (Survey of young peasants' ideology), *Nongye jingji congkan* 1983: 2, p. 43.

18. Ibid.

19. Quoted in Stanley Rosen, "Prosperity, Privatization, and China's Youth," *Problems of Communism* 34 (March-April 1985), p. 3.

20. Hebei Tangshan, p. 43.

21. Hebei shengwei, p. 41.

more painfully with a dilemma. It had to support the new, materialistic values embodied in privatization in order to reach the leadership's core domestic policy goals. But in promoting these values the Party was undermining its own appeal as the pathway to success for ambitious, resourceful peasants.

Repudiating the Ghost of a Peasant Constituency

Reform and privatization undermined a third base of state power in the countryside by encouraging the state to renounce its traditional peasant constituency. Since Land Reform (1946–52), the movement that completed the Revolution by destroying the landlord class, the state had proclaimed an alliance with what the Party called the "poor and lower-middle peasants." This part of the peasantry had then formed the Party's bedrock of support. The poor and lower-middle peasants were also the chief beneficiaries of Land Reform, which endowed them with an enduring sense of gratitude and loyalty. As dissident journalist Liu Binyan said, for years after Land Reform, "peasants would do *anything* for the Communist Party, even against their own interests."[22] The state reinforced this alliance with the poor and lower-middle peasants in the ensuing decades by granting privileged status, easier Party entrance, local office, and relative safety during political campaigns to people with this "good" class status. For decades the state relied on this minimally privileged majority (within a peasantry sorely underprivileged in wider Chinese society) as its mainstay of support in the countryside.

Problems arose when the class analysis on which this alliance was based drifted away from reality over the years. Land Reform undermined the old class divisions within the peasantry. In time the people called poor and lower-middle peasants became less of a real economic class and more of an ascriptive status group. People were poor and lower-middle peasants because they had been labeled so during Land Reform or because they were later born to parents with that status. The label stuck, however, for decades—with deep personal consequences, since the state preserved the old class designations for political purposes.[23] People with poor and lower-middle peasant status

22. Liu Binyan, speech in Minneapolis, Minnesota, October 1990.
23. On the politics of class after the Revolution, see Richard Curt Kraus,

continued to enjoy the Party's good graces through the 1960s and 1970s, even though this class label had little to do with the new social reality. Each succeeding political campaign attacked the same "rich peasants" and "landlords," and as these perennial targets grew old and died out, their children and grandchildren were victimized as surrogates.

By the time Deng Xiaoping came to power, reformers in the Party were disenchanted with both the class designations and the theory of political alliance based on them. For the state, attempts to shore up its rural power on a phantom social class of poor and lower-middle peasants looked ever more untenable. In the collective period the fiction had been an ongoing nightmare for peasants stuck with the bad class labels of rich peasant and landlord. In the reform period, with individuals making and losing their own fortunes despite fanciful class labels, the fiction would have been impossible to maintain. The Third Plenum therefore scrapped the whole irrational, vindictive system of class labels in 1978. Yet in repudiating the invidious class labels of rich peasant and landlord, the reformers also jettisoned the state's traditional approach to rural politics. Burying the old class enemy destroyed the political meaning of the state's supposed class alliance with the poor and lower-middle peasants. "Since the landlord and rich peasant class has been wiped out," theorists realized, "the poor and lower-middle peasants have also lost their original significance."[24] The volatile, shifting patterns of wealth, income, and status among the peasantry in the ensuing period of privatization left the state with a serious problem. The collective structure was weakened. The Party had lost much of its appeal. And now the state had to find a new social basis for power to replace the alliance with the poor and lower-middle peasants.

Class Conflict in Chinese Socialism (New York: Columbia University Press, 1981); Gordon White, *The Politics of Class and Class Origin: The Case of the Cultural Revolution,* Contemporary China Papers no. 9 (Canberra: Australian National University, 1976); and Hong Yung Lee, *The Politics of the Chinese Cultural Revolution* (Berkeley: University of California Press, 1978).

24. Hubei sheng nonghui, shehui kexue yuan diaocha zu (Investigative Group of the Hubei Provincial Peasant Association and the Hubei Provincial Academy of Social Sciences), "Dui xian jieduan nongmin duiwu de guji" (An appraisal of the peasant ranks in the present stage), *Nongye jingji congkan* 1983: 2, p. 33.

A New Social Basis for State Power

In coping with the changed setting for state power, Deng Xiaoping's coalition combined a dispassionate assessment of rural politics with some soul-searching on the proper function of the state. The reformers wanted to break decisively from the politically divisive leadership style of the Cultural Revolution decade. They sought a new style that would cool the overheated political life of rural China. Deng's leftist predecessors had made the countryside the grand stage of social experimentation. The program of the Left had required an enormous political effort in campaigns playing up rural class conflicts. Repudiating that legacy, the reform leaders tried to find a new way to enforce state policies without aggravating political tensions. They discarded the Left's ambitious social agenda and groped toward a rural society that would be stable without ceaseless political campaigns. They wanted a calm political order roughly akin to the self-regulating farm economy they tried to create. As part of the new style of leadership, the state began to practice more refined price, tax, and credit policies. With privatization, the state also turned over authority for an array of decisions to individuals and enterprises.

This less intrusive method of state control reinforced the basic tenet of privatization: that heavy state intervention in rural life was counterproductive. Eschewing mass mobilization, the state promoted a new vision of public-spirited activism. This new activism would be economic rather than political, and private rather than collective. Hoping to wed this private activism to the public cause, the reformers sought people whose skills could promote economic progress. The state needed people through whom to exercise its control over the peasantry, and both the Party and the local bureaucracy needed recruits. The question was who these new activists would be. As the Hubei Peasant Association asked, "Under the new historical conditions, who in the villages should the Party ultimately rely on to rally the broad mass of peasants to carry out socialist modernized construction?"[25]

25. Ibid., p. 36.

The reformers set out to answer this question in a deliberate way, for they had no confidence that peasants would naturally follow state policies. After all, the reformers had openly declared their distrust of the "natural peasant economy" and its tendencies, which were reviving under reform. Therefore the leadership consciously set about finding the new type of peasant activist. In 1982, Deng Liqun (then Party propaganda chief) first identified the rural constituency and recruitment target on which the Party would concentrate: "With the great changes that have occurred in the countryside, it is no longer appropriate to continue the class line of 'relying on the poor and lower-middle peasants.' What should our work line be, then? Some comrades have suggested that we rally and organize the advanced element (*xianjin fenzi*) in the villages and rely on them. . . . I think that until we have a better method we should try this."[26]

Provincial officials following Deng Liqun's lead were more precise about who was to be included in this "advanced element." In 1983, the Hebei Provincial Party Committee (which had been one of the most resistant to reform) targeted peasants who launched enterprises, contracted for bigger sales to the state, produced more, and adapted modern technology for rural use—the people who "are getting wealthy through their own labor."[27] Meanwhile, Hubei Province sought out "the village's skilled people, the craftsmen, the middle school graduates, the young people returning to the village after getting an education, the demobilized soldiers, and so on, [who] all have some scientific, technical, or intellectual knowledge."[28]

The overlap of this group targeted for recruitment and the people who prospered under reform was hard to miss. The new entrepreneurs

26. In all likelihood Deng Liqun himself, never a strong reformist, had misgivings about offering Party support to this part of the peasantry, and his reluctance shows in his speech. The quotation is from the speech he gave on November 1, 1982, at the National Conference on Rural Ideological and Political Work. Deng Liqun, "Jiaqiang he gaijin nongcun sixiang zhengzhi gongzuo de ji dian yijian" (Some opinions on strengthening and improving rural ideological and political work), *Jingji yanjiu cankao ziliao* 1983: 1 (Jan. 1), p. 16.

27. Hebei shengwei yanjiu shi, p. 40.

28. Fan Zuogang, "Dangdai nongmin xianjin ceng de xingqi ji qi jiben tezheng" (The rise and basic characteristics of the contemporary advanced stratum of the peasantry), *Shehui kexue dongtai [Hubei]* 1983: 2 (Jan. 10), p. 15.

and the more successful farmers had the skills and characteristics the Party said it was seeking. Both groups had technical backgrounds, better education, higher incomes, and experience with more creative forms of management. Targeting such people offered several advantages to the reform leaders. First, the entrepreneurs and bigger farmers were perfect models: other peasants could be expected to envy their wealth and emulate their success. Second, the state could assume that these richer households were politically dependable. They had an overwhelming personal stake in consolidating the reforms. The entrepreneurs in particular acted as the unconscious champions of reform policy throughout the process of privatization. Finally, these technically skilled, better-educated people represented an alternative to the older cohort of rural cadres. In the old commune system, only half the Party members in Hubei at the all-important brigade level (where rural industry was concentrated) had even finished primary school. The provincial Party journal granted that these old-style peasant Party members may have been indispensable in the Revolution, "but under the new situation, because of their low educational level, they are not fully suited to the needs of building the Four Modernizations."[29] Privatization brought to the fore a group with the education, skills, management ability, and technical expertise that suited them to the task of modernization.

The celebration of this new type of activist caused the Party to drastically redefine its self-image during the 1980s. As one theorist said, "This is clearly a profound, historic change from past reliance on simple class feeling, on the philosophical faith that the poorer you are the more revolutionary you are, on traditional forms of manual labor, and on an asceticism which is only concerned with plowing and weeding and not with results." Now rural cadres were being told to unite with an "advanced stratum" of the peasantry (xianjin ceng), "principally the model households and the activists, including the specialized households."[30] State leaders calculated that these "people

29. Tu Zhaojing, "Xianning xian Henggou gongshe dangwei zhuyi fazhan you wenhua de nongmin rudang" (The Party Committee of Henggou Commune in Xianning County pays attention to recruiting educated peasants into the Party), Dangyuan shenghuo [Hubei] 1981: 2, p. 30.
30. Fan, "Dangdai nongmin," pp. 16, 12.

in the advanced stratum are staunch supporters and vigorous practitioners of the Party's line, guiding principles, and policies."[31] Many rural cadres were unswayed by the new line—even repulsed by it. They feared that the Party was betraying its anti-elitist traditions, embracing people with a more urban, even anti-peasant profile. The disparity between the traditional profile of a recruit and the new one went beyond the rancorous debate over whether Party members should be "red" or "expert." It raised the raw question of the state's philosophy toward individual wealth. In a period of modernization and economic growth, should official policy favor the wealthy? Should the privileged be welcomed into official position, and even actively recruited for it?

Many officials, particularly older ones, rejected richer recruits out of hand, especially entrepreneurs. The press highlighted many instances of specialized households who were turned away from the Party because of their entrepreneurial status and their relative wealth. The older cadres' opposition had foundations in both prejudice and principle. But the state center repudiated this opposition, and the Party made special overtures to entrepreneurs and richer farmers. An official from the cadre school at the Ministry of Agriculture said it was time for "the powers of administrative leadership to be transferred from older, poorly educated cadres to the young, educated, specialized households."[32] Editorial policy at the *People's Daily* favored stories of rural officials who led the way in innovation and entrepreneurship. Headlines proclaimed that "rural Party members should serve as models for working hard to get rich."[33] Theorists labored to make sense of the unfamiliar territory. The Provincial Propaganda Department of Liaoning reasoned that when peasants got rich, they also made greater contributions to the state and the collective. And since "politics is the concentrated expression of economics," when people

31. Hubei sheng nonghui, shehui kexue yuan diaocha zu, p. 36.

32. Zhou Ruchang, of the Rural Economics Cadre School of the Ministry of Agriculture, Animal Husbandry, and Fishery, quoted in "Zai jingji tizhi gaige beijing xia kan nongcun fazhan de xianshi, wenti he qushi" (Viewing realities, problems, and trends in rural development against the background of reform in the economic system), *Nongye jingji wenti* 1985: 1, p. 23.

33. *Renmin ribao*, Mar. 20, 1984, p. 2.

are economically successful, it "determines their advanced status in political life."[34] The rural Communist Youth League seized on this new equation of political enlightenment with economic success as the magic to revive its moribund recruitment effort. In some areas the League tried to pose as the gateway to financial success for ambitious young peasants; in others it cemented the association between wealth and eventual Party membership by setting high income minima for new League members.[35]

This heavily publicized effort to find a new kind of activist for official positions left the traditional pool of recruits feeling abandoned. In the course of privatization the leadership became disenchanted with the small peasant farm and with the semiliterate recruit that such farms traditionally produced for the Party. Some farmers felt keenly that the Party was no longer interested in them. Peasants of ordinary means complained that the Party regularly "contacts the rich but not the poor, the families strong in labor power but not those weak in labor power, and those who are doing well but not those who are having trouble."[36] Grain farmers—who gained less from reform than any other peasant group—felt particularly excluded, observing that officials devoted their most assiduous attention to successful entrepreneurs: "The great majority of cadres want to maintain close links with the specialized households who run industrial and sideline enterprises or grow economic crops. But they aren't willing to be in contact with grain-growing households. The reason is that the economic benefits of grain production are low—you can't draw attention to yourself or get rich growing grain. There is no prestige in it."[37] Some farmers also resented the official honors bestowed upon more prosperous families: "We used to think the idea was to take work in the fields as

34. Zhang Li'an, "Bu ying hushi xian fu nongmin de zhengzhi diwei he zuoyong" (Don't neglect the political status and function of peasants who get rich first), Lilun yu shijian [Shenyang] 1985: 8, p. 22.
35. Rosen, "Prosperity," pp. 9–10, 23–24.
36. Xianning xian Tingsiqiao gongshe dangwei hui (Tingsiqiao Commune Party Committee, Xianning County), "Yanjiu xin qingkuang, jiejue xin wenti" (Study the new situation, solve new problems), Dangyuan shenghuo [Hubei] 1983: 7, p. 22.
37. Xu Jinbiao et al., "Nongmin weishenme bu yuanyi zhongtian" (Why aren't the peasants willing to till the land?) Nongye jingji congkan 1984: 1, p. 58.

the fundamental thing. But as soon as we saw the attitude of the people at the top, our hearts sank. . . . When they hold model worker meetings they invite the 10,000-yuan households over and over again. It's only the people who grow grain who are always left out in the cold."[38]

The reform coalition regarded such resentment as an acceptable price to pay for its attempt to modernize the rural bureaucrats and rejuvenate the Party. Reform, privatization, and the coalition's own activist leadership shook the official ranks in the provinces as nothing had since the Cultural Revolution. By 1983 two-thirds of the nation's top fourteen hundred provincial officials had already been retired, with reverberations down to the village level.[39] But the reformers were dissatisfied still, and launched a massive rectification campaign that ran from the end of 1983 through the spring of 1987. The effort to recruit a new rural leadership cadre was just part of this much larger regeneration of the Communist Party, but it reflected the goals of the national campaign. Rectification specifically targeted four qualities to be encouraged: the Party would recruit and promote "younger, better educated, more professionally competent and revolutionary cadres."[40]

The new kind of activist that privatization nurtured in the countryside possessed exactly these qualities. Assuming that the fourth quality ("revolutionary") had only a symbolic meaning, there was a remarkable congruence between the people favored by privatization and those the state now wanted to cultivate. The temptation here is to jump at the irony of a communist state embracing an activist type distinguished by individual material success and some degree of privilege. But the irony may be illusory. Privatization and the strange political alliances it produces may flow naturally from the course of state socialism in a poor agrarian country.

38. Zhou Yegao, "Yao zhongshi jiejue liangshi zhuanye hu, zhongdian hu fazhan yudao de wenti" (Pay attention to solving the problems that specialized grain households and keypoint grain households run into in the course of development), *Nongye jingji congkan* 1983: 5, p. 61.

39. Christopher M. Clarke, "The Shakeup Moves Down," *The China Business Review* 10 (September-October 1983), p. 9.

40. *Jiefang ribao*, July 15, 1987, translated in JPRS-CAR-87–036 (Aug. 21, 1987), p. 111.

Privatization and State Socialism

To understand why privatization might become a normal part of state socialism in a poor agrarian country like China, one must step back and look at the whole life-course of state socialism.

The Chinese Revolution brought a measure of social justice, safety, and material improvement to rural areas. These accomplishments were real and important, though modest when considered against the long time-frame in which they occurred—the first several decades of the People's Republic. Especially after 1958, when the Great Leap began, the new government stopped matching the splendid record of improvement it showed peasants during the first decade following Liberation. From a political point of view, the Revolution's more impressive (though unromantic) achievement was the assertion of state power in the countryside. Centralized government in the prerevolutionary dynasties of China had barely existed below the county level. The People's Republic did what no previous government of China had: it established state power with complete lines of command reaching beneath the county into every village of the nation. Collectivized agriculture was a crucial part of this intrusive state structure.

Collectivization in a poor agrarian economy springs as much from political motives as from economic motives. In China, where a vast human population was lodged on a relatively small amount arable land, collectivization had few economic advantages. With exceptions like the sparsely populated plains of Manchuria, the overburdened farmland could barely be expected to yield more as a result of the collectivization undertaken in 1955–56. The rudimentary farm technology was no more productive when applied by people working collectively than it was when used by individual farmers. It may even have been less productive, given the intense labor that individual farmers anxiously poured into their garden-sized plots. What the People's Republic did achieve with collectivization in the 1950s was not agricultural abundance but political control. For over a century rural China had been a violent, nightmarish land only intermittently and tenuously under any government's dominion. With collectivization, state authority suddenly intruded everywhere, even into the most vital activity of rural life, farming. Collectivization enabled policies formulated at the state center to govern the daily work of peasants in the most remote villages; it gave the state an organization to compete for control of the harvest; and it created an apparatus for inculcating state ideology that touched all peasants, whether Party members or not.

After a generation passed in the strict confines of this collective structure, the intrusion of state power ceased to be an unstable experiment. The People's Republic was secure as China's first truly national government of the twentieth century. State power in the countryside was a fact of life—for many peasants an oppressive fact, but not something that anyone questioned. With this achievement, by the late 1970s collectivization had fulfilled its political function. Reform leaders then turned the government's primary attention to the economy for the first time since the Cultural Revolution interregnum, and loyal officials began to doubt the economic efficacy of collective farming. In certain regions and localities of rural China, collectivism was a wonderful step forward. But as a national policy, uniformly enforced, collectivism lost the promise it would have had if applied more selectively. Given the dismal poverty in most of the Chinese countryside after more than twenty years of collective farming, collectivization nationwide could only weakly claim to be economically beneficial to China. With its political mission completed, collectivization fell unceremoniously from the scene after only a few years of reform. Privatization then had its heyday.

Looking at the *economic* trajectory of state socialism, one is not surprised that privatization should arise after collectivism runs its political course—at least in a poor country. In a richer nation with more advanced technology, collectivism might be a lasting success. But in a poor agrarian country like China, a return to private farming can be considered a predictable event once state power is installed in rural areas. This occurs because the state, having achieved political security, may be eager to accelerate economic development. At this point privatization might be a natural and attractive alternative.

What is surprising, however, is how readily privatization meets the political needs of the state. The *political* trajectory of state socialism, running parallel to economic development, also brings the state to a point where its political foundation would benefit from privatization. In China the government came to power through a violent revolution, and its style of governance remained combative, coercive, and, for long spells, violent. The metaphors of Chinese political discourse were still military even decades after the revolutionary battlefield was won. The trouble with this coercive style of government is that force preempts all other potential bases for state power. Governing rural China through campaigns, political attacks, intimidation, and scapegoating of "class enemies," the Maoist state cultivated only a very small social base of support. Except for the local cadres, the state's only constituency among the peasantry was the ill-defined poor and lower-middle peasants, whose chief benefit from their privileged status was exemption from attack in the repeated political campaigns. For a stable foundation of uncoerced, active support, the state developed only the narrowest rural constituency.

Privatization is a potential solution to the problem of thin social support, which, as Eastern Europe showed in the late 1980s, may be endemic in state socialism. Privatization creates a constituency of entrepreneurs and richer farmers whose fortunes are directly tied to the survival of a reform government. As the state withdraws from direct administration of the economy, it may come to rely on these key non-state groups to lead rural development in the direction it desires. The state may become particularly attentive to groups promoting commercialization and economic revival, and less sympathetic toward peasants pursuing a traditional farm life that reformers regard as a dead end. In other words, in its search for new allies in the changing peasantry, the state may act to reinforce the logic of privatization, bestowing political and economic preference upon peasants who play the most active part in privatizing the economy. For a state eager to retire from the exhausting effort of using coercion to enforce its will, finding this constituency is a blessing. By coming fairly close to such a course in the 1980s, China demonstrated that privatization is not merely a tool seized upon to repair the economic woes of state socialism, but a political choice, embraced because it meets the needs of the evolving state.

Chapter Nine

Peasant Power under a Strong State

Peasants customarily are invisible in political analysis. Anyone familiar with the field of third-world politics can readily think of books on predominantly agrarian countries that barely mention the peasantry. This blindness to peasants is not necessarily the product of urban cultural prejudice. It arises from cold analysis of the facts: peasants are usually disenfranchised, weak, and unorganized. Thus political analysts omit the peasantry not out of neglect but because peasants are reckoned to have a negligible effect on political processes. In instances of revolution, of course, peasants attract concentrated, if short-lived, attention. Under normal circumstances, however, much analysis treats peasants as nearly irrelevant to political outcomes, reinforcing our cultural vision of peasants as passive victims.

This book has challenged the assumption that peasants are politically irrelevant by looking at peasant power under the circumstances that favor it least—that is, under a strong state. Do peasants under a strong state have any significant power? An answer can be constructed from the evidence in China's post-Mao reforms.

In trying to distill more precisely what the Chinese case tells us about peasant power, the first problem is interpreting the evidence. The evidence from China's decade of reform is extremely varied. It has given rise to interpretations with quite different conclusions about the balance of power between peasant and state in instigating change. The three case histories of reform I have presented—family farming, marketing, and privatization—all contain variations on a pattern of change in which peasant initiative led state policy. This view of the evidence places peasants at the forefront of change. Before making the jump from this interpretation of the Chinese evidence to a more general statement about peasant power, however, I want to make it clear that the jumping-off point is solid ground, and not merely an idiosyncratic construction of the Chinese case. The preliminary task, therefore, is to show where this interpretation stands among three main alternatives.

Alternative versions of China's rural transformation have varied in how much they credit Deng Xiaoping's government with conceiving and directing the reforms. The version most adulatory of the Chinese government appeared in the press. Both Chinese and Western news organs portrayed reform as a textbook case of successful policy implementation. In this telling, Deng and his associates first analyzed the shortcomings of the collective economy and attacked the ideological underpinnings of leftist rural policy. Then, to test their ideas for a market-oriented alternative, they conducted experiments at the village level. Finally, the government synthesized these experiences in carefully prepared policy packages. According to this first interpretation, then, the state directed a series of brilliant policy changes that dazzled observers and won the hearts of the peasants.

A second interpretation challenges this vision of textbook-perfect policy design, pointing out that Deng's policy announcements all came after peasants were already widely practicing whatever "new" policy the state was ordering. Andrew Watson, for example, argued that "throughout the period of the growth of the production responsibility system . . . the central authorities and theoreticians have been in the position of reacting to and sanctioning developments that had already taken place."[1] The creative force that preceded the celebrated central documents actually came from people at the local level. According to Watson, "the pressures came from below and proceeded to force the pace of change thereafter."[2] Other scholars also noted that

1. Andrew Watson, "Agriculture Looks for 'Shoes that Fit': The Production Responsibility System and Its Implications," *World Development* 11: 8 (1983), p. 714.

2. Ibid., p. 712. See also Andrew Watson, "New Structures in the Organi-

at times the state center seemed to be reacting to local demands. David Zweig, for example, summarized the movement away from collective farming this way: "As soon as the opposition acceded to one step on the path to decollectivization, new demands for another change arose from the localities, keeping up the pressure on the policy process in Beijing until collective agriculture was dismantled."[3]

A third interpretation denies that peasants had such a part in instigating reform. Kathleen Hartford argued against seeing reform as "a massive spontaneous surge of the peasantry back to family farming."[4] Emphasizing peasant resistance to the destruction of the collectives, she pointed out that her rural informants perceived family farming as a change forced upon the villages by high officials.[5] Jonathan Unger also challenged the idea that peasants went back to family farms "by popular grassroots demand." Although Unger's work suggested that peasants may have been more attracted to reform than Hartford indicated, his findings still corroborated her argument that peasants had no choice in decollectivization. Nearly all of his interviewing sample (predominantly from Guangdong) reported that "in their own villages the decision as to precisely what type of system would be adopted was made exclusively by officials at levels far above the village."[6] However popular or unpopular reform may have been in the end, this third interpretation rejects the notion of peasants inventing reform. Rather, reform was imposed upon peasants by a state apparatus that controlled the whole process of change.

The evidence I have presented in this book clearly contravenes the first of these three alternative versions of how reform occurred.

zation of Chinese Agriculture: A Variable Model," *Pacific Affairs* 57 (Winter 1984–85), pp. 621–45.

3. David Zweig, *Agrarian Radicalism in China, 1968–1981* (Cambridge: Harvard University Press, 1989), p. 174.

4. Kathleen Hartford, "Socialist Agriculture is Dead; Long Live Socialist Agriculture! Organizational Transformations in Rural China," in Elizabeth J. Perry and Christine Wong, eds., *The Political Economy of Reform in Post-Mao China* (Cambridge: Harvard University Press, 1985), p. 38.

5. Hartford said of her rural informants, "The significant point is that they *did* perceive the household contracting system to be required from on (often very) high." Hartford, pp. 39–43.

6. Jonathan Unger, "The Decollectivization of the Chinese Countryside: A Survey of Twenty-eight Villages," *Pacific Affairs* 58 (Winter 1985–86), p. 587.

Chinese and Western press portraits of the state as the benign and omnipotent promulgator of reform do not stand up. But what of the second version, which emphasizes peasant involvement in reform, and the third, which denies peasant involvement? The evidence gathered here clearly endorses the second interpretation: peasants did indeed create China's reforms. This book largely disagrees with the third interpretation's dismissal of peasant instigation in reform. Yet it is important to acknowledge the fieldwork on which this third interpretation is based, specifically the testimony of peasant passivity or even resistance to reform. It is irrefutable that some peasants resisted. Different ecological settings, cropping patterns, procurement quotas, and commercial opportunities in each village created a disjointed movement of reform across rural China, with some communities pressing for change and others resisting it. As Helen Siu showed in her ethnography of a Pearl River delta community, even peasants of neighboring brigades within the same commune responded differently to the hopes and dangers presented by change.[7] But the evidence suggests, across the diversity of peasant response, a pattern—a distinct interpretation—that accounts for both activism promoting reform and passivity or resistance.

The interpretation advanced by the evidence I have presented here clarifies the essential pattern by distinguishing between the *innovation* of new policies in reform-era China and their eventual *implementation*. The core of the matter is this: local people innovated; the state implemented.

Peasants did lead the way, for the fundamental changes were their inventions. It was peasants who made family farms, who hired labor, who lent money, started businesses, sold company shares, ducked barriers to trade, rented land, finessed the price system, and defied the state plan. There is nothing in the documentary record to indicate that the state advocated any of these ideas before peasants started putting them to work. And there is a mountain of documentary evidence showing that key organs of the state (in both Party and government) opposed all of these practices when peasants first tried them out.

Some observers have discounted peasant innovation by imagining

7. Helen F. Siu, *Agents and Victims in South China: Accomplices in Rural Revolution* (New Haven: Yale University Press, 1989), chap. 12.

a prescient reform leadership pulling all the strings from behind the scenes—cleverly giving peasants room to innovate, *knowing* all the changes peasants would make, and thereby bringing about a complex radical reform program that they could not endorse publicly. There is a small amount of truth in this: Wan Li in Anhui, Zhao Ziyang in Sichuan, and Deng Xiaoping in Beijing all encouraged experimentation; perhaps they hoped for radical change. But the vision of a coterie of mastermind reformers manipulating the peasantry to perform their will is based on speculation rather than hard evidence. Indeed, it contradicts the concrete evidence at hand, claiming that the state was somehow surreptitiously promoting everything that it loudly condemned and outlawed in the late 1970s and early 1980s.[8] The preponderance of evidence, from the villages to the state center, tells a different story—a story that does not credit state leaders with omniscience or deny the human agency of the ordinary Chinese who created changes with their own hands. The evidence shows peasants consciously going against state policy with practices that would later become the backbone of reform.

Implementation was another matter, however. Facing immense pressure from below, the state surveyed the thousands of variants of basic innovations and chose what it was prepared to accept. The main criterion for backing an innovation was productivity. The imperative in implementing policy was national uniformity. Repeatedly the state made national policy of peasant practices that it had initially condemned—after these new practices showed promise for raising production. Once the state adopted a peasant innovation, it forced the new policy upon all rural communities, whether they were willing or not. Both Unger's and Hartford's fieldwork showed this heavy-handed implementation in action. In Unger's surveys, hapless villagers may have wanted to dismantle the collectives, but they finally did so only in obedience to orders from above. Especially in northern China, this same state insistence on unified reform policy violated the wishes of communities that would have preferred to stick to collectives.

Thus the evidence clearly supports the vision of a peasant-led

8. Even assuming that radical reformers at the state center were muzzled until the last remnant of the Left fell with the "little gang of four" in 1980, it is impossible to argue that until then they were in complete control, manipulating the peasantry to carry out their secret desires.

reform, but it does not reject reports that the state finally forced reform upon unwilling peasants. In the creative stage, local people had enormous influence, making virtually all the elements of new policy while manipulating and reshaping old policy. In the final stage of implementation, however, the state retained all of the coercive power, which it readily used against peasants in order to achieve uniform national policy.

With this interpretation of a rural transformation whose genesis mixed both peasant strength and peasant weakness, what conclusions can be drawn about peasant power under a strong state?

Power as Coercion

The first conclusion is that peasant power under a strong state is small. And if power is conceived of as coercion—that is, the capacity to force another agent to perform an action unwillingly—then this conclusion can be pushed much further: peasant power under a strong state is not only small, but negligible. The imbalance of coercive force between a strong state and a weak society is so lopsided that "peasant power" is hardly worth analyzing. The strong state has legitimacy, a working ideology, an information and propaganda network, controls over the economy, organizations reaching down to the most local level of social life, and, often, a constituency of rural dwellers whose own interests impel them to back state policy with their personal support. And all of these advantages the strong state enjoys *prior* to any resort to the overtly coercive forces it also controls: army, militia, and police. Under these conditions, coercion in the state-peasant relationship operates in one direction only. If power is equated with coercion, therefore, peasants under a strong state are virtually bereft of power.

The case of Chinese reform clearly bears out this conclusion. Coercion was strictly the state's prerogative under Deng Xiaoping. The state forced peasants to act against their will throughout the reform period. The basic rural system forced peasants to sell goods to the state at discount prices, to plant grain instead of profitable economic crops; and to submit to a set of exchanges that built relative prosperity in the cities while confining peasants to the penurious countryside. In the reform process itself, the state retained sole power over final decisions, and in some regions forced them upon communities that did not welcome the order to change.

On the other side, the reform period contains evidence of little that peasants forced the state to do against *its* will. Overt peasant attempts at coercion were rare, sporadic, and ineffectual. Only the most local, minimal, and temporary gains came from the odd attack on procurement officials or the occasional storming of a county storehouse containing scarce fertilizer. Peasants could cheat, lie, and steal, of course, to squeeze unintended results out of state policy, but they could not compel state leaders to change policy itself. They never had that degree of coercive power.

Power as the Alteration of Political Outcomes

Coercion is not the only form power takes, however. Peasants exercise power in ways that are more subtle than either coercion or legitimate participation in political processes. With none of the trappings of organized politics, peasant power in a weak society wins neither electoral contests nor armed battles and it enjoys no public celebrations when it succeeds. What peasant power achieves is purely practical: it changes political outcomes.

The first way in which peasants change political outcomes is *manipulation of policy*. Policy manipulation is the lowest order of peasant power, but it is a step above what people usually see when they look at peasant politics. Social scientists generally look upon resistance as the quintessential political action of peasants in daily life. But peasant action even under a strong state is often more positive than mere resistance, noncompliance, or noncooperation. Policy manipulation is distinguished from resistance by its creative element. Peasants do not merely resist state policy (a passive act); they reshape policy into something new, something the state never intended (a creative act).

In China manipulation of policy for creative ends took several forms. One was deliberate misconstruing of policy, which occurred repeatedly as peasants pushed to dismantle the collectives. Peasants and local cadres gave creative misreadings to central documents, using (in one example) the state's approval of work groups as a pretext for creating single-surname landholdings or for breaking up the collective structure. Manipulation also took the form of finding weaknesses in new rules that could be exploited for gains against the state. Price manipulation exemplified this form. Peasants basically followed the new procurement policies, but in a selective way, marketing their crops narrowly within specific new procurement categories to effect an overall rise in average farm-gate prices. Here again, peasants were not merely resisting the state—they were not just refusing to sell—but were instead twisting central policy to produce outcomes that they wanted and the state did not. Policy manipulation can thus be a positive action, an exercise of power (however illegitimate) that transforms state policy and creates something new. It is active rather than inert, hence distinct from foot-dragging and other traditional expressions of peasant resistance. Policy manipulation is the first, if crudest, way in which peasants exercise power.

At the other end of the spectrum is the *original creation of policy*. This is the highest order of peasant power under a strong state. Peasants have no coercive power to force the state to initiate policy change. In fact, under many strong states they do not even have a legitimate avenue for peacefully expressing their policy preferences. Nevertheless, peasants can sometimes create new policy choices that the state previously neglected or even actively opposed. Peasants make new policy options by adopting practices without permission or by defying established rules. The effect of widespread rule-breaking is the creation of a policy experiment: a different way of doing things, nestled quietly inside the officially mandated system. Given enough room to flourish through secrecy or benign neglect by local authorities, these unsanctioned peasant initiatives can prove superior to the state's original policy preference.

In China this surreptitious experimentation created the most radical changes of the reform period. Some experiments were complex affairs that required local conspiracies to ward off official repression until they could prove their productive potential. Illegal experiments with family farming, for example, thrived with clandestine pacts among many villagers and with the protection of cadre conspirators. Other radical policy departures grew in pedestrian, undramatic ways, through habit and corner-cutting. Peasants broke strictures against land transfers, for example, merely because the rules were cumbersome and inconvenient. Peasants had no thought of a national movement. But with everyone skirting the rules in the same way, a rental market in land became a fact of life. Similarly, private entrepreneurship required no conspiracy to nurture it. Entrepreneurship blossomed simply because so many peasants turned to it for the mundane purpose of increasing family income. When peasants under a strong state deviate from policy in great numbers, as the Chinese did, they push policy choices back into the realm of possibility, from which the state had attempted to banish them.

For peasants' original creation of policy to have any effect, however, they must have some way of influencing the state to select the policy choices which they pioneer. Peasants exert this influence through two other expressions of peasant power: aggressive productivity and inflating the cost of undesirable state preferences.

Peasants practice *aggressive productivity* when they throw their energies into policy alternatives banned by the state, raising production to the point where state leaders can no longer resist the attractiveness of an outlawed practice. In China, under the looser policy enforcement in many areas of the countryside in the late 1970s, peasants aggressively boosted production through methods known to be illegal, winning the attention of officials who were attuned to the new leadership's sensitivity to production. Early on, peasants broke the rules on expanded sidelines, sowing of economic crops, and family farming. They pressed each of these unsanctioned activities to achieve new levels of output. Were peasants deliberately influencing the state here? The degree to which they were consciously trying to demonstrate to the leadership the productivity of these policy alternatives is hard to ascertain, for in pursuing these practices peasants were obviously following their personal interest in raising their own income. Later in the reform period, however, peasants became more aware of the alacrity with which the state was abandoning restrictions on activities that were demonstrably more productive. By the time peasants were illegally exceeding restrictions on the number of laborers an entrepreneur could hire, for example, they did so with confidence that state policy would follow the scent of the resultant production increase—which it did.

The companion to aggressive productivity is *inflating the cost of state preferences*. Of the types of peasant power I have outlined here, this is the least creative. It is barely distinguishable from simple resistance. In China, however, inflating the cost of state preferences was of great importance in moving the state to acquiesce in policy alternatives created by peasants. Passivity, sabotage, and deliberate lethargy on the part of peasants, for example, undermined the state's uncertain effort to keep the collective system afloat in the early reform period. The state could certainly have used coercion to sustain the collectives over peasant objections indefinitely. But peasants in some areas inflated the cost to the state of doing so by making the collectives too unproductive compared to the peasant-made alternative of family farming. Later, the same inflation of cost to the state subverted central planning in agriculture. Without question, the state could have forced peasants to plant whatever it wanted them to plant. But again peasants made the cost of such enforcement too high for the state to pay willingly. Peasant defiance of the state plan actually became more attractive to the state in the early 1980s, for it offered an explosive burst of productivity in China's chief economic crops.

In summary, the Chinese case suggests that peasants affect political outcomes in at least four ways: manipulation of policy, original creation of policy, aggressive productivity, and inflating the cost of state policy preferences. Scrutiny of the four ways in which peasants exercise power under a strong state quickly shows that each one lacks any substantial coercive force. Even taken together, these four means add up to a peasant power which is small relative to the power of a strong state. It is also immediately evident that every one of these expressions of peasant power is illegitimate. In each case, what power the peasants can bring to bear is unsanctioned; it intrudes on state policy deliberations surreptitiously, covertly, illegally. What kind of efficacy can such peasant power have?

Efficacy of Peasant Power

Weapons of the Weak, by James C. Scott, is a pioneering study of the ways peasants assert themselves through unsanctioned, illegitimate means.[9] Comparing my findings from China with what Scott found in the Malaysian village of Sedaka will help to illuminate the efficacy of peasant power against overwhelming force. Whereas my study of China has concentrated on peasants contending against the state, Scott focused on class struggle between the village rich and poor. The state was nevertheless a large presence in Sedaka, for peasants were fighting to maintain their position "against the effects of state-fostered capitalist development in the countryside."[10] The immediate objects of the struggle in Sedaka, like those in China, were all local. And in that struggle, Sedaka's peasants were clearly losing ground against the superior power of the rich.

The parallels between the means of fighting superior force used by the Malaysian peasants and by Chinese peasants were many: dissimulation, sabotage, foot-dragging, fraud, theft, and so on. I want to draw attention, however, not to the many parallels between these two cases, but to a contrast in the outcome. The fight between rich and poor in Sedaka was a struggle at the margins. As Scott put it, "On both sides—landlord-tenant, farmer–wage laborer—there is a never-ending attempt to seize each small advantage and press it home, to probe the limits of the existing relationships, to see precisely what can be gotten away with at the margin, and to include this margin as part of an accepted, or at least tolerated territorial claim."[11] Sedaka peasants mostly lost in this struggle, and what they won was marginal—a small gain at the edge of what they had before. In most circumstances, this sort of small gain, eating away at the edges of the territory claimed by a superior force, is all that peasants aim for in politics and the limit of what they can get. Scott does briefly discuss historical examples of petty resistance resulting in major changes, even revolutionary ones.[12] Except for successful resistance to the Is-

9. James C. Scott, *Weapons of the Weak: Everyday Forms of Peasant Resistance* (New Haven: Yale University Press, 1985).
10. Ibid., p. 241.
11. Ibid., p. 255.
12. Ibid., pp. 30–32, 293–94. Cf. James C. Scott, "Resistance without Pro-

lamic tithe enforced by the state, however, the "weapons of the weak" that Sedaka peasants wielded won only piecemeal gains. The small power of subordinate peasants did not produce a larger social effect outside the village. Peasant power did not touch national policy.

But in China it did: peasants acting with the same sort of marginal goals and local intentions as in Sedaka had a telling impact on national policy. The genealogies of all the radical changes of China's rural reform (such as family farming, commercial practices, and entrepreneurship) can be traced back to peasant innovations. The state had to approve these peasant initiatives before they could become national policy, to be sure. But these radical choices finally became preferable to the state because of peasants' widespread actions—their manipulation of policy, their creation of new possibilities, and their productive enthusiasm for certain banned practices. In contrast to Sedaka and most instances of peasant struggle, the disparate acts of millions of Chinese peasants added up to an effective challenge against the superior force of the state. The contrast here is one of efficacy, not magnitude. Individual Chinese peasants had no more power than their Malaysian counterparts, and in organization they were even more impoverished. In both cases subordinate peasants were terribly weak relative to their adversary, whether it was Malaysia's richer rural class or the Chinese state. But in China peasant power, however small, was more effective. The problem therefore is to specify the conditions that increase the efficacy of small peasant power.

Although the evidence from China's rural reform cannot be generalized to cover all cases, it is extremely useful in analyzing peasant power when rural society is weak. A weak society lacks alternative organizations to compete against the state—and this immediately creates a novel analytical problem. Analyses of peasant politics are always looking for organizational capacity. But Chinese peasants in the People's Republic had none. Not only did they lack alternative organizations, but the political system choked any hope that peasants could create such organizations, legally or illegally. Yet nearly all

test and without Organization: Peasant Opposition to the Islamic *Zakat* and the Christian Tithe," *Comparative Studies in Society and History* 29 (July 1987), pp. 417–452.

scholarly analysis of peasant politics has rested on precisely this point: when scholars think of peasants in politics, they look to see whether there are structures in agrarian life that might facilitate peasant organization against the state or against class adversaries. As Theda Skocpol put it, "The really important question is what transforms the peasantry, if only at local levels, into a collective force capable of striking out against its oppressors."[13]

This question of collective force and organization has dominated influential books on peasant politics. Scholars who disagree on nearly everything else agree that collective capacity is the core issue. Skocpol, for example, focused on the conditions that maximize peasants' community solidarity and autonomy from landlords and that simultaneously minimize the power of state coercion against peasant revolts. She was looking for conditions that would give peasants "some organized capacity for collective action."[14] Jeffrey Paige, writing from a perspective with which Skocpol disagreed, also sought the roots of peasant political action in organizational capacity. Examining the structures of rural production, he looked to see whether peasants' work created the community, solidarity, and common interests necessary for collective movements.[15] From another point of view, which shares little with either Skocpol or Paige, Samuel Popkin analyzed peasants' rational-choice decisions to engage in collective action in Vietnam.[16] In each case—and the list could go on—the assumption is that effective peasant action depends on conditions favoring organizational capacity.[17]

The difficulty with this focus on collective action is that it leaves

13. Theda Skocpol, *States and Social Revolutions: A Comparative Analysis of France, Russia, and China* (Cambridge: Cambridge University Press, 1979), p. 115.

14. Ibid.

15. Jeffrey M. Paige, *Agrarian Revolution* (New York, Free Press, 1975). For Skocpol's disagreement with Paige, see Skocpol, *States and Social Revolutions*, p. 319 n.

16. Samuel L. Popkin, *The Rational Peasant* (Berkeley: University of California Press, 1979).

17. See also Eric R. Wolf, *Peasant Wars of the Twentieth Century* (New York: Harper and Row, 1969). Wolf took a different approach, analyzing peasant class structure to identify segments of the peasantry with the "tactical mobility" to engage freely in political activity (pp. 290–94).

out all the typically disorganized ways in which peasants press their interests against oppressive states and classes. What about cases where peasants have no organizational capacity? What if peasants' actions are collective—in the sense of being duplicated and multiplied on a massive scale—with almost no conscious organization? The impulse of most political scientists would be to ignore such cases. Yet disorganized peasant action can, as in China, have an enormous impact on political outcomes—and these outcomes must be explained. The solution to this analytical problem is to seek the source of peasant capacity in aspects of the state-peasant relationship other than organizational potential. The goal is still to identify the conditions that increase the efficacy of the peasantry's small power, but without resort to organization as a variable. For in China, organization was not what enabled peasants to affect state policy as they did in the reform period.

The evidence from China shows two conditions conducive to peasant power. The first condition involves the basic project pursued by the state. A strong state (like that of China) is one that can remake society and culture. This remaking implies a goal, or a basic enterprise, that the state seeks to achieve. Strong states with large peasantries have been guided by such basic projects as rapid industrialization, social transformation, or balanced economic growth. The evidence from China suggests that peasant power is at its height when the state's basic project is balanced economic growth—that is, when the state puts the economy as a whole before other domestic goals and gives balanced support to major sectors within the economy.

Because peasants derive almost all their leverage over the state from their position in agriculture, their small power is greatest when the state is bent on balanced economic growth. This is why peasant power in the People's Republic bloomed only under Deng Xiaoping. In the Maoist era, the government did not pursue balanced growth. Mao Zedong's government created severe sectoral imbalances in its quest for rapid industrialization, displaying a practical indifference to the plight of agriculture. During repeated ideological campaigning, Maoism also prized political and social advances over agricultural growth. Under these circumstances, peasants could exert almost no leverage from their strategic position in agriculture. In contrast, Deng's reform government staked its hopes for greatness on an economic program that required record expansion in the farm sector. Deng's coalition feared that peasant dissatisfaction, expressed in traditional modes like passivity and noncooperation, could doom the whole enterprise. Consequently, Deng's government displayed unprecedented restraint toward peasant defiance, an urge to accommodate peasant desires, and, above all, an openness to peasant initiatives. Hence the degree to which the peasants' experiments, innovations, and changing economic habits shaped state policy.

The second requisite for the efficacy of peasant power is something to provide cohesion to otherwise disparate peasant actions. To exert a force concerted enough to sway state policy, peasants need to compensate for the organizational vacuum a repressive state forces upon a weak society. The evidence from China suggests that the enforced uniformity of the peasant condition under state socialism can have this unifying effect. The irony of state socialism is that instead of doing away with class it makes class into an even more deterministic definition of individual social existence. For Chinese peasants this was certainly the case. Barred from residing in cities, peasants were not only locked into a rural existence, they were in effect tied to the land in a specific commune. The collective structure was universal, regardless of its aptness for local ecological conditions. Thus peasants in a given region often faced similar problems and reacted to them in similar ways. As a result, dispersed, disconnected peasants with no organization acted with a unity that mimicked organized, collective action. The evidence from the reform period is full of examples: the rush to family farming in Anhui, the steady dismantling of the collective structure in Hubei, the embrace of entrepreneurship nationwide, the development of private credit and private employment practices, and the colossal effort to twist farm-good price policies to serve the peasantry's own ends. All of these inadvertently united peasant endeavors quietly moved the state, and in some cases created what would become state policy.

In addition to specifying these two conditions for the efficacy of peasant power, the Chinese case suggests a caveat. Even under the best of conditions, peasant power under a strong state remains small.

As the price war between the peasantry and the Chinese state showed, peasants had no coercive power to oppose the state once the battle carried them into domains that state leaders considered inviolable. Peasants could not stop the backlash of 1985 after they aroused the conservative leaders' obsession with finance and control. To use their power, then, peasants must work within the substantial terrain of policy issues that the state does not regard as threatening its own survival. Within those limits peasant power has the potential to help change a nation's fundamental policies.

Privatization and the State's Response to Peasant Power

Privatization plays a peculiar role in the contest between state and peasant, both in the assertion of peasant power and in the state's response. As a vehicle of peasant innovation, privatization is only partly the expression of peasants' free will. The creative impulse behind privatization in rural China did indeed come from the peasantry, and some innovations (such as private entrepreneurship) greatly rewarded those daring enough to pioneer them. But peasants who led the way in privatization did not always embrace it the way they did family farming or price manipulation. Instead, many peasants undertook privatization under the compulsion of circumstance. Some were caught in a relentless tide of privatization that kept encroaching on the old collective economy. Instead of innovating in an aggressive, creative way, as they had when they reinvented family farming, peasants acted defensively, taking successive steps out of necessity to keep their households afloat in the unforgiving individual economy. Farmers who turned to tenancy and private credit, for example, resorted to these innovations with little choice. Even though peasants clearly led the way in privatization, with the state adopting their creations as policy after the fact, peasant innovators were sometimes bowing to economic imperatives that neither they nor the state seemed able to control.

If privatization was thus only partly an assertion of peasant power, the state's acquiescence to it was not entirely a surrender to peasant will. On the contrary, privatization played an additional role in the contest for power: it gave the state a special way to respond to the peasant challenge while increasing the state's political power.

In what way did the Chinese state need this augmentation of political power? A strong state with unchecked power over a weak peasant society has an unseen political vulnerability. On the one hand, the state's superiority appears irresistible: what power the peasants can muster is disorganized and amorphous, clearly no match for state coercion. But on the other hand, the state's continuing resort to coercion (that is, ordering people to act against their will) bespeaks its failure to foster a dependable, voluntary base of support within rural society. This is not a mild oversight in the political development of state socialism—it is a calamity, as evinced in the 1980s collapse of the Eastern European governments that had failed to engender any real social support.

Rural privatization solves this political problem for the state in two ways. First, privatization creates a rural constituency whose fortunes ride on the perpetuation of the liberalizing state. This constituency includes successful farmers, entrepreneurs, and even smaller property holders who fear that their well-being would decline with a reversion to collectivist policies. Second, privatization tends to crack the cohesion upon which peasant power rests. Remember that one of the main conditions for peasant power is something to create unity of action by peasants who lack organization. The compulsive rigidity of state socialism creates unity of action among peasants by forcing them into like circumstances, even in so a vast country as China. But privatization divides the peasantry, breaking its unity of action into the disparate acts of different types of people—individual farmers, traders, hired laborers, moneylenders, investors, entrepreneurs, shareholders, middlemen, and so on. Thus privatization not only delivers to state socialism a rural constituency, it also weakens one of the main bases for disorganized peasant power. Privatization is not merely an economic strategy in which the state acquiesces; it is a political response to peasant power.

The history of state socialism in the 1980s can be read (among other ways) as the tale of the states that learned this lesson in time and those that did not. Privatization swept through the state-socialist world by the end of the 1980s, either under the state's direction or over its dead body. China, the world's largest state-socialist system, seemed to lead the stampede toward privatization. The Chinese state survived the upsurge of the democracy movement in 1989 partly because it had accepted rural privatization over the previous decade. When China's urban political crisis struck in 1989, peasants were off pursuing their own personal fortunes rather than adding their collective grievances to the urbanites' challenge to the government. The third-largest state-socialist system, Vietnam, followed China's lead with its own program of privatization and more individual farming beginning in 1981. In Europe, the most instantaneous disintegration befell the states with the most inflexible systems, such as East Germany and Czechoslovakia. The smoothest transition, on the other hand, occurred in Hungary. The Hungarian state had created perhaps the least unpopular social system in Eastern Europe after many years of highly developed privatization in the countryside, where a surprisingly large part of the population continued not only to reside, but to live in relative prosperity.[18] And finally, in the Soviet Union, the decade closed in 1990 with Mikhail Gorbachev failing to obtain privatizing reforms in time to win an economic recovery and a grateful constituency to go with it.

Thus the connection between privatization and state socialism may be deeper and more political than it appears, especially in peasant countries. As a political tactic, privatization gives the state a new foundation of social support even as it eliminates one of the main bases of peasant power. For the state to give itself up to a tide of privatization, as China did in its rural policy of the 1980s, is therefore less a surrender of power than a means for clinging to it.

Peasant Politics

Is peasant power under a strong state really political? In the Chinese case, peasants fought the struggles of the reform era strictly through illegitimate means. The Chinese

18. On the family economy of rural Hungary and its political consequences, see Ivan Szelenyi, *Socialist Entrepreneurs: Embourgeoisement in Rural Hungary* (Madison: University of Wisconsin Press, 1988).

system of government offered peasants no real political role. Peasants were completely uninvolved in public decision-making. Even in their unsanctioned behavior outside the system, they acted mostly in disorganized ways, often without consciousness that they were crashing the gates of public policy. Chinese peasants in the 1980s apparently fit Eric Hobsbawm's famous characterization of "*pre-political* people who have not yet found, or only begun to find, a specific language in which to express their aspirations about the world."[19]

The tendency to see peasants as nonpolitical has often banished them from analysis unless they are revolutionaries. The trouble with the dazzling light concentrated on peasant revolution is that it casts a shadow over the much larger terrain of ordinary peasant politics—a phenomenon that has been criticized before.[20] Once analysts step outside the narrow strip of history where peasants have been revolutionaries, however, they are likely to see peasants as victims, helplessly suffering the epochal changes that have modernized the world. Karl Marx's chilling chapters in *Capital* on the destruction of England's peasant proprietors helped to establish this image of peasants as victims.[21] Later, Barrington Moore's hugely influential *Social Origins of Dictatorship and Democracy* tried to capture "the dying wail of a class over whom the wave of progress is about to roll."[22] Following Moore, most scholarly writing on traumatic change in rural societies has portrayed peasants as the victims of world economic forces they can neither comprehend nor resist. The dreary historical truths that have created this image of peasants as victims are beyond dispute. But the image itself—of peasants being swallowed by fate—is badly misleading. It suggests that peasants have no effect on politics, no role in shaping the aftermath of their many defeats, no hand in making the new world of their children even as their own world collapses around

19. E. J. Hobsbawm, *Primitive Rebels* (New York: W. W. Norton and Co., 1959), p. 2. Emphasis in the original.

20. See, for example, Scott, *Weapons of the Weak*, pp. 28–29.

21. Karl Marx, *Capital: A Critique of Political Economy*, vol. 1: *The Process of Capitalist Production*, trans. Ben Fowkes (New York: Vintage, 1977), chaps. 26–32.

22. Barrington Moore, Jr., *Social Origins of Dictatorship and Democracy: Lord and Peasant in the Making of the Modern World* (Boston: Beacon Press, 1966), p. 505.

them. Assigning peasants the role of history's passive victims denies them any political efficacy. They can contribute nothing to the making of politics.

The evidence presented in this book contradicts the idea that ordinary peasants have no part in creating political outcomes. Yet there is a danger that even the case of reform-era China could be used to reinforce the image of peasants as politically ineffectual. As Bruce Cumings has written, much of the best literature on peasant politics is "prepolitical, apolitical, or extrapolitical."[23] This same characterization might carelessly be applied to Chinese peasants in the reform era, whose individual acts and motives would fall below the threshold of what many people consider political. This could yield a conclusion that I believe is misleading: namely, that peasants did not play a causal role in China's reforms and had a negligible part in the politics of the era. The mistake here lies in seeing only individual peasants and small communities. In isolation, any one of the actions that peasants took during the reform years truly was inconsequential. For the real strength of the peasantry lay in great numbers. It was the *cumulative effect* of peasants' barely political actions that had such an impact on Chinese politics. Only by beholding the totality of peasant action is it possible to see the efficacy of peasant power.

Recognition of this peasant power is essential—not to achieve a romanticized communion with the downtrodden, but to understand politics. For if the cumulative power of small acts is dismissed as apolitical, then political outcomes become mysterious and inexplicable. To prevent this we must bring peasant actions with barely any claim to being conventionally political—and thus peasant power in its cumulative form—back into the realm of recognized political efficacy.

This is why the case of reform-era China is so important. It demonstrates the effect that the most mundane forms of peasant power can have on politics. Disenfranchised Chinese peasants committed small acts of innovation and disobedience. Any one of these acts could only be judged meaningless by itself. But compounded in countless numbers, countless places and repetitions, these small actions

23. Bruce Cumings, "Interest and Ideology in the Study of Agrarian Politics," *Politics and Society* 10: 4 (1981), p. 469.

achieved a level of political efficacy unrecognizable in any one of them seen alone. The combined power of millions of peasants helped to accelerate China toward family farming, liberalized markets, and privatization, all ahead of the wishes of a reluctant government. A vast change overtook rural China, driven by peasants who were neither victims nor revolutionaries.

Index

Administration, rural: levels of, xvi; in communes, 9; conflict in, 33–34, 91, 170–72; reform of, 56, 214–18. *See also* Collectives; *Xiang* government

Agriculture: in modernization plan, 4, 13–14, 16–17, 43, 45–51; under Mao, 8–9, 10, 15–16, 29; and industry, 16–17, 46–47, 72–73, 142–48; as threat to modernization plan, 41–42, 43, 45; growth and output in, 43, 50, 121, *table 1,* 139–40, 140, *table 7,* 168; and capital accumulation, 148–58

Anhui Province: as leading reform center, x, 60, 105, 154; family farming in, 60–64, 247; collective funds collapse in, 190, 190*n*; mentioned, 31, 65, 68, 69, 78, 88, 170, 185, 206, 207, 237

Backlash reform of *1985,* 109–10, 119, 134–41, 143, 164–65, 174. *See also* Procurement prices

Balanced economic growth: as state's basic project, 29–30; as condition for peasant power, 100–101, 172–73, 246–47

Banks, 167, 191–93, 208. *See also* Credit; Credit cooperatives

Basic state project, 27–30, 246–47

Budget. *See* State finance and budget

Cadres, rural: conflicting role of, 56, 81, 135; attitudes toward reform, 61–63, 81–88, 95, 216; and policy confusion, 62–63, 86–88, 205; effectiveness of, 68, 82, 86–88, 88*n*, 218; collusion against the state by, 68, 82, 104, 129–30, 135, 159; as entrepreneurs, 81, 205–6; and ideology, 83–85, 220; relations with peasants, 88, 93–95; and corruption, 167–68

Capital accumulation from agriculture, 4, 28, 46, 47, 142, 148–58

Central planning. *See* Planning

Chen Pixian: as Hubei leader, 65; on unreliability of peasants, 116

Chen Yun: career of, 1, 3, 3*n*; on development strategy, 3–4, 16–17; on capital accumulation, 4, 149–52; as conservative leader, 11, 141, 163–65; and critique of Mao, 15–16; on peasant income and state finance, 55, 116, 149–50; versus petroleum faction, 72–74; versus liberals and markets, 74, 78, 163–65; mentioned, 47, 120, 174

Cities: dependence on grain, 46; peasants barred from, 103; in conflict with countryside, 158; protected by price subsidies, 142–46; unrest in, 143–44, 145*n,* 250

Class: in state socialism, 31–32, 103; and state power, 222–23, 224–29, 232; class labels, 214, 222–23, 224. *See also* Social stratification; Rich versus poor